بِسْمِ اللهِ الرَّحْمٰنِ الرَّحِيْم

Hadith of the Prophet

Peace and Blessings be Upon Him

Sahih Al-Bukhari

Volume 8

Book 73 to 82

Copyright
K.F. National Library Cataloging-in-Publication Data
Edition. 2022
Editors/Writers Imam Ahmad and Noah Ibn Kathir

Other Great Books to Read

ISBN	9798774942602
ISBN	9798774942602
ISBN	9798517657411
ISBN	9798515913731
ISBN	9798515149253
ISBN	9798782321932
ISBN	9798782033439
ISBN	9781643542775
ISBN	9798418408044
ISBN	9781643544342
ISBN	9781727812718
ISBN	9781798285466
ISBN	9781643544328
ISBN	9781643544311
ISBN	9781643544236
ISBN	9781643544229
ISBN	9781643544212
ISBN	9781643544205

Content

About this Book

Sahīh Al-Bukhārī is a collection of deeds and sayings of the Prophet, Mūhammad (Peace and Blessings Be Upon Him), also known as the Sunnah. The reports of the Prophet's deeds and sayings are called ahadith.

Al-Bukhārī worked extremely hard to collect the Prophet's ahadith. Al-Bukhārī and the author checked each report for accuracy and compatibility with the Quran, and the authenticity of the chain of reporters was painstakingly done. The reports in this book have been recognized by the majority of all Muslims to be one of the most authentic collections of the Sunnah of the Messenger of Allâh (Peace and Blessings Be Upon Him).

VOLUME 8

Book 73: Good Manners and Form (Al-Adab)

Volume 8, Book 73, Number 1:

Narrated Al-Walid bin 'Aizar:

I heard Abi Amr 'Ash-Shaibani saying, "The owner of this house." he pointed to 'Abdullah's house, "said, 'I asked the Prophet 'Which deed is loved most by Allah?'" He replied, 'To offer prayers at their early (very first) stated times.' " 'Abdullah asked, "What is the next (in goodness)?" The Prophet said, "To be good and dutiful to one's parents," 'Abdullah asked, "What is the next (in goodness)?" The Prophet said, To participate in Jihad for Allah's Cause." 'Abdullah added, "The Prophet narrated to me these three things, and if I had asked more, he would have told me more."

Volume 8, Book 73, Number 2:

Narrated Abu Huraira:

A man came to Allah's Apostle and said, "O Allah's Apostle! Who is more entitled to be treated with the best companionship by me?" The Prophet said, "Your mother." The man said. "Who is next?" The Prophet said, "Your mother." The man further said, "Who is next?" The Prophet said, "Your mother." The man asked for the fourth time, "Who is next?" The Prophet said, "Your father. "

Volume 8, Book 73, Number 3:

Narrated 'Abdullah bin 'Amr:

A man said to the Prophet, "Shall I participate in Jihad?" The Prophet said, "Are your parents living?" The man said, "Yes." the Prophet said, "Do Jihad for their benefit."

Volume 8, Book 73, Number 4:

Narrated 'Abdullah bin 'Amr:

Allah's Apostle said. "It is one of the greatest sins that a man should curse his parents." It was asked (by the people), "O Allah's Apostle! How does a man curse his parents?" The Prophet said, "'The man abuses the father of another man and the latter abuses the father of the former and abuses his mother."

Volume 8, Book 73, Number 5:

Narrated Ibn 'Umar:

Allah's Apostle said, "While three persons were traveling, they were overtaken by rain and they took shelter in a cave in a mountain. A big rock fell from the mountain over the mouth of the cave and blocked it. They said to each other. 'Think of such good (righteous) deeds which, you did for Allah's sake only, and invoke Allah by giving reference to those deeds so that Allah may relieve you from your difficulty. one of them said, 'O Allah! I had my parents who were very old and I had small children for whose sake I used to work as a shepherd. When I returned to them at night and milked (the sheep), I used to start giving the milk to my parents first before giving to my children. And one day I went far away in search of a grazing place (for my sheep), and didn't return home till late at night and found that my parents had slept. I milked (my livestock) as usual and brought the milk vessel and stood at their heads, and I disliked to wake them up from their sleep, and I also disliked to give the milk to my children before my parents though my children were crying (from hunger) at my feet.

So this state of mine and theirs continued till the day dawned. (O Allah!) If you considered that I had done that only for seeking Your pleasure, then please let there be an opening through which we can see the sky.' So Allah made for them an opening through which they could see the sky. Then the second person said, 'O Allah! I had a she-cousin whom I loved as much as a passionate man love a woman. I tried to seduce her but she refused till I paid her one-hundred Dinars So I worked hard till I collected one hundred Dinars and went to her with that But when I sat in between her legs (to have sexual intercourse with her), she said, 'O Allah's slave! Be afraid of Allah ! Do not deflower me except legally (by marriage contract). So I left her O Allah! If you considered that I had done that only for seeking Your pleasure then please let the rock move a little to have a (wider) opening.'

So Allah shifted that rock to make the opening wider for them. And the last (third) person said 'O Allah ! I employed a laborer for wages equal to a Faraq (a certain measure: of rice, and when he had finished his job he demanded his wages, but when I presented his due to him, he gave it up and refused to take it. Then I kept on sowing that rice for him (several times) till managed to buy with the price of the yield, some cows and their shepherd Later on the laborer came to me an said. '(O Allah's slave!) Be afraid o Allah, and do not be unjust to me an give me my due.' I said (to him). 'Go and take those cows and their shepherd. So he took them and went away. (So, O Allah!) If You considered that I had done that for seeking Your pleasure, then please remove the remaining part of the rock.' And so Allah released them (from their difficulty)."

Volume 8, Book 73, Number 6:

Narrated Al-Mughira:

The Prophet said, "Allah has forbidden you (1) to be undutiful to your mothers (2) to withhold (what you should give) or (3) demand (what you do not deserve), and (4) to bury your daughters alive. And Allah has disliked that (A) you talk too much about others (B), ask too many questions (in religion), or (C) waste your property."

Volume 8, Book 73, Number 7:

Narrated Abu Bakra:

Allah's Apostle said thrice, "Shall I not inform you of the biggest of the great sins?" We said, "Yes, O Allah's Apostle" He said, "To join partners in worship with Allah: to be undutiful to one's parents." The Prophet sat up after he had been reclining and added, "And I warn you against giving forged statement and a false witness; I warn you against giving a forged statement and a false witness." The Prophet kept on saying that warning till we thought that he would not stop.

Volume 8, Book 73, Number 8:

Narrated Anas bin Malik:

Allah's Apostle mentioned the greatest sins or he was asked about the greatest sins. He said, "To join partners in worship with Allah; to kill a soul which Allah has forbidden to kill; and to be undutiful or unkind to one's parents." The Prophet added, "Shall I inform you of the biggest of the great sins? That is the forged statement or the false witness." Shu'ba (the sub-narrator) states that most probably the Prophet said, "the false witness."

Volume 8, Book 73, Number 9:

Narrated Asma' bint Abu Bakr:

My mother came to me, hoping (for my favor) during the lifetime of the Prophet asked the Prophet, "May I treat her kindly?" He replied, "Yes." Ibn 'Uyaina said, "Then Allah revealed: 'Allah forbids you not with regards to those who fought not against you because of religion, and drove you not out from your homes, that you should show them kindness and deal justly with them.'.......(60.8)

Volume 8, Book 73, Number 10:

Narrated Abu Sufyan:

That Heraclius sent for him and said, "What did he, i.e. the Prophet order you?" I replied, "He orders us to offer prayers; to give alms; to be chaste; and to keep good relations with our relatives.

Volume 8, Book 73, Number 11:

Narrated Ibn 'Umar:

My father, seeing a silken cloak being sold, said, "O Allah's Apostle! Buy this and wear it on Fridays and when the foreign delegates pay a visit to you." He said, "This is worn only by that person who will have no share in the Hereafter." Later a few silken cloaks were given to the Prophet as a gift, and he sent one of those cloaks to 'Umar. 'Umar said (to the Prophet), "How can I wear it while you have said about it what you said?" The Prophet said, "I did not give it to you to wear but to sell or to give to someone else to wear." So 'Umar sent it to his (pagan) brother who was from the inhabitants of Mecca before he ('Umar's brother) embraced Islam.

Volume 8, Book 73, Number 12.

Narrated Abu Aiyub Al-Ansari:

A man said, "O Allah's Apostle! Inform me of a deed which will make me enter Paradise." The people said, "What is the matter with him? What is the matter with him?" Allah's Apostle said, "He has something to ask (what he needs greatly)." The Prophet said (to him), (In order to enter Paradise) you should worship Allah and join none in worship with Him. You should offer prayers perfectly, give obligatory charity (Zakat), and keep good relations with your Kith and kin." He then said, "Leave it!" (The sub-narrator said, "It seems that the Prophet was riding his she camel."

Volume 8, Book 73, Number 13.

Narrated Jubair bin Mut'im:

That he heard the Prophet saying, "The person who severs the bond of kinship will not enter Paradise."

Volume 8, Book 73, Number 14.

Narrated Abu Huraira:

I heard Allah's Apostle saying, "Who ever is pleased that he be granted more wealth and that his lease of life be pro longed, then he should keep good relations with his Kith and kin."

Volume 8, Book 73, Number 15.

Narrated Anas bin Malik:

Allah 's Apostle said, "Whoever loves that he be granted more wealth and that his lease of life be prolonged then he should keep good relations with his Kith and kin."

Volume 8, Book 73, Number 16.

Narrated Abu Huraira:

The Prophet said, "Allah created the creations, and when He finished from His creations, Ar-Rahm i.e., womb said, "(O Allah) at this place I seek refuge with You from all those who sever me (i.e. sever the ties of Kith and kin). Allah said, 'Yes, won't you be pleased that I will keep good relations with the one who will keep good relations with you, and I will sever the relation with the one who will sever the relations with you.' It said, 'Yes, O my Lord.' Allah said, 'Then that is for you ' " Allah's Apostle added. "Read (in the Qur'an) if you wish, the Statement of Allah: 'Would you then, if you were given the authority, do mischief in the land and sever your ties of kinship?' (47.22)

Volume 8, Book 73, Number 17:

Narrated Abu Huraira:

The Prophet said, "The word 'Ar-Rahm (womb) derives its name from Ar-Rahman (i.e., one of the names of Allah) and Allah said: 'I will keep good relation with the one who will keep good relation with you, (womb i.e. Kith and Kin) and sever the relation with him who will sever the relation with you, (womb, i.e. Kith and Kin).

Volume 8, Book 73, Number 18:

Narrated 'Aisha:

(the wife of the Prophet) The Prophet said, "The word 'Ar-Rahm' (womb) derives its name from 'Ar-Rahman' (i.e. Allah). So whosoever keeps good relations with it (womb i.e. Kith and kin), Allah will keep good relations with him, and whosoever will sever it (i.e. severs his bonds of Kith and kin) Allah too will sever His relations with him.

Volume 8, Book 73, Number 19:

Narrated 'Amr bin Al-'As:

I heard the Prophet saying openly not secretly, "The family of Abu so-and-so (i.e. Talib) are not among my protectors." 'Amr said that there was a blank space (1) in the Book of Muhammad bin Ja'-far. He added, "My Protector is Allah and the righteous believing people." 'Amr bin Al-'As added: I heard the Prophet saying, 'But they (that family) have kinship (Rahm) with me and I will be good and dutiful to them. "

Volume 8, Book 73, Number 20:

Narrated Abdullah bin 'Amr:

The Prophet said, "Al-Wasil is not the one who recompenses the good done to him by his relatives, but Al-Wasil is the one who keeps good relations with those relatives who had severed the bond of kinship with him."

Volume 8, Book 73, Number 21:

Narrated Hakim bin Hizam:

That he said, "O Allah's Apostle! What do you think about my good deeds which I used to do during the period of ignorance (before embracing Islam) like keeping good relations with my Kith and kin, manumitting of slaves and giving alms etc; Shall I receive the reward for that?" Allah's Apostle said, "You have embraced Islam with all those good deeds which you did.

Volume 8, Book 73, Number 22:

Narrated Sa'id:

Um Khalid bint Khalid bin Said said, "I came to Allah's Apostle along with my father and I was wearing a yellow shirt. Allah's Apostle said, "Sanah Sanah!" ('Abdullah, the sub-narrator said, "It means, 'Nice, nice!' in the Ethiopian language.") Um Khalid added, "Then I started playing with the seal of Prophethood. My father admonished me. But Allah's Apostle said (to my father), "Leave her," Allah's Apostle (then addressing me) said, "May you live so long that your dress gets worn out, and you will mend it many times, and then wear another till it gets worn out (i.e. May Allah prolong your life)." (The sub-narrator, 'Abdullah aid, "That garment (which she was wearing remained usable for a long

Volume 8, Book 73, Number 23:

Narrated Ibn Abi Na'm:

-smelling flowers in this world."

Volume 8, Book 73, Number 24:

Narrated 'Aisha:

(the wife of the Prophet) A lady along with her two daughters came to me asking me (for some alms), but she found nothing with me except one date which I gave to her and she divided it between her two daughters, and then she got up and went away. Then the Prophet came in and I informed him about this story. He said, "Whoever is in charge of (put to test by) these daughters and treats them generously, then they will act as a shield for him from the (Hell) Fire."

Volume 8, Book 73, Number 25:

Narrated Abu Qatada:

The Prophet came out towards us, while carrying Umamah, the daughter of Abi Al-As (his granddaughter) over his shoulder. He prayed, and when he wanted to bow, he put her down, and when he stood up, he lifted her up.

Volume 8, Book 73, Number 26:

Narrated Abu Huraira:

Allah's Apostle kissed Al-Hasan bin Ali while Al-Aqra' bin Habis At-Tamim was sitting beside him. Al-Aqra said, "I have ten children and I have never kissed anyone of them," Allah's Apostle cast a look at him and said, "Whoever is not merciful to others will not be treated mercifully."

Volume 8, Book 73, Number 27:

Narrated 'Aisha:

A bedouin came to the Prophet and said, "You (people) kiss the boys! We don't kiss them." The Prophet said, "I cannot put mercy in your heart after Allah has taken it away from it."

Volume 8, Book 73, Number 28:

Narrated 'Umar bin Al-Khattab:

Some Sabi (i.e. war prisoners, children and woman only) were brought before the Prophet and behold, a woman amongst them was milking her breasts to feed and whenever she found a child amongst the captives, she took it over her chest and nursed it (she had lost her child but later she found him) the Prophet said to us, "Do you think that this lady can throw her son in the fire?" We replied, "No, if she has the power not to throw it (in the fire)." The Prophet then said, "Allah is more merciful to His slaves than this lady to her son."

Volume 8, Book 73, Number 29:

Narrated Abu Huraira:

I heard Allah's Apostle saying, Allah divided Mercy into one-hundred parts and He kept its ninety-nine parts with Him and sent down its one part on the earth, and because of that, its one single part, His creations are Merciful to each other, so that even the mare lifts up its hoofs away from its baby animal, lest it should trample on it."

Volume 8, Book 73, Number 30:

Narrated 'Abdullah:

I said 'O Allah's Apostle! Which sin is the greatest?" He said, "To set up a rival unto Allah, though He Alone created you." I said, "What next?" He said, "To kill your son lest he should share your food with you." I further asked, "What next?" He said, "To commit illegal sexual intercourse with the wife of your neighbor." And then Allah revealed as proof of the statement of the Prophet: 'Those who invoke not with Allah any other god)................ (to end of verse)...' (25.68)

Volume 8, Book 73, Number 31:

Narrated 'Aisha:

The Prophet took a child in his lap for Tahnik (i.e. he chewed a date in his mouth and put its juice in the mouth of the child). The child urinated on him, so he asked for water and poured it over the place of the urine.

Volume 8, Book 73, Number 32:

Narrated Usama bin Zaid:

Allah's Apostle used to put me on (one of) his thighs and put Al-Hasan bin 'Ali on his other thigh, and then embrace us and say, "O Allah! Please be Merciful to them, as I am merciful to them. "

Volume 8, Book 73, Number 33:

Narrated 'Aisha:

I never felt so jealous of any woman as I did of Khadija, though she had died three years before the Prophet married me, and that was because I heard him mentioning her too often, and because his Lord had ordered him to give her the glad tidings that she would have a palace in Paradise, made of Qasab and because he used to slaughter a sheep and distribute its meat among her friends.

Volume 8, Book 73, Number 34:

Narrated Sahl bin Sa'd:

The Prophet said, "I and the person who looks after an orphan and provides for him, will be in Paradise like this," putting his index and middle fingers together.

Volume 8, Book 73, Number 35:

Narrated Safwan bin Salim:

The Prophet said "The one who looks after and works for a widow and for a poor person, is like a warrior fighting for Allah's Cause or like a person who fasts during the day and prays all the night." Narrated Abu Huraira that the Prophet said as above.

Volume 8, Book 73, Number 36:

Narrated Abu Huraira:

Allah's Apostle said, "The one who looks after and works for a widow and for a poor person is like a warrior fighting for Allah's Cause." (The narrator Al-Qa'nabi is not sure whether he also said "Like the one who prays all the night without slackness and fasts continuously and never breaks his fast.")

Volume 8, Book 73, Number 37:

Narrated Abu Sulaiman and Malik bin Huwairith:

We came to the Prophet and we were (a few) young men of approximately equal age and stayed with him for twenty nights. Then he thought that we were anxious for our families, and he asked us whom we had left behind to look after our families, and we told him. He was kindhearted and merciful, so he said, "Return to your families and teach them (religious knowledge) and order them (to do good deeds) and offer your prayers in the way you saw me offering my prayers, and when the stated time for the prayer becomes due, then one of you should pronounce its call (i.e. the Adhan), and the eldest of you should lead you in prayer.

Volume 8, Book 73, Number 38:

Narrated Abu Huraira:

Allah's Apostle said, "While a man was walking on a road. he became very thirsty. Then he came across a well, got down into it, drank (of its water) and then came out. Meanwhile he saw a dog panting and licking mud because of excessive thirst. The man said to himself "This dog is suffering from the same state of thirst as I did." So he went down the well (again) and filled his shoe (with water) and held it in his mouth and watered the dog. Allah thanked him for that deed and forgave him." The people asked, "O Allah's Apostle! Is there a reward for us in serving the animals?" He said, "(Yes) There is a reward for serving any animate (living being) ."

Volume 8, Book 73, Number 39:

Narrated Abu Huraira:

Allah's Apostle stood up for the prayer and we too stood up along with him. Then a bedouin shouted while offering prayer. "O Allah! Bestow Your Mercy on me and Muhammad only and do not bestow it on anybody else along with us." When the Prophet had finished his prayer with Taslim, he said to the Bedouin, "You have limited (narrowed) a very vast (thing)," meaning Allah's Mercy.

Volume 8, Book 73, Number 40:

Narrated An-Nu'man bin Bashir:

Allah's Apostle said, "You see the believers as regards their being merciful among themselves and showing love among themselves and being kind, resembling one body, so that, if any part of the body is not well then the whole body shares the sleeplessness (insomnia) and fever with it."

Volume 8, Book 73, Number 41:

Narrated Anas bin Malik:

The Prophet said, "If any Muslim plants any plant and a human being or an animal eats of it, he will be rewarded as if he had given that much in charity."

Volume 8, Book 73, Number 42:

Narrated Jarir bin 'Abdullah:

The Prophet said, "He who is not merciful to others, will not be treated mercifully.

Volume 8, Book 73, Number 43:

Narrated 'Aisha:

The Prophet said "Gabriel continued to recommend me about treating the neighbors Kindly and politely so much so that I thought he would order me to make them as my heirs.

Volume 8, Book 73, Number 44:

Narrates Ibn Umar:

Allah' Apostle said, Gabriel kept on recommending me about treating the neighbors in a kind and polite manner, so much so that I thought that he would order (me) to make them (my) heirs."

Volume 8, Book 73, Number 45:

Narrated Abu Shuraih:

The Prophet said, "By Allah, he does not believe! By Allah, he does not believe! By Allah, he does not believe!" It was said, "Who is that, O Allah's Apostle?" He said, "That person whose neighbor does not feel safe from his evil."

Volume 8, Book 73, Number 46:

Narrated Abu Huraira:

The Prophet used to say, "O Muslim ladies! A neighbouress should not look down upon the present of her neighbouress even it were the hooves of a sheep."

Volume 8, Book 73, Number 47:

Narrated Abu Huraira:

Allah's Apostle said, "Anybody who believes in Allah and the Last Day should not harm his neighbor, and anybody who believes in Allah and the Last Day should entertain his guest generously and anybody who believes in Allah and the Last Day should talk what is good or keep quiet. (i.e. abstain from all kinds of evil and dirty talk).

Volume 8, Book 73, Number 48:

Narrated Abu Shuraih Al-Adawi:

My ears heard and my eyes saw the Prophet when he spoke, "Anybody who believes in Allah and the Last Day, should serve his neighbor generously, and anybody who believes in Allah and the Last Day should serve his guest generously by giving him his reward." It was asked. "What is his reward, O Allah's Apostle?" He said, "(To be entertained generously) for a day and a night with high quality of food and the guest has the right to be entertained for three days (with ordinary food) and if he stays longer, what he will be provided with will be regarded as Sadaqa (a charitable gift). And anybody who believes in Allah and the Last Day should talk what is good or keep quite (i.e. abstain from all kinds of dirty and evil talks)."

Volume 8, Book 73, Number 49:

Narrated 'Aisha:

I said, "O Allah's Apostle! I have two neighbors! To whom shall I send my gifts?" He said, "To the one whose gate in nearer to you."

Volume 8, Book 73, Number 50:

Narrated Jabir bin 'Abdullah:

The Prophet said, Enjoining, all that is good is a Sadaqa."

Volume 8, Book 73, Number 51:

Narrated Abu Musa Al-Ash'ari:

The Prophet said, "On every Muslim there is enjoined (a compulsory) Sadaqa (alms)." They (the people) said, "If one has nothing?' He said, "He should work with his hands so that he may benefit himself and give in charity." They said, "If he cannot work or does not work?" He said, "Then he should help the oppressed unhappy person (by word or action or both)." They said, "If he does not do it?" He said, "Then he should enjoin what is good (or said what is reasonable).' They said, "If he does not do that'" He said, "Then he should refrain from doing evil, for that will be considered for Him as a Sadaqa (charity) . "

Volume 8, Book 73, Number 52:

Narrated 'Adi bin Hatim:

The Prophet mentioned the (Hell) Fire and sought refuge (with Allah) from it, and turned his face to the other side. He mentioned the (Hell) Fire again and took refuge (with Allah) from it and turned his face to the other side. (Shu'ba, the sub-narrator, said, "I have no doubt that the Prophet repeated it twice.") The Prophet then said, "(O people!) Save yourselves from the (Hell) Fire even if with one half of a date fruit (given in charity), and if this is not available, then (save yourselves) by saying a good pleasant friendly word."

Volume 8, Book 73, Number 53:

Narrated 'Aisha:

(the wife of the Prophet) A group of Jews entered upon the Prophet and said, "As-Samu-Alaikum." (i.e. death be upon you). I understood it and said, "Wa-Alaikum As-Samu wal-la'n. (death and the curse of Allah be Upon you)." Allah's Apostle said "Be calm, O 'Aisha! Allah loves that on, should be kind and lenient in all matters." I said, "O Allah's Apostle! Haven't you heard what they (the Jews) have said?" Allah's Apostle said "I have (already) said (to them) "And upon you ! "

Volume 8, Book 73, Number 54:

Narrated Anas bin Malik:

A bedouin urinated in the mosque and the people ran to (beat) him. Allah's Apostle said, "Do not interrupt his urination (i.e. let him finish)." Then the Prophet asked for a tumbler of water and poured the water over the place of urine.

Volume 8, Book 73, Number 55:

Narrated Abu Musa:

The Prophet said, "A believer to another believer is like a building whose different parts enforce each other." The Prophet then clasped his hands with the fingers interlaced. (At that time) the Prophet was sitting and a man came and begged or asked for something. The Prophet faced us and said, "Help and recommend him and you will receive the reward for it, and Allah will bring about what He will through His Prophet's tongue."

Volume 8, Book 73, Number 560:

Narrated Abu Musa:

Whenever a beggar or a person in need came to the Prophet, the Prophet would say "Help and recommend him and you will receive the reward for it, and Allah will bring about what he will through His Prophet's tongue

Volume 8, Book 73, Number 56:

Narrated Masruq:

Abdullah bin 'Amr mentioned Allah's Apostle saying that he was neither a Fahish nor a Mutafahish. Abdullah bin 'Amr added, Allah's Apostle said, 'The best among you are those who have the best manners and character.'

Volume 8, Book 73, Number 57:

Narrated 'Abdullah bin Mulaika:

'Aisha said that the Jews came to the Prophet and said, "As-Samu 'Alaikum" (death be on you). 'Aisha said (to them), "(Death) be on you, and may Allah curse you and shower His wrath upon you!" The Prophet said, "Be calm, O 'Aisha ! You should be kind and lenient, and beware of harshness and Fuhsh (i.e. bad words)." She said (to the Prophet), "Haven't you heard what they (Jews) have said?" He said, "Haven't you heard what I have said (to them)? I said the same to them, and my invocation against them will be accepted while theirs against me will be rejected (by Allah). "

Volume 8, Book 73, Number 58:

Narrated Anas bin Malik:

The Prophet was not one who would abuse (others) or say obscene words, or curse (others), and if he wanted to admonish anyone of us, he used to say: "What is wrong with him, his forehead be dusted!"

Volume 8, Book 73, Number 590:

Narrated 'Aisha:

A man asked permission to enter upon the Prophet. When the Prophet saw him, he said, "What an evil brother of his tribe! And what an evil son of his tribe!" When that man sat down, the Prophet behaved with him in a nice and polite manner and was completely at ease with him. When that person had left, 'Aisha said (to the Prophet). "O Allah's Apostle! When you saw that man, you said so-and-so about him, then you showed him a kind and polite behavior, and you enjoyed his company?" Allah's

Apostle said, "O 'Aisha! Have you ever seen me speaking a bad and dirty language? (Remember that) the worst people in Allah's sight on the Day of Resurrection will be those whom the people leave (undisturbed) to be away from their evil (deeds)."

Volume 8, Book 73, Number 59i:

Narrated Anas:

The Prophet was the best among the people (both in shape and character) and was the most generous of them, and was the bravest of them. Once, during the night, the people of Medina got afraid (of a sound). So the people went towards that sound, but the Prophet having gone to that sound before them, met them while he was saying, "Don't be afraid, don't be afraid." (At that time) he was riding a horse belonging to Abu Talha and it was naked without a saddle, and he was carrying a sword slung at his neck. The Prophet said, "I found it (the horse) like a sea, or, it is the sea indeed."

Volume 8, Book 73, Number 60:

Narrated Jabir:

Never was the Prophet asked for a thing to be given for which his answer was 'no'.

Volume 8, Book 73, Number 61:

Narrated Masruq:

We were sitting with 'Abdullah bin 'Amr who was narrating to us (Hadith). He said, "Allah's Apostle was neither a Fahish nor a Mutafahhish, and he used to say, 'The best among you are the best in character (having good manners).'"

Volume 8, Book 73, Number 62:

Narrated Abu Hazim:

Sahl bin Sa'd said that a woman brought a Burda (sheet) to the Prophet. Sahl asked the people, "Do you know what is a Burda?" The people replied, "It is a 'Shamla', a sheet with a fringe." That woman said, "O Allah's Apostle! I have brought it so that you may wear it." So the Prophet took it because he was in need of it and wore it. A man among his companions, seeing him wearing it, said, "O Allah's Apostle! Please give it to me to wear." The Prophet said, "Yes." (and gave him that sheet). When the Prophet left, the man was blamed by his companions who said, "It was not nice on your part to ask the Prophet for it while you know that he took it because he was in need of it, and you also know that he (the Prophet) never turns down anybody's request that he might be asked for." That man said, "I just wanted to have its blessings as the Prophet had put it on, so I hoped that I might be shrouded in it."

Volume 8, Book 73, Number 63:

Narrated Abu Huraira:

Allah's Apostle said, "Time will pass rapidly, good deeds will decrease, and miserliness will be thrown (in the hearts of the people), and the Harj (will increase)." They asked, "What is the Harj?" He replied, "(It is) killing (murdering), (it is) murdering (killing).

Volume 8, Book 73, Number 64:

Narrated Anas:

I served the Prophet for ten years, and he never said to me, "Uf" (a minor harsh word denoting impatience) and never blamed me by saying, "Why did you do so or why didn't you do so?"

Volume 8, Book 73, Number 65:

Narrated Al-Aswad:

I asked 'Aisha what did the Prophet use to do at home. She replied. "He used to keep himself busy serving his family and when it was time for the prayer, he would get up for prayer."

Volume 8, Book 73, Number 66:

Narrated Abu Huraira:

The Prophet said, "If Allah loves a person, He calls Gabriel saying. 'Allah loves so and so; O Gabriel, love him.' Gabriel would love him, and then Gabriel would make an announcement among the residents of the Heaven, 'Allah loves so-and-so, therefore, you should love him also.' So, all the residents of the Heavens would love him and then he is granted the pleasure of the people of the earth."

Volume 8, Book 73, Number 67:

Narrated Anas bin Malik:

The Prophet said, "None will have the sweetness (delight) of Faith (a) till he loves a person and loves him only for Allah's sake, (b) and till it becomes dearer to him to be thrown in the fire than to revert to disbelief (Heathenism) after Allah has brought him out of it, (c) and till Allah and His Apostle become dearer to him than anything else."

Volume 8, Book 73, Number 68:

Narrated 'Abdullah bin Zam'a:

The Prophet forbade laughing at a person who passes wind, and said, "How does anyone of you beat his wife as he beats the stallion camel and then he may embrace (sleep with) her?" And Hisham said, "As he beats his slave"

Volume 8, Book 73, Number 69:

Narrated Ibn 'Umar:

The Prophet said at Mina, "Do you know what day is today?" They (the people) replied, "Allah and His Apostle know better." He said "Today is 10th of Dhul-Hijja, the sacred (forbidden) day. Do you know what town is this town?" They (the people) replied, "Allah and His Apostle know better." He said, "This is the (forbidden) Sacred town (Mecca a sanctuary)." And do you know which month is this month?" They (the People) replied, "Allah and His Apostle know better." He said, "This is the Sacred (forbidden) month ." He added, "Allah has made your blood, your properties and your honor Sacred to one another (i.e. Muslims) like the sanctity of this day of yours in this month of yours, in this town of yours." (See Hadith No. 797, Vol. 2.)

Volume 8, Book 73, Number 70:

Narrated 'Abdullah:

Allah's Apostle said, "Abusing a Muslim is Fusuq (i.e., an evil-doing), and killing him is Kufr (disbelief)."

Volume 8, Book 73, Number 71:

Narrated Abu Dhar:

That he heard the Prophet saying, "If somebody accuses another of Fusuq (by calling him 'Fasiq' i.e. a wicked person) or accuses him of Kufr, such an accusation will revert to him (i.e. the accuser) if his companion (the accused) is innocent."

Volume 8, Book 73, Number 72:

Narrated Anas:

Allah's Apostle was neither a Fahish (one who had a bad tongue) nor a Sabbaba (one who abuses others) and he used to say while admonishing somebody, "What is wrong with him? May dust be on his forehead!"

Volume 8, Book 73, Number 73:

Narrated Thabit bin Ad-Dahhak:

(who was one of the companions who gave the pledge of allegiance to the Prophet underneath the tree (Al-Hudaibiya)) Allah's Apostle said, "Whoever swears by a religion other than Islam (i.e. if somebody swears by saying that he is a non-Muslim e.g., a Jew or a Christian, etc.) in case he is telling a lie, he is really so if his oath is false, and a person is not bound to fulfill a vow about a thing which he does not possess. And if somebody commits suicide with anything in this world, he will be tortured with that very thing on the Day of Resurrection; And if somebody curses a believer, then his sin will be as if he murdered him; And whoever accuses a believer of Kufr (disbelief), then it is as if he killed him."

Volume 8, Book 73, Number 74:

Narrated Sulaiman bin Surad:

A man from the companions of the Prophet said, "Two men abused each other in front of the Prophet and one of them became angry and his anger became so intense that his face became swollen and changed. The Prophet said, "I know a word the saying of which will cause him to relax if he does say it." Then a man went to him and informed him of the statement of the Prophet and said, "Seek refuge with Allah from Satan." On that, angry man said, 'Do you find anything wrong with me? Am I insane? Go away!'"

Volume 8, Book 73, Number 75:

Narrated 'Ubada bin As-Samit:

Allah's Apostle went out to inform the people about the (date of the Night of decree (Al-Qadr). There happened a quarrel between two Muslim men. The Prophet said, "I came out to inform you about the Night of Al-Qadr, but as so-and-so and so-and-so quarrelled, so the news about it had been taken away; and may be it was better for you. So look for it in the ninth, the seventh, or the fifth (of the last ten days of Ramadan)."

Volume 8, Book 73, Number 76:

Narrated Ma'rur:

I saw Abu Dhar wearing a Burd (garment) and his slave too was wearing a Burd, so I said (to Abu Dhar), "If you take this (Burda of your slave) and wear it (along with yours), you will have a nice suit (costume) and you may give him another garment." Abu Dhar said, "There was a quarrel between me and another man whose mother was a non-Arab and I called her bad names. The man mentioned (complained about) me to the Prophet. The Prophet said, "Did you abuse so-and-so?" I said, "Yes" He said, "Did you call his mother bad names?" I said, "Yes". He said, "You still have the traits of (the Pre-Islamic period of) ignorance." I said. "(Do I still have ignorance) even now in my old age?" He said, "Yes, they (slaves or servants) are your brothers, and Allah has put them under your command. So the one under whose hand Allah has put his brother, should feed him of what he eats, and give him dresses of what he wears, and should not ask him to do a thing beyond his capacity. And if at all he asks him to do a hard task, he should help him therein."

Volume 8, Book 73, Number 77:

Narrated Abu Huraira:

The Prophet led us in the Zuhr prayer, offering only two Rakat and then (finished it) with Taslim, and went to a piece of wood in front of the mosque and put his hand over it. Abu Bakr and 'Umar were also present among the people on that day but dared not talk to him (about his unfinished prayer). And the hasty people went away, wondering. "Has the prayer been shortened" Among the people there was a man whom the Prophet used to call Dhul-Yadain (the longarmed). He said, "O Allah's Prophet! Have you forgotten or has the prayer been shortened?" The Prophet said, "Neither have I forgotten, nor has it been shortened." They (the people) said, "Surely, you have forgotten, O Allah's Apostle!" The Prophet said, Dhul-Yadain has told the truth." So the Prophet got up and offered other two Rakat and finished his prayer with Taslim. Then he said Takbir, performed a prostration of ordinary duration or longer, then he raised his head and said Takbir and performed another prostration of ordinary duration or longer and then raised his head and said Takbir (i.e. he performed the two prostrations of Sahu, i.e., forgetfulness)."

Volume 8, Book 73, Number 78:

Narrated Ibn 'Abbas:

Allah's Apostle passed by two graves and said, "Both of them (persons in the grave) are being tortured, and they are not being tortured for a major sin. This one used not to save himself from being soiled with his urine, and the other used to go about with calumnies (among the people to rouse hostilities, e.g., one goes to a person and tells him that so-and-so says about him such-and-such evil things). The Prophet then asked for a green leaf of a date-palm tree, split it into two pieces and planted one on each grave and said, "It is hoped that their punishment may be abated till those two pieces of the leaf get dried." (See Hadith No 215, Vol 1).

Volume 8, Book 73, Number 79:

Narrated Abu Usaid As-Sa'idi:

The Prophet said, "The best family among the Ansar is the Banu An-Najjar. "

Volume 8, Book 73, Number 80:

Narrated 'Aisha:

A man asked permission to enter upon Allah's Apostle. The Prophet said, "Admit him. What an evil brother of his people or a son of his people." But when the man entered, the Prophet spoke to him in a very polite manner. (And when that person left) I said, "O Allah's Apostle! You had said what you had said, yet you spoke to him in a very polite manner?" The Prophet said, "O 'Aisha! The worst people are those whom the people desert or leave in order to save themselves from their dirty language or from their transgression."

Volume 8, Book 73, Number 81:

Narrated Ibn 'Abbas:

Once the Prophet went through the grave-yards of Medina and heard the voices of two humans who were being tortured in their graves. The Prophet said, "They are being punished, but they are not being punished because of a major sin, yet their sins are great. One of them used not to save himself from (being soiled with) the urine, and the other used to go about with calumnies (Namima)." Then the Prophet asked for a green palm tree leaf and split it into two pieces and placed one piece on each grave, saying, "I hope that their punishment may be abated as long as these pieces of the leaf are not dried."

Volume 8, Book 73, Number 82:

Narrated Hudhaifa:

I heard the Prophet saying, "A Qattat will not enter Paradise."

Volume 8, Book 73, Number 83:

Narrated Abu Huraira:

The Prophet said, "Whoever does not give up false statements (i.e. telling lies), and evil deeds, and speaking bad words to others, Allah is not in need of his (fasting) leaving his food and drink."

Volume 8, Book 73, Number 84:

Narrated Abu Huraira:

The Prophet said, "The worst people in the Sight of Allah on the Day of Resurrection will be the double faced people who appear to some people with one face and to other people with another face."

Volume 8, Book 73, Number 85:

Narrated Ibn Mas'ud:

Once Allah's Apostle divided and distributed (the war booty). An Ansar man said, "By Allah ! Muhammad, by this distribution, did not intend to please Allah." So I came to Allah's Apostle and informed him about it whereupon his face became changed with anger and he said, "May Allah bestow His Mercy on Moses for he was hurt with more than this, yet he remained patient."

Volume 8, Book 73, Number 86:

Narrated Abu Musa:

The Prophet heard a man praising another man and he was exaggerating in his praise. The Prophet said (to him). "You have destroyed (or cut) the back of the man."

Volume 8, Book 73, Number 87:

Narrated Abu Bakra:

A man was mentioned before the Prophet and another man praised him greatly The Prophet said, "May Allah's Mercy be on you ! You have cut the neck of your friend." The Prophet repeated this sentence many times and said, "If it is indispensable for anyone of you to praise someone, then he should say, 'I think that he is so-and-so," if he really thinks that he is such. Allah is the One Who will take his accounts (as He knows his reality) and no-one can sanctify anybody before Allah." (Khalid said, "Woe to you," instead of "Allah's Mercy be on you.")

Volume 8, Book 73, Number 88:

Narrated Salim:

that his father said; "When Allah's Apostle mentioned wh at he mentioned about (the hanging of) the Izar (waist sheet), Abu Bakr said, "O Allah's Apostle! My Izar slackens on one side (without my intention)." The Prophet said, "You are not among those (who, out of pride) drag their Izars behind them."

Volume 8, Book 73, Number 89:

Narrated 'Aisha:

The Prophet continued for such-and-such period imagining that he has slept (had sexual relations) with his wives, and in fact he did not. One day he said, to me, "O 'Aisha! Allah has instructed me regarding a matter about which I had asked Him. There came to me two men, one of them sat near my feet and the other near my head. The one near my feet, asked the one near my head (pointing at me), 'What is wrong with this man? The latter replied, 'He is under the effect of magic.' The first one asked, 'Who had worked magic on him?' The other replied, 'Lubaid bin Asam.' The first one asked, 'What material (did he use)?' The other replied, 'The skin of the pollen of a male date tree with a comb and the hair stuck to it, kept under a stone in the well of Dharwan."' Then the Prophet went to that well and said, "This is the same well which was shown to me in the dream. The tops of its date-palm trees look like the heads of the devils, and its water looks like the Henna infusion." Then the Prophet ordered that those things be taken out. I said, "O Allah's Apostle! Won't you disclose (the magic object)?" The Prophet said, "Allah has cured me and I hate to circulate the evil among the people." 'Aisha added, "(The magician) Lubaid bin Asam was a man from Bani Zuraiq, an ally of the Jews."

Volume 8, Book 73, Number 90:

Narrated Abu Huraira:

The Prophet said, "Beware of suspicion, for suspicion is the worst of false tales; and do not look for the others' faults and do not spy, and do not be jealous of one another, and do not desert (cut your relation with) one another, and do not hate one another; and O Allah's worshipers! Be brothers (as Allah has ordered you!")

Volume 8, Book 73, Number 91:

Narrated Anas bin Malik:

Allah's Apostle said, "Do not hate one another, and do not be jealous of one another, and do not desert each other, and O, Allah's worshipers! Be brothers. Lo! It is not permissible for any Muslim to desert (not talk to) his brother (Muslim) for more than three days."

Volume 8, Book 73, Number 92:

Narrated Abu Huraira:

Allah's Apostle said, "Beware of suspicion, for suspicion is the worst of false tales. and do not look for the others' faults, and do not do spying on one another, and do not practice Najsh, and do not be jealous of one another and do not hate one another, and do not desert (stop talking to) one another. And O, Allah's worshipers! Be brothers!"

Volume 8, Book 73, Number 93:

Narrated 'Aisha:

The Prophet said, "I do not think that so-and-so and so-and-so know anything of our religion." (And Al-Laith said, "These two persons were among the hypocrites.")

Volume 8, Book 73, Number 94:

Narrated Al-Laith:

'Aisha said "The Prophet entered upon me one day and said, 'O 'Aisha! I do not think that so-and-so and so-and-so know anything of our religion which we follow."'

Volume 8, Book 73, Number 95:

Narrated Abu Huraira:

I heard Allah's Apostle saying. "All the sins of my followers will be forgiven except those of the Mujahirin (those who commit a sin openly or disclose their sins to the people). An example of such disclosure is that a person commits a sin at night and though Allah screens it from the public, then he comes in the morning, and says, 'O so-and-so, I did such-and-such (evil) deed yesterday,' though he spent his night screened by his Lord (none knowing about his sin) and in the morning he removes Allah's screen from himself."

Volume 8, Book 73, Number 96:

Narrated Safwan bin Muhriz:

A man asked Ibn 'Umar, "What did you hear Allah's Apostle saying regarding An-Najwa (secret talk between Allah and His believing worshipper on the Day of Judgment)?" He said, "(The Prophet said), "One of you will come close to his Lord till He will shelter him in His screen and say: Did you commit such-and-such sin? He will say, 'Yes.' Then Allah will say: Did you commit such and such sin? He will say, 'Yes.' So Allah will make him confess (all his sins) and He will say, 'I screened them (your sins) for you in the world, and today I forgive them for you."'

Volume 8, Book 73, Number 97:

Narrated Haritha bin Wahb:

Al-Khuzai: The Prophet said, "Shall I inform you about the people of Paradise? They comprise every obscure unimportant humble person, and if he takes Allah's Oath that he will do that thing, Allah will fulfill his oath (by doing that). Shall I inform you about the people of the Fire? They comprise every cruel, violent, proud and conceited person." Anas bin Malik said, "Any of the female slaves of Medina could take hold of the hand of Allah's Apostle and take him wherever she wished."

Volume 8, Book 73, Number 98:

Narrated 'Aisha:

(the wife of the Prophet) that she was told that 'Abdullah bin Az-Zubair (on hearing that she was selling or giving something as a gift) said, "By Allah, if 'Aisha does not give up this, I will declare her incompetent to dispose of her wealth." I said, "Did he ('Abdullah bin Az-Zubair) say so?" They (people) said, "Yes." 'Aisha said, "I vow to Allah that I will never speak to Ibn Az-Zubair." When this desertion lasted long, 'Abdullah bin Az-Zubair sought intercession with her, but she said, "By Allah, I will not accept the intercession of anyone for him, and will not commit a sin by breaking my vow." When this state of affairs was prolonged on Ibn Az-Zubair (he felt it hard on him), he said to Al-Miswar bin Makhrama and 'Abdur-Rahman bin Al-Aswad bin 'Abu Yaghuth, who were from the tribe of Bani Zahra, "I beseech you, by Allah, to let me enter upon 'Aisha, for it is unlawful for her to vow to cut the relation with me." So Al-Miswar and 'Abdur-Rahman, wrapping their sheets around themselves, asked 'Aisha's permission saying, "Peace and Allah's Mercy and Blessings be upon you! Shall we come in?" 'Aisha said, "Come in." They said, "All of us?" She said, "Yes, come in all of you," not knowing that Ibn Az-Zubair was also with them. So when they entered, Ibn Az-Zubair entered the screened place and got hold of 'Aisha and started requesting her to excuse him, and wept. Al-Miswar and 'Abdur Rahman also started requesting her to speak to him and to accept his repentance. They said (to her), "The Prophet forbade what you know of deserting (not speaking to your Muslim Brethren), for it is unlawful for any Muslim not to talk to his brother for more than three nights (days)." So when they increased their reminding her (of the superiority of having good relation with Kith and kin, and of excusing others' sins), and brought her down to a critical situation, she started reminding them, and wept, saying, "I have made a vow, and (the question of) vow is a difficult one." They (Al-Miswar and 'Abdur-Rahman) persisted in their appeal till she spoke with 'Abdullah bin Az-Zubair and she manumitted forty slaves as an expiation for her vow. Later on, whenever she remembered her vow, she used to weep so much that her veil used to become wet with her tears.

Volume 8, Book 73, Number 99:

Narrated Anas bin Malik:

Allah's Apostle said, "Do not hate one another, nor be jealous of one another; and do not desert one another, but O Allah's worshipers! Be Brothers! And it is unlawful for a Muslim to desert his brother Muslim (and not to talk to him) for more than three nights."

Volume 8, Book 73, Number 100:

Narrated Abu Aiyub Al-Ansari:

Allah's Apostle said, "It is not lawful for a man to desert his brother Muslim for more than three nights. (It is unlawful for them that) when they meet, one of them turns his face away from the other, and the other turns his face from the former, and the better of the two will be the one who greets the other first."

Volume 8, Book 73, Number 101:

Narrated 'Aisha:

Allah's Apostle said, " I know whether you are angry or pleased." I said, "How do you know that, Allah's Apostle?" He said, "When you are pleased, you say, "Yes, by the Lord of Muhammad,' but when you are angry, you say, 'No, by the Lord of Abraham!' " I said, "Yes, I do not leave, except your name."

Volume 8, Book 73, Number 102:

Narrated 'Aisha:

(the wife of the Prophet) "I do not remember my parents believing in any religion other than the Religion (of Islam), and our being visited by Allah's Apostle in the morning and in the evening. One day, while we were sitting in the house of Abu Bakr (my father) at noon, someone said, 'This is Allah's Apostle coming at an hour at which he never used to visit us.' Abu Bakr said, 'There must be something very urgent that has brought him at this hour.' The Prophet said, 'I have been allowed to go out (of Mecca) to migrate.' "

Volume 8, Book 73, Number 103:

Narrated Anas bin Malik:

Allah's Apostle visited a household among the Ansars, and he took a meal with them. When he intended to leave, he asked for a place in that house for him, to pray so a mat sprinkled with water was put and he offered prayer over it, and invoked for Allah's Blessing upon them (his hosts).

Volume 8, Book 73, Number 104:

Narrated 'Abdullah:

'Umar saw a silken cloak over a man (for sale) so he took it to the Prophet and said, 'O Allah's Apostle! Buy this and wear it when the delegate come to you.' He said, 'The silk is worn by one who will have no share (in the Here-after).' Some time passed after this event, and then the Prophet sent a (similar) cloak to him. 'Umar brought that cloak back to the Prophet and said, 'You have sent this to me, and you said about a similar one what you said?' The Prophet said, 'I have sent it to you so that you may get money by selling it.' Because of this, Ibn 'Umar used to hate the silken markings on the garments.

Volume 8, Book 73, Number 105:

Narrated Anas:

When 'Abdur-Rahman came to us, the Prophet established a bond of brotherhood between him and Sa'd bin Ar-Rabi'. Once the Prophet said, "As you (O 'Abdur-Rahman) have married, give a wedding banquet even if with one sheep."

Volume 8, Book 73, Number 106:

Narrated 'Asim:

I said to Anas bin Malik, "Did it reach you that the Prophet said, "There is no treaty of brotherhood in Islam'?" Anas said, "The Prophet made a treaty (of brotherhood) between the Ansar and the Quraish in my home."

Volume 8, Book 73, Number 107:

Narrated 'Aisha:

Rifa'a Al-Qurazi divorced his wife irrevocably (i.e. that divorce was the final). Later on 'Abdur-Rahman bin Az-Zubair married her after him. She came to the Prophet and said, "O Allah's Apostle! I was Rifa'a's wife and he divorced me thrice, and then I was married to 'Abdur-Rahman bin AzZubair, who, by Allah has nothing with him except something like this fringe, O Allah's Apostle," showing a fringe she had taken from her covering sheet. Abu Bakr was sitting with the Prophet while Khalid Ibn Said bin Al-As was sitting at the gate of the room waiting for admission. Khalid started calling Abu Bakr, "O Abu Bakr! Why don't you reprove this lady from what she is openly saying before Allah's Apostle?" Allah's Apostle did nothing except smiling, and then said (to the lady), "Perhaps you want to go back to Rifa'a? No, (it is not possible), unless and until you enjoy the sexual relation with him ('Abdur Rahman), and he enjoys the sexual relation with you."

Volume 8, Book 73, Number 108:

Narrated Sa'd:

'Umar bin Al-Khattab asked permission of Allah's Apostle to see him while some Quraishi women were sitting with him and they were asking him to give them more financial support while raising their voices over the voice of the Prophet. When 'Umar asked permission to enter, all of them hurried to screen themselves the Prophet admitted 'Umar and he entered, while the Prophet was smiling. 'Umar said, "May Allah always keep you smiling, O Allah's Apostle! Let my father and mother be sacrificed for you !" The Prophet said, "I am astonished at these women who were with me. As soon as they heard your voice, they hastened to screen themselves." 'Umar said, "You have more right, that they should be afraid of you, O Allah's Apostle!" And then he ('Umar) turned towards them and said, "O enemies of your souls! You are afraid of me and not of Allah's Apostle?" The women replied, "Yes, for you are sterner and harsher than Allah's Apostle." Allah's Apostle said, "O Ibn Al-Khattab! By Him in Whose Hands my life is, whenever Satan sees you taking a way, he follows a way other than yours!"

Volume 8, Book 73, Number 109:

Narrated 'Abdullah bin 'Umar:

When Allah Apostle was in Ta'if (trying to conquer it), he said to his companions, "Tomorrow we will return (to Medina), if Allah wills." Some of the companions of Allah's Apostle said, "We will not leave till we conquer it." The Prophet said, "Therefore, be ready to fight tomorrow." On the following day, they (Muslims) fought fiercely (with the people of Ta'if) and suffered many wounds. Then Allah's Apostle said, "Tomorrow we will return (to Medina), if Allah wills." His companions kept quiet this time. Allah's Apostle then smiled.

Volume 8, Book 73, Number 110:

Narrated Abu Huraira:

A man came to the Prophet and said, "I have been ruined for I have had sexual relation with my wife in Ramadan (while I was fasting)" The Prophet said (to him), "Manumit a slave." The man said, " I cannot afford that." The Prophet said, "(Then) fast for two successive months continuously". The man said, "I cannot do that." The Prophet said, "(Then) feed sixty poor persons." The man said, "I have nothing (to feed them with)." Then a big basket full of dates was brought to the Prophet. The Prophet said, "Where is the questioner? Go and give this in charity." The man said, "(Shall I give this in charity) to a poorer person than I? By Allah, there is no family in between these two mountains (of Medina) who are poorer than we." The Prophet then smiled till his premolar teeth became visible, and said, "Then (feed) your (family with it)."

Volume 8, Book 73, Number 111:

Narrated Anas bin Malik:

While I was going along with Allah's Apostle who was wearing a Najrani Burd (sheet) with a thick border, a bedouin overtook the Prophet and pulled his Rida' (sheet) forcibly. I looked at the side of the shoulder of the Prophet and noticed that the edge of the Rida' had left a mark on it because of the violence of his pull. The bedouin said, "O Muhammad! Order for me some of Allah's property which you have." The Prophet turned towards him, (smiled) and ordered that he be given something.

Volume 8, Book 73, Number 112:

Narrated Jarir:

The Prophet did not screen himself from me (had never prevented me from entering upon him) since I embraced Islam, and whenever he saw me, he would receive me with a smile. Once I told him that I could not sit firm on horses. He stroked me on the chest with his hand, and said, "O Allah! Make him firm and make him a guiding and a rightly guided man.

Volume 8, Book 73, Number 113:

Narrated Zainab bint Um Salama:

Um Sulaim said, "O Allah's Apostle! Verily Allah is not shy of (telling you) the truth. Is it essential for a woman to take a bath after she had a wet dream (nocturnal sexual discharge)?" He said, "Yes, if she notices discharge. On that Um Salama laughed and said, "Does a woman get a (nocturnal sexual) discharge?" He said, "How then does (her) son resemble her (his mother)?"

Volume 8, Book 73, Number 114:

Narrated 'Aisha:

I never saw the Prophet laughing to an extent that one could see his palate, but he always used to smile only.

Volume 8, Book 73, Number 115:

Narrated Anas:

A man came to the Prophet on a Friday while he (the Prophet) was delivering a sermon at Medina, and said, "There is lack of rain, so please invoke your Lord to bless us with the rain." The Prophet looked at the sky when no cloud could be detected. Then he invoked Allah for rain. Clouds started gathering together and it rained till the Medina valleys started flowing with water. It continued raining till the next Friday. Then that man (or some other man) stood up while the Prophet was delivering the Friday sermon, and said, "We are drowned; Please invoke your Lord to withhold it (rain) from us" The Prophet smiled and said twice or thrice, "O Allah! Please let it rain round about us and not upon us." The clouds started dispersing over Medina to the right and to the left, and it rained round about Medina and not upon Medina. Allah showed them (the people) the miracle of His Prophet and His response to his invocation.

Volume 8, Book 73, Number 116:

Narrated 'Abdullah:

The Prophet said, "Truthfulness leads to righteousness, and righteousness leads to Paradise. And a man keeps on telling the truth until he becomes a truthful person. Falsehood leads to Al-Fajur (i.e.

wickedness, evil-doing), and Al-Fajur (wickedness) leads to the (Hell) Fire, and a man may keep on telling lies till he is written before Allah, a liar."

Volume 8, Book 73, Number 117:

Narrated Abu Huraira:

Allah's Apostle said, "The signs of a hypocrite are three: Whenever he speaks, he tells a lie; and whenever he promises, he breaks his promise; and whenever he is entrusted, he betrays (proves to be dishonest)".

Volume 8, Book 73, Number 118:

Narrated Samura bin Jundub:

The Prophet said, "I saw (in a dream), two men came to me." Then the Prophet narrated the story (saying), "They said, 'The person, the one whose cheek you saw being torn away (from the mouth to the ear) was a liar and used to tell lies and the people would report those lies on his authority till they spread all over the world. So he will be punished like that till the Day of Resurrection.'"

Volume 8, Book 73, Number 119:

Narrated Hudhaifa:

From among the people, Ibn Um 'Abd greatly resembled Allah's Apostles in solemn gate and good appearance of piety and in calmness and sobriety from the time he goes out of his house till he returns to it. But we do not know how he behaves with his family when he is alone with them.

Volume 8, Book 73, Number 120:

Narrated Tariq:

'Abdullah said, "The best talk is Allah's Book (Qur'an), and the best guidance is the guidance of Muhammad."

Volume 8, Book 73, Number 121:

Narrated Abu Musa:

The Prophet said: None is more patient than Allah against the harmful saying. He hears from the people they ascribe children to Him, yet He gives them health and (supplies them with) provision."

Volume 8, Book 73, Number 122.

Narrated 'Abdullah:

The Prophet divided and distributed something as he used to do for some of his distributions. A man from the Ansar said, "By Allah, in this division the pleasure of Allah has not been intended." I said, "I will definitely tell this to the Prophet ." So I went to him while he was sitting with his companions and told him of it secretly. That was hard upon the Prophet and the color of his face changed, and he became so angry that I wished I had not told him. The Prophet then said, "Moses was harmed with more than this, yet he remained patient."

Volume 8, Book 73, Number 123.

Narrated 'Aisha:

The Prophet did something and allowed his people to do it, but some people refrained from doing it. When the Prophet learned of that, he delivered a sermon, and after having sent Praises to Allah, he said, "What is wrong with such people as refrain from doing a thing that I do? By Allah, I know Allah better than they, and I am more afraid of Him than they."

Volume 8, Book 73, Number 124.

Narrated Abu Said Al-Khudri:

The Prophet was more shy than a virgin in her separate room. And if he saw a thing which he disliked, we would recognize that (feeling) in his face.

Volume 8, Book 73, Number 125d.

Narrated Abu Huraira:

Allah's Apostle said, "If a man says to his brother, O Kafir (disbeliever)!' Then surely one of them is such (i.e., a Kifir). "

Volume 8, Book 73, Number 125m.

Narrated 'Abdullah bin 'Umar:

Allah's Apostle said, 'If anyone says to his brother, 'O misbeliever! Then surely, one of them such."

Volume 8, Book 73, Number 126.

Narrated Thabit bin Ad-Dahhak:

The Prophet said, "Whoever swears by a religion other than Islam (i.e. if he swears by saying that he is a non-Muslim in case he is telling a lie), then he is as he says if his oath is false and whoever commits suicide with something, will be punished with the same thing in the (Hell) fire, and cursing a believer is like murdering him, and whoever accuses a believer of disbelief, then it is as if he had killed him."

Volume 8, Book 73, Number 127:

Narrated Jabir bin 'Abdullah:

Mu'adh bin Jabal used to pray with the Prophet and then go to lead his people in prayer. Once he led the people in prayer and recited Surat-al-Baqara. A man left (the row of the praying people) and offered (light) prayer (separately) and went away. When Mu'adh came to know about it, he said. "He (that man) is a hypocrite." Later that man heard what Mu'adh said about him, so he came to the Prophet and said, "O Allah's Apostle! We are people who work with our own hands and irrigate (our farms) with our camels. Last night Mu'adh led us in the (night) prayer and he recited Sura-al-Baqara, so I offered my prayer separately, and because of that, he accused me of being a hypocrite." The Prophet called Mu'adh and said thrice, "O Mu'adh! You are putting the people to trials? Recite 'Wash-shamsi wad-uhaha' (91) or'Sabbih isma Rabbi ka-l-A'la' (87) or the like."

Volume 8, Book 73, Number 128:

Narrated Abu Huraira:

Allah's Apostle said: "Whoever amongst you swears, (saying by error) in his oath 'By Al-Lat and Al-Uzza', then he should say, 'None has the right to be worshipped but Allah.' And whoever says to his companions, 'Come let me gamble' with you, then he must give something in charity (as an expiation for such a sin)." (See Hadith No. 645)

Volume 8, Book 73, Number 129:

Narrated Ibn 'Umar:

that he found 'Umar bin Al-Khattab in a group of people and he was swearing by his father. So Allah's Apostle called them, saying, "Verily! Allah forbids you to swear by your fathers. If one has to take an oath, he should swear by Allah or otherwise keep quiet."

Volume 8, Book 73, Number 130:

Narrated 'Aisha:

The Prophet entered upon me while there was a curtain having pictures (of animals) in the house. His face got red with anger, and then he got hold of the curtain and tore it into pieces. The Prophet said, "Such people as paint these pictures will receive the severest punishment on the Day of Resurrection ."

Volume 8, Book 73, Number 131:

Narrated Abu Mas'ud:

A man came to the Prophet and said "I keep away from the morning prayer only because such and such person prolongs the prayer when he leads us in it. The narrator added: I had never seen Allah's Apostle more furious in giving advice than he was on that day. He said, "O people! There are some among you who make others dislike good deeds) cause the others to have aversion (to congregational prayers). Beware! Whoever among you leads the people in prayer should not prolong it, because among them there are the sick, the old, and the needy." (See Hadith No. 670, Vol 1)

Volume 8, Book 73, Number 132:

Narrated 'Abdullah bin 'Umar:

While the Prophet was praying, he saw sputum (on the wall) of the mosque, in the direction of the Qibla, and so he scraped it off with his hand, and the sign of disgust (was apparent from his face) and then said, "Whenever anyone of you is in prayer, he should not spit in front of him (in prayer) because Allah is in front of him."

Volume 8, Book 73, Number 133:

Narrated Zaid bin Khalid Al-Juhani:

A man asked Allah's Apostle about "Al-Luqata" (a lost fallen purse or a thing picked up by somebody). The Prophet said, "You should announce it publicly for one year, and then remember and recognize the tying material of its container, and then you can spend it. If its owner came to you, then you should pay him its equivalent." The man said, "O Allah's Apostle! What about a lost sheep?" The Prophet said, "Take it because it is for you, for your brother, or for the wolf." The man again said, "O Allah's Apostle! What about a lost camel?" Allah's Apostle became very angry and furious and his cheeks became red (or his face became red), and he said, "You have nothing to do with it (the camel) for it has its food and its water container with it till it meets its owner."

Volume 8, Book 73, Number 134:

Narrated Zaid bin Thabit:

Allah's Apostle made a small room (with a palm leaf mat). Allah's Apostle came out (of his house) and prayed in it. Some men came and joined him in his prayer. Then again the next night they came for the prayer, but Allah's Apostle delayed and did not come out to them. So they raised their voices and knocked the door with small stones (to draw his attention). He came out to them in a state of anger, saying, "You are still insisting (on your deed, i.e. Tarawih prayer in the mosque) that I thought that this prayer (Tarawih) might become obligatory on you. So you people, offer this prayer at your homes, for the best prayer of a person is the one which he offers at home, except the compulsory (congregational) prayer."

Volume 8, Book 73, Number 135:

Narrated Abu Huraira:

Allah's Apostle said, "The strong is not the one who overcomes the people by his strength, but the strong is the one who controls himself while in anger."

Volume 8, Book 73, Number 136:

Narrated Sulaiman bin Sarad:

Two men abused each other in front of the Prophet while we were sitting with him. One of the two abused his companion furiously and his face became red. The Prophet said, "I know a word (sentence) the saying of which will cause him to relax if this man says it. Only if he said, 'I seek refuge with Allah from Satan, the outcast.' " So they said to that (furious) man, 'Don't you hear what the Prophet is saying?" He said, "I am not mad."

Volume 8, Book 73, Number 137:

Narrated Abu Huraira:

A man said to the Prophet , "Advise me! "The Prophet said, "Do not become angry and furious." The man asked (the same) again and again, and the Prophet said in each case, "Do not become angry and furious."

Volume 8, Book 73, Number 138:

Narrated Abu As-Sawar Al-Adawi:

'Imran bin Husain said, "The Prophet said, 'Haya' does not bring anything except good." Thereupon Bashir bin Ka'b said, 'It is written in the wisdom paper: Haya leads to solemnity; Haya leads to tranquility (peace of mind)." 'Imran said to him, "I am narrating to you the saying of Allah's Apostle and you are speaking about your paper (wisdom book)?"

Volume 8, Book 73, Number 139:

Narrated 'Abdullah bin 'Umar:

The Prophet passed by a man who was admonishing his brother regarding Haya and was saying, "You are very shy, and I am afraid that might harm you." On that, Allah's Apostle said, "Leave him, for Haya is (a part) of Faith."

Volume 8, Book 73, Number 140:

Narrated Abu Said:

The Prophet was shier than a veiled virgin girl. (See Hadith No. 762, Vol. 4)

Volume 8, Book 73, Number 141:

Narrated Abu Mas'ud:

The Prophet said, 'One of the sayings of the early Prophets which the people have got is: If you don't feel ashamed do whatever you like." (See Hadith No 690, 691, Vol 4)

Volume 8, Book 73, Number 142:

Narrated Um Salama:

Um Sulaim came to Allah's Apostle and said, "O Allah's Apostle! Verily, Allah does not feel shy to tell the truth. If a woman gets a nocturnal sexual discharge (has a wet dream), is it essential for her to take a bath? He replied, "Yes if she notices a discharge."

Volume 8, Book 73, Number 143:

Narrated Ibn 'Umar:

The Prophet said, "The example of a believer is like a green tree, the leaves of which do not fall." The people said. "It is such-and-such tree. It is such-and-such tree." I intended to say that it was the datepalm tree, but I was a young boy and felt shy (to answer). The Prophet said, "It is the date-palm tree." Ibn 'Umar added, " I told that to 'Umar who said, 'Had you said it, I would have preferred it to such-and such a thing."

Volume 8, Book 73, Number 144:

Narrated Thabit:

that he heard Anas saying, "A woman came to the Prophet offering herself to him in marriage, saying, "Have you got any interest in me (i.e. would you like to marry me?)" Anas's daughter said, "How shameless that woman was!" On that Anas said, "She is better than you for, she presented her-self to Allah's Apostle (for marriage)."

Volume 8, Book 73, Number 145:

Narrated Abu Musa:

that when Allah's Apostle sent him and Mu'adh bin Jabal to Yemen, he said to them, "Facilitate things for the people (treat the people in the most agreeable way), and do not make things difficult for them, and give them glad tidings, and let them not have aversion (i.e. to make the people hate good deeds) and you should both work in cooperation and mutual understanding, obey each other." Abu Musa said, "O Allah's Apostle! We are in a land in which a drink named Al Bit' is prepared from honey, and another drink named Al-Mizr is prepared from barley." On that, Allah's Apostle said, "All intoxicants (i.e. all alcoholic drinks) are prohibited."

Volume 8, Book 73, Number 146:

Narrated Anas bin Malik:

The Prophet said, "Make things easy for the people, and do not make it difficult for them, and make them calm (with glad tidings) and do not repulse (them)."

Volume 8, Book 73, Number 147:

Narrated 'Aisha:

Whenever Allah's Apostle was given the choice of one of two matters he would choose the easier of the two as long as it was not sinful to do so, but if it was sinful, he would not approach it. Allah's Apostle never took revenge over anybody for his own sake but (he did) only when Allah's legal bindings were outraged, in which case he would take revenge for Allah's sake." (See Hadith No. 760. Vol. 4)

Volume 8, Book 73, Number 148:

Narrated Al-Azraq bin Qais:

We were in the city of Al-Ahwaz on the bank of a river which had dried up. Then Abu Barza Al-Aslami came riding a horse and he started praying and let his horse loose. The horse ran away, so Abu Barza interrupted his prayer and went after the horse till he caught it and brought it, and then he offered his prayer. There was a man amongst us who was (from the Khawari) having a different opinion. He came saying. "Look at this old man! He left his prayer because of a horse." On that Abu Barza came to us and said, "Since the time I left Allah's Apostle, nobody has admonished me; My house is very far from this place, and if I had carried on praying and left my horse, I could not have reached my house till night." Then Abu Barza mentioned that he had been in the company of the Prophet, and that he had seen his leniency.

Volume 8, Book 73, Number 149:

Narrated Abu Huraira:

A bedouin urinated in the mosque, and the people rushed to beat him. Allah's Apostle ordered them to leave him and pour a bucket or a tumbler (full) of water over the place where he has passed urine. The Prophet then said, " You have been sent to make things easy (for the people) and you have not been sent to make things difficult for them."

Volume 8, Book 73, Number 150:

Narrated Anas bin Malik:

The Prophet used to mix with us to the extent that he would say to a younger brother of mine, 'O father of 'Umar! What did the Nughair (a kind of bird) do?"

Volume 8, Book 73, Number 151:

Narrated 'Aisha:

I used to play with the dolls in the presence of the Prophet, and my girl friends also used to play with me. When Allah's Apostle used to enter (my dwelling place) they used to hide themselves, but the Prophet would call them to join and play with me. (The playing with the dolls and similar images is forbidden, but it was allowed for 'Aisha at that time, as she was a little girl, not yet reached the age of puberty.) (Fateh-al-Bari page 143, Vol.13)

Volume 8, Book 73, Number 152:

Narrated Aisha:

A man asked permission to see the Prophet. He said, "Let Him come in; What an evil man of the tribe he is! (Or, What an evil brother of the tribe he is)."

But when he entered, the Prophet spoke to him gently in a polite manner. I said to him, "O Allah's Apostle! You have said what you have said, then you spoke to him in a very gentle and polite manner? The Prophet said, "The worse people, in the sight of Allah are those whom the people leave (undisturbed) to save themselves from their dirty language."

Volume 8, Book 73, Number 153:

Narrated 'Abdullah bin Abu Mulaika:

The Prophet was given a gift of a few silken cloaks with gold buttons. He distributed them amongst some of his companions and put aside one of them for Makhrama. When Makhrama came, the

Prophet said, "I kept this for you." (Aiyub, the sub-narrator held his garment to show how the Prophet showed the cloak to Makhrama who had something unfavorable about his temper.)

Volume 8, Book 73, Number 154:

Narrated Abu Huraira:

The Prophet said, "A believer is not stung twice (by something) out of one and the same hole."

Volume 8, Book 73, Number 155:

Narrated 'Abdullah bin 'Amr:

Allah's Apostle entered upon me and said, "Have I not been informed that you offer prayer all the night and fast the whole day?" I said, "Yes." He said, "Do not do so; Offer prayer at night and also sleep; Fast for a few days and give up fasting for a few days because your body has a right on you, and your eye has a right on you, and your guest has a right on you, and your wife has a right on you. I hope that you will have a long life, and it is sufficient for you to fast for three days a month as the reward of a good deed, is multiplied ten times, that means, as if you fasted the whole year." I insisted (on fasting more) so I was given a hard instruction. I said, "I can do more than that (fasting)" The Prophet said, "Fast three days every week." But as I insisted (on fasting more) so I was burdened. I said, "I can fast more than that." The Prophet said, "Fast as Allah's prophet David used to fast." I said, "How was the fasting of the prophet David?" The Prophet said, "One half of a year (i.e. he used to fast on alternate days). '

Volume 8, Book 73, Number 156:

Narrated Abu Shuraih Al-Ka'bi:

Allah's Apostle said, Whoever believes in Allah and the Last Day, should serve his guest generously. The guest's reward is: To provide him with a superior type of food for a night and a day and a guest is to be entertained with food for three days, and whatever is offered beyond that, is regarded as something given in charity. And it is not lawful for a guest to stay with his host for such a long period so as to put him in a critical position."

Volume 8, Book 73, Number 157:

Narrated Malik:

Similarly as above (156) adding, "Who believes in Allah and the Last Day should talk what is good or keep quiet." (i.e. abstain from dirty and evil talk, and should think before uttering).

Volume 8, Book 73, Number 158:

Narrated Abu Huraira:

The Prophet said, "Whoever believes in Allah and the Last Day, should not hurt his neighbor and whoever believes in Allah and the Last Day, should serve his guest generously and whoever believes in Allah and the Last Day, should talk what is good or keep quiet."

Volume 8, Book 73, Number 159:

Narrated Uqba bin 'Amir:

We said, "O Allah's Apostle! You send us out and it happens that we have to stay with such people as do not entertain us. What do you think about it?" Allah's Apostle said to us, "If you stay with some people and they entertain you as they should for a guest, accept is; but if they do not do then you should take from them the right of the guest, which they ought to give."

Volume 8, Book 73, Number 160:

Narrated Abu Huraira:

The Prophet said, "Whoever believes in Allah and the Last Day, should serve his guest generously; and whoever believes in Allah and the Last Day, should unite the bond of kinship (i.e. keep good relation with his Kith and kin); and whoever believes in Allah and the Last Day, should talk what is good or keep quit. "

Volume 8, Book 73, Number 161:

Narrated Abu Juhaifa:

The Prophet established a bond of brotherhood between Salman and Abu Darda'. Salman paid a visit to Abu ad-Darda and found Um Ad-Darda' dressed in shabby clothes and asked her why she was in that state.?" She replied, "Your brother, Abu Ad-Darda is not interested in the luxuries of this world." In the meantime Abu Ad-Darda came and prepared a meal for him (Salman), and said to him, "(Please) eat for I am fasting." Salman said, "I am not going to eat, unless you eat." So Abu Ad-Darda' ate. When it was night, Abu Ad-Darda' got up (for the night prayer). Salman said (to him), "Sleep," and he slept. Again Abu-Ad-Darda' got up (for the prayer), and Salman said (to him), "Sleep." When it was the last part of the night, Salman said to him, "Get up now (for the prayer)." So both of them offered their prayers and Salman said to Abu Ad-Darda','"Your Lord has a right on you; and your soul has a right on you; and your family has a right on you; so you should give the rights of all those who have a right on you). Later on Abu Ad-Darda' visited the Prophet and mentioned that to him. The Prophet, said, "Salman has spoken the truth."

Volume 8, Book 73, Number 162:

Narrated 'Abdur-Rahman bin Abu Bakr:

Abu Bakr invited a group of people and told me, "Look after your guests." Abu Bakr added, I am going to visit the Prophet and you should finish serving them before I return." 'Abdur-Rahman said, So I went at once and served them with what was available at that time in the house and requested them to eat." They said, "Where is the owner of the house (i.e., Abu Bakr)?" 'Abdur-Rahman said, "Take your meal." They said, "We will not eat till the owner of the house comes." 'Abdur-Rahman said, "Accept your meal from us, for if my father comes and finds you not having taken your meal yet, we will be blamed severely by him, but they refused to take their meals . So I was sure that my father would be angry with me. When he came, I went away (to hide myself) from him. He asked, "What have you done (about the guests)?" They informed him the whole story. Abu Bakr called, "O 'Abdur Rahman!" I kept quiet. He then called again. "O 'Abdur-Rahman!" I kept quiet and he called again, "O ignorant (boy)! I beseech you by Allah, if you hear my voice, then come out!" I came out and said, "Please ask your guests (and do not be angry with me)." They said, "He has told the truth; he brought the meal to us." He said, "As you have been waiting for me, by Allah, I will not eat of it tonight." They said, "By Allah, we will not eat of it till you eat of it." He said, I have never seen a night like this night in evil. What is wrong with you? Why don't you accept your meals of hospitality from us?" (He said to me), "Bring your meal." I brought it to him, and he put his hand in it, saying, "In the name of Allah. The first (state of fury) was because of Satan." So Abu Bakr ate and so did his guests.

Volume 8, Book 73, Number 163:

Narrated 'Abdur-Rahman bin Abu Bakr:

Abu Bakr came with a guest or some guests, but he stayed late at night with the Prophet and when he came, my mother said (to him), "Have you been detained from your guest or guests tonight?" He said, "Haven't you served the supper to them?" She replied, "We presented the meal to him (or to them), but he (or they) refused to eat." Abu Bakr became angry, rebuked me and invoked Allah to cause (my) ears to be cut and swore not to eat of it!" I hid myself, and he called me, "O ignorant (boy)!" Abu Bakr's wife swore that she would not eat of it and so the guests or the guest swore that they would not eat of it till he ate of it. Abu Bakr said, "All that happened was from Satan." So he asked for the meals and ate of it, and so did they. Whenever they took a handful of the meal, the meal grew (increased) from underneath more than that mouthful. He said (to his wife), "O, sister of Bani Firas! What is this?" She said, "O, pleasure of my eyes! The meal is now more than it had been before we started eating" So they ate of it and sent the rest of that meal to the Prophet. It is said that the Prophet also ate of it.

Volume 8, Book 73, Number 164:

Narrated Rafi bin Khadij and Sahl bin Abu Hathma:

'Abdullah bin Sahl and Muhaiyisa bin Mas'ud went to Khaibar and they dispersed in the gardens of the date-palm trees. 'Abdullah bin Sahl was murdered. Then 'Abdur-Rahman bin Sahl, Huwaiyisa and Muhaiyisa, the two sons of Mas'ud, came to the Prophet and spoke about the case of their (murdered) friend. 'Abdur-Rahman who was the youngest of them all, started talking. The Prophet said, "Let the older (among you) speak first." So they spoke about the case of their (murdered) friend. The Prophet said, "Will fifty of you take an oath whereby you will have the right to receive the blood money of your murdered man," (or said, "..your companion"). They said, "O Allah's Apostle! The murder was a thing we did not witness." The Prophet said, "Then the Jews will release you from the oath, if fifty of them (the Jews) should take an oath to contradict your claim." They said, "O Allah's Apostle! They are disbelievers (and they will take a false oath)." Then Allah's Apostle himself paid the blood money to them.

Volume 8, Book 73, Number 165:

Narrated Ibn 'Umar:

Allah's Apostle said, "Inform me of a tree which resembles a Muslim, giving its fruits at every season by the permission of its Lord, and the leaves of which do not fall." I thought of the date-palm tree, but I disliked to speak because Abu Bakr and 'Umar were present there. When nobody spoke, the Prophet said, "It is the date-palm tree" When I came out with my father, I said, "O father! It came to my mind that it was the date-palm tree." He said, "What prevented you from saying it?" Had you said it, it would have been more dearer to me than such-and-such a thing (fortune)." I said, "Nothing prevented me but the fact that neither you nor Abu Bakr spoke, so I disliked to speak (in your presence)."

Volume 8, Book 73, Number 166:

Narrated Ubai bin Ka'b:

Allah's Apostle said, "Some poetry contains wisdom."

Volume 8, Book 73, Number 167:

Narrated Jundub:

While the Prophet was walking, a stone hit his foot and stumbled and his toe was injured. He then (quoting a poetic verse) said, "You are not more than a toe which

Volume 8, Book 73, Number 168:

Narrated Abu Huraira:

The Prophet said, "The most true words said by a poet were the words of Labid. He said, i.e. 'Verily, everything except Allah is perishable and Umaiya bin Abi As-Salt was about to embrace Islam '

Volume 8, Book 73, Number 169:

Narrated Salama bin Al-Aqwa:

We went out with Allah's Apostle to Khaibar and we travelled during the night. A man amongst the people said to 'Amir bin Al-Aqwa', "Won't you let us hear your poetry?" 'Amir was a poet, and so he got down and started (chanting Huda) reciting for the people, poetry that keep pace with the camel's foot steps, saying, "O Allah! Without You we would not have been guided on the right path, neither would we have given in charity, nor would we have prayed. So please forgive us what we have committed. Let all of us be sacrificed for Your cause and when we meet our enemy, make our feet firm and bestow peace and calmness on us and if they (our enemy) will call us towards an unjust thing we will refuse.

The infidels have made a hue and cry to ask others help against us. Allah's Apostle said, "Who is that driver (of the camels)?" They said, "He is 'Amir bin Al-Aqwa." He said, "May Allah bestow His mercy on him." A man among the people said, Has Martyrdom been granted to him, O Allah's Prophet! Would that you let us enjoy his company longer." We reached (the people of) Khaibar and besieged them till we were stricken with severe hunger but Allah helped the Muslims conquer Khaibar. In the evening of its conquest the people made many fires. Allah's Apostle asked, "What are those fires? For what are you making fires?" They said, "For cooking meat." He asked, "What kind of meat?" They said, "Donkeys' meat." Allah's Apostle said, "Throw away the meat and break the cooking pots." A man said, O Allah's Apostle! Shall we throw away the meat and wash the cooking pots?" He said, "You can do that too." When the army files aligned in rows (for the battle), 'Amir's sword was a short one, and while attacking a Jew with it in order to hit him, the sharp edge of the sword turned back and hit 'Amir's knee and caused him to die.

When the Muslims returned (from the battle), Salama said, Allah's Apostle saw me pale and said, 'What is wrong with you?" I said, "Let my parents be sacrificed for you! The people claim that all the deeds of Amir have been annulled." The Prophet asked, "Who said so?" I replied, "So-and-so and so-and-so and Usaid bin Al-Hudair Al-Ansari said, 'Whoever says so is telling a lie. Verily, 'Amir will have double reward."' (While speaking) the Prophet put two of his fingers together to indicate that, and added, "He was really a hard-working man and a Mujahid (devout fighter in Allah's Cause) and rarely have there lived in it (i.e., Medina or the battle-field) an "Arab like him."

Volume 8, Book 73, Number 170:

Narrated Anas bin Malik:

The Prophet came to some of his wives among whom there was Um Sulaim, and said, "May Allah be merciful to you, O Anjasha! Drive the camels slowly, as they are carrying glass vessels!" Abu Qalaba said, "The Prophet said a sentence (i.e. the above metaphor) which, had anyone of you said it, you would have admonished him for it".

Volume 8, Book 73, Number 171:

Narrated 'Aisha:

Hassan bin Thabit asked the permission of Allah's Apostle to lampoon the pagans (in verse). Allah's Apostle said, "What about my fore-fathers (ancestry)?" Hassan said (to the Prophet) "I will take you out of them as a hair is taken out of dough."

Narrated Hisham bin 'Urwa that his father said, "I called Hassan with bad names in front of 'Aisha." She said, "Don't call him with bad names because he used to defend Allah's Apostle (against the pagans)."

Volume 8, Book 73, Number 172:

Narrated Al-Haitham bin Abu Sinan:

that he heard Abu Huraira in his narration, mentioning that the Prophet said, "A Muslim brother of yours who does not say dirty words." and by that he meant Ibn Rawaha, "said (in verse): 'We have Allah's Apostle with us who recites the Holy Qur'an in the early morning time. He gave us guidance and light while we were blind and astray, so our hearts are sure that whatever he says, will certainly happen. He does not touch his bed at night, being busy in worshipping Allah while the pagans are sound asleep in their beds.' "

Volume 8, Book 73, Number 173:

Narrated Abu Salama bin 'Abdur-Rahman bin 'Auf:

that he heard Hassan bin Thabit Al-Ansari asking the witness of Abu Huraira, saying, "O Abu-Huraira! I beseech you by Allah (to tell me). Did you hear Allah's Apostle saying' 'O Hassan ! Reply on behalf of Allah's Apostle. O Allah ! Support him (Hassan) with the Holy Spirit (Gabriel).'?" Abu Huraira said, "Yes."

Volume 8, Book 73, Number 174:

Narrated Al-Bara:

The Prophet said to Hassan, "Lampoon them (the pagans) in verse, and Gabriel is with you."

Volume 8, Book 73, Number 175:

Narrated Ibn 'Umar:

The Prophet said, "It is better for a man to fill the inside of his body with pus than to fill it with poetry."

Volume 8, Book 73, Number 176:

Narrated Abu Huraira:

Allah's Apostle; said, "It is better for anyone of you that the inside of his body be filled with pus which may consume his body, than it be filled with poetry."

Volume 8, Book 73, Number 177:

Narrated 'Aisha:

Allah, the brother of Abu Al-Qu'ais asked my permission to enter after the verses of Al-Hijab (veiling the ladies) was revealed, and I said, "By Allah, I will not admit him unless I take permission of Allah's Apostle for it was not the brother of Al-Qu'ais who had suckled me, but it was the wife of Al-Qu'ais, who had suckled me." Then Allah's Apostle entered upon me, and I said, "O Allah's Apostle! The man has not nursed me but his wife has nursed me." He said, "Admit him because he is your uncle (not from blood relation, but because you have been nursed by his wife), Taribat Yaminuki." 'Urwa said, "Because of this reason, ' Aisha used to say: Foster suckling relations render all those things (marriages etc.) illegal which are illegal because of the corresponding blood relations." (See Hadith No. 36, Vol. 7)

Volume 8, Book 73, Number 178:

Narrated 'Aisha:

The Prophet intended to return home after the performance of the Hajj, and he saw Safiya standing at the entrance of her tent, depressed and sad because she got her menses. The Prophet said, "Aqra Halqa! --An expression used in the Quraish dialect--"You will detain us." The Prophet then asked (her), "Did you perform the Tawaf Al-Ifada on the Day of Sacrifice (10th of Dhul-Hijja)?" She said, "Yes." The Prophet said, "Then you can leave (with us)."

Volume 8, Book 73, Number 179:

Narrated Um Hani:

(the daughter of Abu Talib) I visited Allah's Apostle in the year of the Conquest of Mecca and found him taking a bath, and his daughter, Fatima was screening him. When I greeted him, he said, "Who is it?" I replied, "I am Um Hani, the daughter of Abu Talib." He said, "Welcome, O Um Hani ! " When the Prophet had finished his bath, he stood up and offered eight Rakat of prayer while he was wrapped in a single garment. When he had finished his prayer, I said, "O Allah's Apostle! My maternal brother assumes (or claims) that he will murder some man whom I have given shelter, i.e., so-and-so bin Hubaira." Allah's Apostle said, "O Um Hani! We shelter him whom you have sheltered." Um Hani added, "That happened in the forenoon."

Volume 8, Book 73, Number 180:

Narrated Anas:

The Prophet saw a man driving a Badana (a camel for sacrifice) and said (to him). "Ride it." The man said, "It is a Bandana." The Prophet said, "Ride on it." The man said, "It is a Bandana." The Prophet said, Ride on it, woe to you!"

Volume 8, Book 73, Number 181:

Narrated Abu Huraira:

Allah's Apostle saw a man driving a Badana (a camel for sacrifice) and said to him, "Ride on it." The man said, "O Allah's Apostle! It is a Bandana." The Prophet said, "Ride on it, woe to you!" on the second or third time.

Volume 8, Book 73, Number 182:

Narrated Anas bin Malik:

Allah's Apostle was on a journey and he had a black slave called Anjasha, and he was driving the camels (very fast, and there were women riding on those camels). Allah's Apostle said, "Waihaka (May Allah be merciful to you), O Anjasha! Drive slowly (the camels) with the glass vessels (women)!"

Volume 8, Book 73, Number 183:

Narrated Abu Bakra:

A man praised another man in front of the Prophet. The Prophet said thrice, "Wailaka (Woe on you) ! You have cut the neck of your brother!" The Prophet added, "If it is indispensable for anyone of you to praise a person, then he should say, "I think that such-and-such person (is so-and-so), and Allah is the one who will take his accounts (as he knows his reality) and none can sanctify anybody before Allah (and that only if he knows well about that person.)".

Volume 8, Book 73, Number 184:

Narrated Abu Said Al-Khudri:

While the Prophet was distributing (war booty etc.) one day, Dhul Khawaisira, a man from the tribe of Bani Tamim, said, "O Allah's Apostle! Act justly." The Prophets said, "Woe to you! Who else would act justly if I did not act justly?" 'Umar said (to the Prophet), "Allow me to chop his neck off." The Prophet said, "No, for he has companions (who are apparently so pious that) if anyone of (you compares his prayer with) their prayer, he will consider his prayer inferior to theirs, and similarly his fasting inferior to theirs, but they will desert Islam (go out of religion) as an arrow goes through the victim's body (games etc.) in which case if its Nasl is examined nothing will be seen thereon, and if its Nady is examined, nothing will be seen thereon, and if its Qudhadh is examined, nothing will be seen thereon, for the arrow has gone out too fast even for the excretions and blood to smear over it. Such people will come out at the time of difference among the (Muslim) people and the sign by which they will be recognized, will be a man whose one of the two hands will look like the breast of a woman or a lump of flesh moving loosely." Abu Said added, "I testify that I heard that from the Prophet and also testify that I was with 'Ali when 'Ali fought against those people. The man described by the Prophet was searched for among the killed, and was found, and he was exactly as the Prophet had described him." (See Hadith No. 807, Vol. 4)

Volume 8, Book 73, Number 185:

Narrated Abu Huraira:

A man came to Allah's Apostle and said, "O Allah's Apostle! I am ruined!" The Prophet said, "Waihaka (May Allah be merciful to you) !" The man said, "I have done sexual intercourse with my wife while fasting in Ramadan." The Prophet said, "Manumit a slave." The man said, " I cannot afford that. " The Prophet said; "Then fast for two successive months." The man said, " I have no power to do so." The Prophet said, "Then feed sixty poor persons." The man said, "I have nothing (to feed sixty persons). Later a basket full of dates were brought to the Prophet and he said (to the man), "Take it and give it in charity." The man said, "O Allah's Apostle! Shall I give it to people other than my family? By Him in Whose Hand my life is, there is nobody poorer than me in the whole city of Medina." The Prophet smiled till his premolar teeth became visible, and said, "Take it." Az-Zuhri said (that the Prophet said). "Wailaka."

Volume 8, Book 73, Number 186:

Narrated Abu Sa'id Al-Khudri:

A bedouin said, "O Allah's Apostle! Inform me about the emigration." The Prophet said, "Waihaka (May Allah be merciful to you)! The question of emigration is a difficult one. Have you got some camels?" The bedouin said, "Yes." The Prophet said, "Do you pay their Zakat?" He said, "Yes." The

Prophet said, "Go on doing like this from beyond the seas, for Allah will not let your deeds go in vain."

Volume 8, Book 73, Number 187:

Narrated Ibn 'Umar:

The Prophet said, "Wailakum" (woe to you) or "waihakum" (May Allah be merciful to you)." Shu'ba is not sure as to which was the right word. "Do not become disbelievers after me by cutting the necks of one another."

Volume 8, Book 73, Number 188:

Narrated Anas:

A bedouin came to the Prophet and said, "O Allah's Apostle! When will The Hour be established?" The Prophet said, "Wailaka (Woe to you), What have you prepared for it?" The bedouin said, "I have not prepared anything for it, except that I love Allah and H is Apostle." The Prophet said, "You will be with those whom you love." We (the companions of the Prophet) said, "And will we too be so? The Prophet said, "Yes." So we became very glad on that day. In the meantime, a slave of Al-Mughira passed by, and he was of the same age as I was. The Prophet said. "If this (slave) should live long, he will not reach the geriatric old age, but the Hour will be established."

Volume 8, Book 73, Number 189:

Narrated 'Abdullah:

The Prophet said, "Everyone will be with those whom he loves."

Volume 8, Book 73, Number 190:

Narrated 'Abdullah bin Mas'ud:

A man came to Allah's Apostle and said, "O Allah's Apostle! What do you say about a man who loves some people but cannot catch up with their good deeds?" Allah's Apostle said, "Everyone will be with those whom he loves."

Volume 8, Book 73, Number 191:

Narrated Abu Musa:

It was said to the Prophet; , "A man may love some people but he cannot catch up with their good deeds?" The Prophet said, "Everyone will be with those whom he loves."

Volume 8, Book 73, Number 192.

Narrated Anas bin Malik.

A man asked the Prophet "When will the Hour be established O Allah's Apostle?" The Prophet . said, "What have you prepared for it?" The man said, " I haven't prepared for it much of prayers or fast or alms, but I love Allah and His Apostle." The Prophet said, "You will be with those whom you love."

Volume 8, Book 73, Number 193.

Narrated Ibn 'Abbas.

Allah's Apostle said to Ibn Saiyad "I have hidden something for you in my mind; What is it?" He said, "Ad-Dukh." The Prophet said, "Ikhsa."

Volume 8, Book 73, Number 194.

Narrated 'Abdullah bin 'Umar.

'Umar bin Al-Khattab set out with Allah's Apostle, and a group of his companions to Ibn Saiyad. They found him playing with the boys in the fort or near the Hillocks of Bani Maghala. Ibn Saiyad was nearing his puberty at that time, and he did not notice the arrival of the Prophet till Allah's Apostle stroked him on the back with his hand and said, "Do you testify that I am Allah's Apostle?" Ibn Saiyad looked at him and said, "I testify that you are the Apostle of the unlettered ones (illiterates)". Then Ibn Saiyad said to the Prophets . "Do you testify that I am Allah's Apostle?" The Prophet denied that, saying, "I believe in Allah and all His Apostles," and then said to Ibn Saiyad, "What do you see?" Ibn Saiyad said, "True people and liars visit me." The Prophet said, "You have been confused as to this matter." Allah's Apostle added, "I have kept something for you (in my mind)." Ibn Saiyad said, "Ad-Dukh." The Prophet said, "Ikhsa (you should be ashamed) for you can not cross your limits." 'Umar said, "O Allah's Apostle! Allow me to chop off h is neck." Allah's Apostle said (to Umar). "Should this person be him (i.e. Ad-Dajjal) then you cannot over-power him; and should he be someone else, then it will be no use your killing him." 'Abdullah bin 'Umar added. Later on Allah's Apostle and Ubai bin Ka'b Al-Ansari (once again) went to the garden in which Ibn Saiyad was present.

When Allah's Apostle entered the garden, he started hiding behind the trunks of the date-palms intending to hear something from Ibn Saiyad before the latter could see him. Ibn Saiyad was Lying on his bed, covered with a velvet sheet from where his mumur were heard. Ibn Saiyad's mother saw the Prophet and said, "O Saf (the nickname of Ibn Saiyad)! Here is Muhammad!" Ibn Saiyad stopped his murmuring. The Prophet said, "If his mother had kept quiet, then I would have learnt more about him." 'Abdullah added. Allah's Apostle stood up before the people (delivering a sermon), and after praising and glorifying Allah as He deserved, he mentioned the Ad-Dajjal saying, "I warn you against him, and there has been no prophet but warned his followers against him. Noah warned his followers against him but I am telling you about him, something which no prophet has told his people of, and that is: Know that he is blind in one eye where as Allah is not so."

Volume 8, Book 73, Number 195:

Narrated Ibn 'Abbas:

When the delegation of 'Abdul Qais came to the Prophet, he said, "Welcome, O the delegation who have come! Neither you will have disgrace, nor you will regret." They said, "O Allah's Apostle! We are a group from the tribe of Ar-Rabi'a, and between you and us there is the tribe of Mudar and we cannot come to you except in the sacred months. So please order us to do something good (religious deeds) so that we may enter Paradise by doing that, and also that we may order our people who are behind us (whom we have left behind at home) to follow it." He said, "Four and four:" offer prayers perfectly , pay the Zakat, (obligatory charity), fast the month of Ramadan, and give one-fifth of the war booty (in Allah's cause), and do not drink in (containers called) Ad-Duba,' Al-Hantam, An-Naqir and Al-Muzaffat."

Volume 8, Book 73, Number 196:

Narrated Ibn 'Umar:

The Prophet said, "For every betrayer (perfidious person), a flag will be raised on the Day of Resurrection, and it will be announced (publicly) 'This is the betrayal (perfidy) of so-and-so, the son of so-and-so.' "

Volume 8, Book 73, Number 197:

Narrated Ibn 'Umar:

Allah's Apostle said, "A flag will be fixed on the Day of Resurrection for every betrayer, and it will be announced (publicly in front of everybody), 'This is the betrayal (perfidy) so-and-so, the son of so-and-so."

Volume 8, Book 73, Number 198:

Narrated 'Aisha:

The Prophet said, "None of you should say Khabuthat Nafsi, but he is recommended to say 'Laqisat Nafsi."

Volume 8, Book 73, Number 199:

Narrated Sal:

The Prophet said, "None of you should say Khabuthat Nafsi but he is recommended to say 'Laqisat Nafsi (See Hadith No. 202)

Volume 8, Book 73, Number 200:

Narrated Abu Huraira:

Allah's Apostle said, "Allah said, "The offspring of Adam abuse the Dahr (Time), and I am the Dahr; in My Hands are the night and the day." !

Volume 8, Book 73, Number 201:

Narrated Abu Huraira: The Prophet said, "Don't call the grapes Al-Karm, and don't say 'Khai

Volume 8, Book 73, Number 202:

Narrated Abu Huraira:

Allah's Apostle said, "They say Al-Karm (the generous), and in fact Al-Karm is the heart of a be-liever."

Volume 8, Book 73, Number 203:

Narrated 'Ali:

I never heard Allah's Apostle saying, "Let my father and mother be sacrificed for you," except for Sa'd (bin Abi Waqqas). I heard him saying, "Throw! (arrows), Let my father and mother be sacrificed for you !" (The sub-narrator added, "I think that was in the battle of Uhud.")

Volume 8, Book 73, Number 204:

Narrated Anas bin Malik:

That he and Abu Talha were coming in the company of the Prophet towards Medina), while Safiya (the Prophet's wife) was riding behind him on his she-camel. After they had covered a portion of the way suddenly the foot of the she-camel slipped and both the Prophet and the woman (i.e., his wife, Safiya) fell down. Abu Talha jumped quickly off his camel and came to the Prophet (saying.) "O Al-lah's Apostle! Let Allah sacrifice me for you! Have you received any injury?" The Prophet said, "No, but take care of the woman (my wife)." Abu Talha covered his face with his garment and went to-wards her and threw his garment over her. Then the woman got up and Abu Talha prepared their she camel (by tightening its saddle, etc.) and both of them (the Prophet and Safiya) mounted it. Then all of them proceeded and when they approached near Medina, or saw Medina, the Prophet said, "Ayibun,' abidun, taibun, liRabbina hamidun (We are coming back (to Medina) with repentance, worshipping (our Lord) and celebrating His (our Lord's) praises". The Prophet continued repeating these words till he entered the city of Medina.

Volume 8, Book 73, Number 205:

Narrated Jabir:

A boy was born for a man among us, and the man named him Al-Qasim. We said to him, "We will not call you Abu-l-Qasim, nor will we respect you for that." The Prophet was informed about that, and he said, "Name your son 'Abdur-Rahman."

Volume 8, Book 73, Number 206:

Narrated Jabi:

A man among us begot a boy whom he named Al-Qasim. The people said, "We will not call him (i.e., the father) by that Kuniya (Abu-l-Qasim) till we ask the Prophet about it. The Prophet said. "Name yourselves by my name, but do not call (yourselves) by my Kuniya."

Volume 8, Book 73, Number 207:

Narrated Abu Huraira:

Abu-l-Qasim (The Prophet) said, "Name yourselves by my name, but do not call yourselves by my Kuniya."

Volume 8, Book 73, Number 208:

Narrated Jabir bin 'Abdullah:

A man among us begot a boy whom he named Al-Qasim. The people said (to him), "We will not call you Abul-1-Qasim, nor will we please you by calling you so." The man came to the Prophet and mentioned that to him. The Prophet said to him, "Name your son 'Abdur-Rahman."

Volume 8, Book 73, Number 209:

Narrated Al-Musaiyab:

That his father (Hazn bin Wahb) went to the Prophet and the Prophet asked (him), "What is your name?" He replied, "My name is Hazn." The Prophet said, "You are Sahl." Hazn said, "I will not change the name with which my father has named me." Ibn Al-Musaiyab added: We have had roughness (in character) ever since.

Volume 8, Book 73, Number 210:

Narrated Al-Musaiyab:

on the authority of his father similarly as above (i.e., 209).

Volume 8, Book 73, Number 211:

Narrated Sahl:

When Al-Mundhir bin Abu Usaid was born, he was brought to the Prophet who placed him on his thigh. While Abu Usaid was sitting there, the Prophet was busy with something in his hands so Abu Usaid told someone to take his son from the thigh of the Prophet . When the Prophet finished his job (with which he was busy), he said, "Where is the boy?" Abu Usaid replied, "We have sent him home." The Prophet said, "What is his name?" Abu Usaid said, "(His name is) so-and-so. " The Prophet said, "No, his name is Al-Mundhir." So he called him Al-Mundhir from that day.

Volume 8, Book 73, Number 212:

Narrated Abu Huraira:

Zainab's original name was "Barrah," but it was said' "By that she is giving herself the prestige of piety." So the Prophet changed her name to Zainab.

Volume 8, Book 73, Number 213:

Narrated Said bin Al-Musaiyab:

That when his grandfather, Hazn visited the Prophet the Prophet said (to him), "What is your name?" He said, "My name is Hazn." The Prophet said, " But you are Sahl." He said, "I will not change my name with which my father named me." Ibn Al-Musaiyab added: So we have had roughness (in character) ever since.

Volume 8, Book 73, Number 214:

Narrated Isma'il:

I asked Abi Aufa, "Did you see Ibrahim, the son of the Prophet ?" He said, "Yes, but he died in his early childhood. Had there been a Prophet after Muhammad then his son would have lived, but there is no Prophet after him."

Volume 8, Book 73, Number 215:

Narrated Al-Bara:

When Ibrahim (the son of the Prophet) died, Allah's Apostle said, "There is a wet nurse for him in Paradise."

Volume 8, Book 73, Number 216:

Narrated Jabir bin 'Abdullah Al-Ansari:

Allah's Apostle said, "Name yourselves after me (by my name) but do not call (yourselves) by my Kuniya (1), for I am Al-Qasim (distributor), and I distribute among you Allah's blessings." This narration has also come on the authority of Anas that the Prophet said so."

Volume 8, Book 73, Number 217:

Narrated Abu Huraira:

The Prophet said, "Name yourselves after me (by my name), but do not call yourselves by my Kuniya, and whoever sees me in a dream, he surely sees me, for Satan cannot impersonate me (appear in my figure). And whoever intentionally ascribes something to me falsely, he will surely take his place in the (Hell) Fire.

Volume 8, Book 73, Number 218:

Narrated Abu Musa:

I got a son and I took him to the Prophet who named him Ibrahim, and put in his mouth the juice of a date fruit (which be himself had chewed?, and invoked for Allah's blessing upon him, and then gave him back to me. He was the eldest son of Abii Musa.

Volume 8, Book 73, Number 219:

Narrated Al-Mughira bin Shuba:

Solar eclipse occurred on the day of Ibrahim's death (the Prophet's son).

Volume 8, Book 73, Number 220:

Narrated 'Aisha:

(the wife the Prophet) Allah's Apostle said, "O Aisha! This is Gabriel sending his greetings to you." I said, "Peace, and Allah's Mercy be on him." 'Aisha added: The Prophet used to see things which we used not to see.

Volume 8, Book 73, Number 221:

Narrated Anas:

Once Um Sulaim was (with the women who were) in charge of the luggage on a journey, and An-jashah, the slave of the Prophet, was driving their camels (very fast). The Prophet said, "O Anjash! Drive slowly (the camels) with the glass vessels (i.e., ladies)."

Volume 8, Book 73, Number 222:

Narrated Anas:

The Prophet was the best of all the people in character. I had a brother called Abu 'Umar, who, I think, had been newly weaned. Whenever he (that child) was brought to the Prophet the Prophet used to say, "O Abu 'Umar! What did Al-Nughair (nightingale) (do)?" It was a nightingale with which he used to play. Sometimes the time of the Prayer became due while he (the Prophet) was in our house. He would order that the carpet underneath him be swept and sprayed with water, and then he would stand up (for the prayer) and we would line up behind him, and he would lead us in prayer.

Volume 8, Book 73, Number 223:

Narrated Sahl bin Sad:

The most beloved names to 'Ali was Abu Turab, and he used to be pleased when we called him by it, for none named him Abu Turab (for the first time), but the Prophet. Once 'Ali got angry with (his wife) Fatima, and went out (of his house) and slept near a wall in the mosque. The Prophet came searching for him, and someone said, "He is there, Lying near the wall." The Prophet came to him while his ('Ali's) back was covered with dust. The Prophet started removing the dust from his back, saying, "Get up, O Abu Turab!"

Volume 8, Book 73, Number 224:

Narrated Abu Huraira:

Allah's Apostle said, "The most awful name in Allah's sight on the Day of Resurrection, will be (that of) a man calling himself Malik Al-Amlak (the king of kings)."

Volume 8, Book 73, Number 225:

Narrated Abu Huraira:

The Prophet said, "The most awful (meanest) name in Allah's sight." Sufyan said more than once, "The most awful (meanest) name in Allah's sight is (that of) a man calling himself king of kings."

Sufyan said, "Somebody else (i.e. other than Abu Az-Zinad, a sub-narrator) says: What is meant by 'The king of kings' is 'Shahan Shah.,"

Volume 8, Book 73, Number 226:

Narrated Usama bin Zaid:

That Allah's Apostle rode over a donkey covered with a Fadakiya (velvet sheet) and Usama was riding behind him. He was visiting Sa'd bin 'Ubada (who was sick) in the dwelling place of Bani Al-Harith bin Al-Khazraj and this incident happened before the battle of Badr. They proceeded till they passed by a gathering in which 'Abdullah bin Ubai bin Salul was present., and that was before 'Abdullah bin Ubat embraced Islam. In that gathering there were Muslims, pagan idolators and Jews, and among the Muslims there was 'Abdullah bin Rawaha.

When a cloud of dust raised by (the movement of) the animal covered that gathering, 'Abdullah bin Ubai covered his nose with his garment and said, "Do not cover us with dust." Allah's Apostle greeted them, stopped, dismounted and invited them to Allah (i.e. to embrace Islam) and recited to them the Holy Qur'an. On that 'Abdullah bin Ubai bin Salul said to him, "O man! There is nothing better than what you say, if it is the truth. So do not trouble us with it in our gatherings, but if somebody comes to you, you can preach to him." On that 'Abdullah bin Rawaha said "Yes, O Allah's Apostle! Call on us in our gathering, for we love that." So the Muslims, the pagans and the Jews started abusing one another till they were about to fight with one another. Allah's Apostle kept on quietening them till all of them became quiet, and then Allah's Apostle rode his animal and proceeded till he entered upon Sa'd bin 'Ubada. Allah's Apostle said, "O Sa'd! Didn't you hear what Abu Habab said?" (meaning 'Abdullah bin Unbar). "He said so-and-so." Sa'd bin Ubada said, "O Allah's Apostle! Let my father be sacrificed for you ! Excuse and forgive him for, by Him Who revealed to you the Book, Allah sent the Truth which was revealed to you at the time when the people of this town had decided to crown him ('Abdullah bin Ubai) as their ruler.

So when Allah had prevented that with the Truth He had given you, he was choked by that, and that caused him to behave in such an impolite manner which you had noticed." So Allah's Apostle excused him. (It was the custom of) Allah's Apostle and his companions to excuse the pagans and the people of the scripture (Christians and Jews) as Allah ordered them, and they used to be patient when annoyed (by them). Allah said: 'You shall certainly hear much that will grieve you from those who received the Scripture before you.....and from the pagans (3.186)

He also said: 'Many of the people of the scripture wish that if they could turn you away as disbelievers after you have believed. .... (2.109) So Allah's Apostle used to apply what Allah had ordered him by excusing them till he was allowed to fight against them. When Allah's Apostle had fought the battle of Badr and Allah killed whomever He killed among the chiefs of the infidels and the nobles of Quraish, and Allah's Apostle and his companions had returned with victory and booty, bringing with them some of the chiefs of the infidels and the nobles of the Quraish as captives. 'Abdullah bin Ubai bin Salul and the pagan idolators who were with him, said, "This matter (Islam) has now brought out its face (triumphed), so give Allah's Apostle the pledge of allegiance (for embracing Islam.)". Then they became Muslims.

Volume 8, Book 73, Number 227.

Narrated 'Abdullah bin Al-Harith bin Naufal.

Abbas bin 'Abdul Muttalib said, "O Allah's Apostle! Did you benefit Abu Talib with anything as he used to protect and take care of you, and used to become angry for you?" The Prophet said, "Yes, he is in a shallow place of Fire. But for me he would have been in the lowest part of the Fire."

Volume 8, Book 73, Number 228.

Narrated Anas bin Malik.

Once the Prophet was on one of his journeys, and the driver of the camels started chanting (to let the camels go fast). The Prophet said to him. "(Take care) Drive slowly with the glass vessels, O Anjasha! Waihaka (May Allah be Merciful to you)."

Volume 8, Book 73, Number 229.

Narrated Anas.

The Prophet was on a journey and a slave named Anjasha was chanting (singing) for the camels to let them go fast (while driving). The Prophet said, "O Anjasha, drive slowly (the camels) with the glass vessels!" Abu Qilaba said, "By the glass vessels' he meant the women (riding the camels)."

Volume 8, Book 73, Number 230.

Narrated Anas bin Malik.

The Prophet had a Had (a camel driver) called Anjasha, and he had a nice voice. The Prophet said to him, "(Drive) slowly, O Anjasha! Do not break the glass vessels!" And Qatada said, "(By vessels') he meant the weak women."

Volume 8, Book 73, Number 231.

Narrated Anas bin Malik.

There was a state of fear in Medina. Allah's Apostle rode a horse belonging to Abu Talha (in order to see the matter). The Prophet said, "We could not see anything, and we found that horse like a sea (fast in speed)."

Volume 8, Book 73, Number 232:

Narrated 'Aisha:

Some people asked Allah's Apostle about the fore-tellers. Allah's Apostle said to them, "They are nothing (i.e., liars)." The people said, 'O Allah's Apostle ! Sometimes they tell something which comes out to be true." Allah's Apostle said, "That word which comes to be true is what a jinx snatches away by stealing and then pours it in the ear of his fore-teller with a sound similar to the cackle of a hen, and then they add to it one-hundred lies."

Volume 8, Book 73, Number 233:

Narrated Jabir bin 'Abdullah:

That he heard Allah's Apostle saying. "Then there was a pause in the revelation of the Divine In-spiration to me. Then while I was walking all of a sudden I heard a voice from the sky, and I raised my sight towards the sky and saw the same angel who had visited me in the cave of Hira,' sitting on a chair between the sky and the earth."

Volume 8, Book 73, Number 234:

Narrated Ibn 'Abbas:

Once I stayed overnight at the house of Maimuna and the Prophet was there with her. When it was the last third of the night, or some part of the night, the Prophet got up looking towards the sky and recited: 'Verily! In the creation of the heavens and the earth, and in the alternation of Night and Day, there are indeed signs for men of u understanding.' (3.190)

Volume 8, Book 73, Number 235:

Narrated Abu Musa:

That he was in the company of the Prophet in one of the gardens of Medina and in the hand of the Prophet there was a stick, and he was striking (slowly) the water and the mud with it. A man came (at the gate of the garden) and asked permission to enter. The Prophet said, "Open the gate for him and give him the glad tidings of entering Paradise. "I went, and behold! It was Abu Bakr. So I opened the gate for him and informed him of the glad tidings of entering Paradise. Then another man came and asked permission to enter. The Prophet said, "Open the gate for him and give him the glad tid-ings of entering Paradise." Behold! It was 'Umar. So I opened the gate for him and gave him the glad tidings of entering Paradise. Then another man came and asked permission to enter.

The Prophet was sitting in a leaning posture, so he sat up and said, "Open the gate for him and give him the glad tidings of entering Paradise with a calamity which will befall him or which will take place." I went, and behold ! It was Uthman. So I opened the gate for him and gave him the glad tidings of entering Paradise and also informed him of what the Prophet had said (about a calamity). 'Uthman said, "Allah Alone Whose Help I seek (against that calamity).

Volume 8, Book 73, Number 236,

Narrated 'Ali,

We were with the Prophet in a funeral procession, and he started scraping the ground with a small stick and said, "There is none amongst you but has been assigned a place (either) in Paradise and (or) in the Hell-Fire." The people said (to him), "Should we not depend upon it?" He said, carry on doing (good) deeds, for everybody will find easy such deeds as will lead him to his destined place. He then recited, "As for him who gives (in charity) and keeps his duty to Allah.." (92.5)

Volume 8, Book 73, Number 237,

Narrated Um Salama,

(One night) the Prophet woke up and said, "Subhan Allah ! How many treasures have been (disclosed) sent down! And how many afflictions have been descended! Who will go and wake the sleeping lady-occupants up of these dwellings (for praying)?" (He meant by this his wives.) The Prophet added, "A well-dressed soul (person) in this world may be naked in the "Hereafter." 'Umar said, "I asked the Prophet, 'Have you divorced your wives?' He said, 'No.' I said, 'Allahu Akbar.' "

Volume 8, Book 73, Number 238,

Narrated Safiya bint Huyai,

The wife of the Prophet that she went to Allah's Apostle while he was in Itikaf (staying in the mosque) during the last ten nights of the month of Ramadan. She spoke to him for an hour (a while) at night and then she got up to return home. The Prophet got up to accompany her, and when they reached the gate of the mosque opposite the dwelling place of Um Salama, the wife of the Prophet, two Ansari men passed by, and greeting Allah's Apostle , they quickly went ahead. Allah's Apostle said to them, "Do not be in a hurry She is Safiya, the daughter of Huyai." They said, "Subhan Allah! O Allah's Apostle (how dare we suspect you)." That was a great thing for both of them. The Prophet then said, "Satan runs in the body of Adam's son (i.e. man) as his blood circulates in it, and I was afraid that he (Satan) might insert an evil thought in your hearts."

Volume 8, Book 73, Number 239,

Narrated 'Abdullah bin Mughaffal Al-Muzani,

The Prophet forbade the throwing of stones (with the thumb and the index or middle finger), and said "It neither hunts a game nor kills (or hurts) an enemy, but it gouges out an eye or breaks a tooth."

Volume 8, Book 73, Number 240:

Narrated Anas bin Malik:

Two men sneezed before the Prophet. The Prophet said to one of them, "May Allah bestow His Mercy on you," but he did not say that to the other. On being asked (why), the Prophet said, "That one praised Allah (at the time of sneezing), while the other did not praise Allah."

Volume 8, Book 73, Number 241:

Narrated Al-Bara:

The Prophet ordered us to do seven (things) and forbade us from seven (other things): He ordered us to pay a visit to the sick, to follow funeral possessions, to say: May Allah be merciful to you to a sneezer, - if he says: Praise be to Allah, to accept invitation (invitation to a wedding banquet), to return greetings, to help the oppressed, and to help others to fulfill their oaths (provided it was not sinful). And he forbade us from seven (things): to wear golden rings or golden bangles, to wear silk (cloth), Dibaj, Sundus and Mayathir.

Volume 8, Book 73, Number 242:

Narrated Abu Huraira:

The Prophet said, "Allah likes sneezing and dislikes yawning, so if someone sneezes and then praises Allah, then it is obligatory on every Muslim who heard him, to say: May Allah be merciful to you (Yar-hamuka-l-lah). But as regards yawning, it is from Satan, so one must try one's best to stop it, if one says 'Ha' when yawning, Satan will laugh at him."

Volume 8, Book 73, Number 243:

Narrated Abu Huraira:

The Prophet said, " If anyone of you sneezes, he should say 'Al-Hamdulillah' (Praise be to Allah), and his (Muslim) brother or companion should say to him, 'Yar-hamuka-l-lah' (May Allah bestow his Mercy on you). When the latter says 'Yar-hamuka-llah", the former should say, 'Yahdikumul-lah wa Yuslih balakum' (May Allah give you guidance and improve your condition)."

Volume 8, Book 73, Number 244,

Narrated Anas,

Two men sneezed before the Prophet and he said Tashmit to one of them, while he did not say Tashmit to the other. So that man said, "O Allah's Apostle! You said Tashmit to that fellow but you did not say Tashmit to me. "The Prophet said, "That man praised Allah, but you did not praise Allah."

Volume 8, Book 73, Number 245,

Narrated Abu Huraira,

The Prophet said, "Allah loves sneezing but dislikes yawning; so if anyone of you sneezes and then praises Allah, every Muslim who hears him (praising Allah) has to say Tashmit to him. But as regards yawning, it is from Satan, so if one of you yawns, he should try his best to stop it, for when anyone of you yawns, Satan laughs at him."

Book 74: Asking Permission

Volume 8, Book 74, Number 246:

Narrated Abu Huraira:

The Prophet said, "Allah created Adam in his complete shape and form (directly), sixty cubits (about 30 meters) in height. When He created him, He said (to him), "Go and greet that group of angels sitting there, and listen what they will say in reply to you, for that will be your greeting and the greeting of your offspring." Adam (went and) said, 'As-Salamu alaikum (Peace be upon you).' They replied, 'AsSalamu-'Alaika wa Rahmatullah (Peace and Allah's Mercy be on you) So they increased 'Wa Rahmatullah' The Prophet added 'So whoever will enter Paradise, will be of the shape and form of Adam. Since then the creation of Adam's (offspring) (i.e. stature of human beings is being diminished continuously) to the present time."

Volume 8, Book 74, Number 247:

Narrated 'Abdullah bin 'Abbas:

Al-Fadl bin 'Abbas rode behind the Prophet as his companion rider on the back portion of his she camel on the Day of Nahr (slaughtering of sacrifice, 10th Dhul-Hijja) and Al-Fadl was a handsome man. The Prophet stopped to give the people verdicts. In the meantime, a beautiful woman From the tribe of Khath'am came, asking the verdict of Allah's Apostle. Al-Fadl started looking at her as her beauty attracted him. The Prophet looked behind while Al-Fadl was looking at her; so the Prophet held out his hand backwards and caught the chin of Al-Fadl and turned his face (to the owner sides in order that he should not gaze at her. She said, "O Allah's Apostle! The obligation of Performing Hajj enjoined by Allah on His worshipers, has become due (compulsory) on my father who is an old man and who cannot sit firmly on the riding animal. Will it be sufficient that I perform Hajj on his behalf?" He said, "Yes."

Volume 8, Book 74, Number 248:

Narrated Abu Said Al-Khudri:

The Prophet said, 'Beware! Avoid sitting on the roads." They (the people) said, "O Allah s Apostle! We can't help sitting (on the roads) as these are (our places) here we have talks." The Prophet said, ' l f you refuse but to sit, then pay the road its right ' They said, "What is the right of the road, O Allah's Apostle?" He said, 'Lowering your gaze, refraining from harming others, returning greeting, and enjoining what is good, and forbidding what is evil."

Volume 8, Book 74, Number 249:

Narrated 'Abdullah:

When we prayed with the Prophet we used to say: As-Salam be on Allah from His worshipers, As-Salam be on Gabriel, As-Salam be on Michael, As-Salam be on so-and-so. When the Prophet finished his prayer, he faced us and said, "Allah Himself is As-Salam (Peace), so when one sits in the prayer, one should say, 'At-Tahiyatu-lillahi Was-Salawatu, Wat-Taiyibatu, As-Salamu 'Alaika aiyuhan-Nabiyyu wa Rah-matul-lahi wa Barakatuhu, As-Salamu 'Alaina wa 'ala 'Ibadillahi assalihin, for if he says so, then it will be for all the pious slave of Allah in the Heavens and the Earth. (Then he should say), 'Ash-hadu an la ilaha illalllahu wa ash-hadu anna Muhammadan 'Abduhu wa rasuluhu,' and then he can choose whatever speech (i.e. invocation) he wishes " (See Hadith No. 797, Vol. 1)

Volume 8, Book 74, Number 250:

Narrated Abu Huraira:

The Prophet said, "The young should greet the old, the passer by should greet the sitting one, and the small group of persons should greet the large group of persons. "

Volume 8, Book 74, Number 251:

Narrated Abu Huraira:

Allah's Apostle said, "The riding one should greet the walking one, and the walking one should greet the sitting one, and the small number of persons should greet the large number of persons."

Volume 8, Book 74, Number 252:

Narrated Abu Huraira:

Allah's Apostle said, "The riding person should greet the walking one, and the walking one should greet the sitting one, and the small number of persons should greet the large number of persons."

Volume 8, Book 74, Number 252e:

Narrated Abu Huraira:

Allah's Apostle said, "The younger person should greet the older one, and the walking person should greet the sitting one, and the small number of persons should greet the large number of persons."

Volume 8, Book 74, Number 253g:

Narrated Al-Bara' bin 'Azib:

Allah's Apostle ordered us to do seven (things): to visit the sick, to follow the funeral processions, to say Tashmit to a sneezer, to help the weak, to help the oppressed ones, to propagate As-Salam (greeting), and to help others to fulfill their oaths (if it is not sinful). He forbade us to drink from silver utensils, to wear gold rings, to ride on silken saddles, to wear silk clothes, Dibaj (thick silk cloth), Qassiy and Istabraq (two kinds of silk). (See Hadith No. 539, Vol. 7)

Volume 8, Book 74, Number 253k:

Narrated 'Abdullah bin 'Amr:

A man asked the Prophet, "What Islamic traits are the best?" The Prophet said, "Feed the people, and greet those whom you know and those whom you do not know."

Volume 8, Book 74, Number 254:

Narrated Abu Aiyub:

The Prophet said, "It is not lawful for a Muslim to desert (not to speak to) his brother Muslim for more than three days while meeting, one turns his face to one side and the other turns his face to the other side. Lo! The better of the two is the one who starts greeting the other."

Volume 8, Book 74, Number 255:

Narrated Anas bin Malik:

that he was a boy of ten at the time when the Prophet emigrated to Medina. He added: I served Allah's Apostle for ten years (the last part of his life time) and I know more than the people about the occasion whereupon the order of Al-Hijab was revealed (to the Prophet). Ubai b n Ka'b used to ask me about it. It was revealed (for the first time) during the marriage of Allah's Apostle with Zainab bint Jahsh. In the morning, the Prophet was a bride-groom of her and he Invited the people, who took their meals and went away, but a group of them remained with Allah's Apostle and they prolonged their stay. Allah's Apostle got up and went out, and I too, went out along with him till he came to the lintel of 'Aisha's dwelling place. Allah's Apostle thought that those people had left by then, so he returned, and I too, returned with him till he entered upon Zainab and found that they were still sitting there and had not yet gone. The Prophet went out again, and so did I with him till he reached the lintel of 'Aisha's dwelling place, and then he thought that those people must have left by then, so he returned, and so did I with him, and found those people had gone. At that time the Divine Verse of Al-Hijab was revealed, and the Prophet set a screen between me and him (his family).

Volume 8, Book 74, Number 256:

Narrated Anas:

When the Prophet married Zainab, the people came and were offered a meal, and then they sat down (after finishing their meals) and started chatting. The Prophet showed as if he wanted to get up, but they did not get up. When he noticed that, he got up, and some of the people also got up and went away, while some others kept on sitting. When the Prophet returned to enter, he found the people still sitting, but then they got up and left. So I told the Prophet of their departure and he came and went in. I intended to go in but the Prophet put a screen between me and him, for Allah revealed.-- 'O you who believe! Enter not the Prophet's houses..' (33.53)

Volume 8, Book 74, Number 257:

Narrated 'Aisha:

(the wife of the Prophet) 'Umar bin Al-Khattab used to say to Allah's Apostle "Let your wives be veiled" But he did not do so. The wives of the Prophet used to go out to answer the call of nature at night only at Al-Manasi.' Once Sauda, the daughter of Zam'a went out and she was a tall woman. 'Umar bin Al-Khattab saw her while he was in a gathering, and said, "I have recognized you, O Sauda!" He ('Umar) said so as he was anxious for some Divine orders regarding the veil (the veiling of women.) So Allah revealed the Verse of veiling. (Al-Hijab; a complete body cover excluding the eyes). (See Hadith No. 148, Vol. 1)

Volume 8, Book 74, Number 258:

Narrated Sahl bin Sa'd:

A man peeped through a round hole into the dwelling place of the Prophet, while the Prophet had a Midray (an iron comb) with which he was scratching his head. the Prophet said, " Had known you were looking (through the hole), I would have pierced your eye with it (i.e., the comb)." Verily! The order of taking permission to enter has been enjoined because of that sight, (that one should not look unlawfully at the state of others). (See Hadith No. 807, Vol. 7)

Volume 8, Book 74, Number 259:

Narrated Anas bin Malik:

A man peeped into a room of the Prophet. The Prophet stood up, holding an arrow head. It is as if I am just looking at him, trying to stab the man.

Volume 8, Book 74, Number 260:

Narrated Ibn 'Abbas:

I have not seen a thing resembling 'lamam' (minor sins) than what Abu Huraira 'narrated from the Prophet who said "Allah has written for Adam's son his share of adultery which he commits inevitably. The adultery of the eyes is the sight (to gaze at a forbidden thing), the adultery of the tongue is the talk, and the inner self wishes and desires and the private parts testify all this or deny it."

Volume 8, Book 74, Number 261:

Narrated Anas:

Whenever Allah's Apostle greeted somebody, he used to greet him three times, and if he spoke a sentence, he used to repeat it thrice.

Volume 8, Book 74, Number 262:

Narrated Abu Said Al-Khudri:

While I was present in one of the gatherings of the Ansar, Abu Musa came as if he was scared, and said, "I asked permission to enter upon 'Umar three times, but I was not given the permission, so I returned." (When 'Umar came to know about it) he said to Abu Musa, "Why did you not enter?'. Abu Musa replied, "I asked permission three times, and I was not given it, so I returned, for Allah's Apostle said, "If anyone of you asks the permission to enter thrice, and the permission is not given, then he should return.' " 'Umar said, "By Allah! We will ask Abu Musa to bring witnesses for it." (Abu Musa went to a gathering of the Ansar and said). "Did anyone of you hear this from the Prophet ?" Ubai bin Ka'b said, "By Allah, none will go with you but the youngest of the people (as a witness)." (Abu Said) was the youngest of them, so I went with Abu Musa and informed 'Umar that the Prophet had said so. (See Hadith No. 277, Vol. 3)

Volume 8, Book 74, Number 263:

Narrated Abu Huraira:

I entered (the house) along with Allah's Apostle . There he found milk in a basin. He said, "O Abu Hirr! Go and call the people of Suffa to me." I went to them and invited them. They came and asked permission to enter, and when it was given, they entered. (See Hadith No. 459 for details)

Volume 8, Book 74, Number 264:

Narrated Anas bin Malik:

that he passed by a group of boys and greeted them and said, "The Prophet used to do so."

Volume 8, Book 74, Number 265:

Narrated Abu Hazim:

Sahl said, "We used to feel happy on Fridays." I asked Sahl, "Why?" He said, "There was an old woman of our acquaintance who used to send somebody to Buda'a (Ibn Maslama said, "Buda'a was a garden of date-palms at Medina). She used to pull out the silq (a kind of vegetable) from its roots and put it in a cooking pot, adding some powdered barley over it (and cook it). After finishing the Jumua (Friday) prayer we used to (pass by her and) greet her, whereupon she would present us with that meal, so we used to feel happy because of that. We used to have neither a midday nap, nor meals, except after the Friday prayer." (See Hadith No. 60, Vol.2)

Volume 8, Book 74, Number 266:

Narrated 'Aisha:

Allah's Apostle said, "O 'Aisha! This is Gabriel sending his greetings to you." I said, "Peace, and Allah's Mercy be on him (Gabriel). You see what we do not see." (She was addressing Allah's Apostle).

Volume 8, Book 74, Number 267:

Narrated Jabir:

I came to the Prophet in order to consult him regarding my father's debt. When I knocked on the door, he asked, "Who is that?" I replied, "I" He said, "I, I?" He repeated it as if he disliked it.

Volume 8, Book 74, Number 268:

Narrated Abu Huraira:

A man entered the mosque while Allah's Apostle was sitting in one side of the mosque. The man prayed, came, and greeted the Prophet. Allah's Apostle said to him, "Wa 'Alaikas Salam (returned his greeting). Go back and pray as you have not prayed (properly)." The man returned, repeated his prayer, came back and greeted the Prophet. The Prophet said, "Wa alaika-s-Salam (returned his greeting). Go back and pray again as you have not prayed (properly)." The man said at the second or third time, "O Allah's Apostle! Kindly teach me how to pray". The Prophet said, "When you stand for prayer, perform ablution properly and then face the Qibla and say Takbir (Allahu-Akbar), and then recite what you know from the Qur'an, and then bow with calmness till you feel at ease then rise from bowing, till you stand straight, and then prostrate calmly (and remain in prostration) till you feel at ease, and then raise (your head) and sit with calmness till you feel at ease and then prostrate with calmness (and remain in prostration) till you feel at ease, and then raise (your head) and sit with calmness till you feel at ease in the sitting position, and do likewise in whole of your prayer." And Abu Usama added, "Till you stand straight." (See Hadith No. 759, Vol.1)

Volume 8, Book 74, Number 269:

Narrated Abu Huraira:

The Prophet said (in the above narration No. 268), "And then raise your head till you feel at ease while sitting. "

Volume 8, Book 74, Number 270:

Narrated 'Aisha: that the Prophet said to her, "Gabriel sends Salam (greetings) to you." She replied, "Wa 'alaihi-s-Salam Wa Rahmatu-l-lah." (Peace and Allah's Mercy be on him).

Volume 8, Book 74, Number 271:

Narrated 'Urwa-bin Az-Zubair:

Usama bin Zaid said, "The Prophet rode over a donkey with a saddle underneath which there was a thick soft Fadakiya velvet sheet. Usama bin Zaid was his companion rider, and he was going to pay a visit to Sa'd bin Ubada (who was sick) at the dwelling place of Bani Al-Harith bin Al-Khazraj, and this incident happened before the battle of Badr. The Prophet passed by a gathering in which there were Muslims and pagan idolators and Jews, and among them there was 'Abdullah bin Ubai bin Sa-lul, and there was 'Abdullah bin Rawaha too. When a cloud of dust raised by the animal covered that gathering, 'Abdullah bin Ubai covered his nose with his Rida (sheet) and said (to the Prophet), "Don't cover us with dust." The Prophet greeted them and then stopped, dismounted and invited them to Al-lah (i.e., to embrace Islam) and also recited to them the Holy Quran. 'Abdullah bin Ubai' bin Salul said, "O man! There is nothing better than what you say, if what you say is the truth. So do not trouble us in our gatherings. Go back to your mount (or house,) and if anyone of us comes to you, tell (your tales) to him." On that 'Abdullah bin Rawaha said, "(O Allah's Apostle!) Come to us and bring it(what you want to say) in our gatherings, for we love that." So the Muslims, the pagans and the Jews started quarreling till they were about to fight and clash with one another. The Prophet kept on quietening them (till they all became quiet). He then rode his animal, and proceeded till he entered upon Sa'd bin 'Ubada, he said, "O Sa'd, didn't you hear what Abu Habbab said? (He meant 'Abdullah bin Ubai). He said so-and-so." Sa'd bin 'Ubada said, "O Allah's Apostle! Excuse and forgive him, for by Allah, Allah has given you what He has given you. The people of this town decided to crown him (as their chief) and make him their king. But when Allah prevented that with the Truth which He had given you, it choked him, and that was what made him behave in the way you saw him behaving." So the Prophet excused him.

Volume 8, Book 74, Number 272:

Narrated 'Abdullah bin Ka'b:

I heard Ka'b bin Malik narrating (when he did not join the battle of Tabuk), Allah's Apostle forbade all the Muslims to speak to us. I would come to Allah's Apostle and greet him, and I would wonder whether the Prophet did move his lips to return to my greetings or not till fifty nights passed away. The Prophet then announced (to the people) Allah's forgiveness for us (acceptance of our repentance) at the time when he had offered the Fajr (morning) prayer.

Volume 8, Book 74, Number 273:

Narrated 'Aisha:

A group of Jews came to Allah's Apostle and said, "As-samu 'Alaika " (Death be on you), and I understood it and said to them, "Alaikum AsSamu wa-l-la'na (Death and curse be on you)." Allah's Apostle said, "Be calm! O 'Aisha, for Allah loves that one should be kind and lenient in all matters." I said. "O Allah's Apostle! Haven't you heard what they have said?" Allah's Apostle said, "I have (already) said (to them), 'Alaikum (upon you).' "

Volume 8, Book 74, Number 274:

Narrated 'Abdullah bin 'Umar:

Allah's Apostle said, "When the Jews greet you, they usually say, 'As-Samu 'alaikum (Death be on you),' so you should say (in reply to them), 'Wa'alaikum (And on you)."

Volume 8, Book 74, Number 275:

Narrated Anas bin Malik:

the Prophet said, "If the people of the Scripture greet you, then you should say (in reply), 'Wa'alaikum (And on you).' "

Volume 8, Book 74, Number 276:

Narrated 'Ali:

Allah's Apostle sent me, Az-Zubair bin Al-Awwam and Abu Marthad Al-Ghanawi, and all of us were horsemen, and he said, "Proceed till you reach Rawdat Khakh, where there is a woman from the pagans carrying a letter sent by Hatib bin Abi Balta'a to the pagans (of Mecca)." So we overtook her while she was proceeding on her camel at the same place as Allah's Apostle told us. We said (to her) "Where is the letter which is with you?" She said, "I have no letter with me." So we made her camel kneel down and searched her mount (baggage etc) but could not find anything. My two companions said, "We do not see any letter." I said, "I know that Allah's Apostle did not tell a lie. By Allah, if you (the lady) do not bring out the letter, I will strip you of your clothes' When she noticed that I was serious, she put her hand into the knot of her waist sheet, for she was tying a sheet round herself, and brought out the letter. So we proceeded to Allah's Apostle with the letter. The Prophet said (to Habib), "What made you o what you have done, O Hatib?" Hatib replied, "I have done nothing except that I believe in Allah and His Apostle, and I have not changed or altered (my religion). But I wanted to do the favor to the people (pagans of Mecca) through which Allah might protect my family and my property, as there is none among your companions but has someone in Mecca through whom Allah protects his property (against harm). The Prophet said, "Habib has told you the truth, so do not say to him (anything) but good." 'Umar bin Al-Khattab said, "Verily he has betrayed Allah, His Apostle, and the believers! Allow me to chop his neck off!" The Prophet said, "O 'Umar! What do you know; perhaps Allah looked upon the Badr warriors and said, 'Do whatever you like, for I have ordained that you will be in Paradise.'" On that 'Umar wept and said, "Allah and His Apostle know best."

Volume 8, Book 74, Number 277:

Narrated Abu Sufyan bin Harb:

that Heraclius had sent for him to come along with a group of the Quraish who were trading in Sha'm, and they came to him. Then Abu Sufyan mentioned the whole narration and said, "Heraclius asked for the letter of Allah's Apostle . When the letter was read, its contents were as follows: 'In the name of Allah, the Beneficent, the Merciful. From Muhammad, Allah's slave and His Apostle to Heraclius, the Chief of Byzantines: Peace be upon him who follows the right path (guidance)! Amma ba'du (to proceed)...' (See Hadith No 6, Vol 1 for details)

Volume 8, Book 74, Number 278:

Narrated Abu Said:

The people of (the tribe of) Quraiza agreed upon to accept the verdict of Sa'd. The Prophet sent for him (Sa'd) and he came. The Prophet said (to those people), "Get up for your chief or the best among you!" Sa'd sat beside the Prophet and the Prophet said (to him), "These people have agreed to accept your verdict." Sa'd said, "So I give my judgment that their warriors should be killed and their women and children should be taken as captives." The Prophet said, "You have judged according to the King's (Allah's) judgment." (See Hadith No. 447, Vol. 5)

Volume 8, Book 74, Number 279:

Narrated Qatada:

I asked Anas, "Was it a custom of the companions of the Prophet to shake hands with one another?" He said, "Yes."

Volume 8, Book 74, Number 280:

Narrated 'Abdullah bin Hisham:

We were in the company of the Prophet and he was holding the hand of 'Umar bin Al-Khattab.

Volume 8, Book 74, Number 281:

Narrated Ibn Mas'ud:

Allah's Apostle taught me the Tashah-hud as he taught me a Sura from the Quran, while my hand was between his hands. (Tashah-hud was) all the best compliments and the prayers and the good things are for Allah. Peace and Allah's Mercy and Blessings be on you, O Prophet! Peace be on us and on the pious slaves of Allah, I testify that none has the right to be worshipped but Allah, and I also testify that Muhammad is Allah's slave and His Apostle. (We used to recite this in the prayer) during the lifetime of the Prophet , but when he had died, we used to say, "Peace be on the Prophet."

Volume 8, Book 74, Number 282:

Narrated 'Abdullah bin 'Abbas:

'Ali bin Abu Talib came out of the house of the Prophet during his fatal ailment. The people asked ('Ali), "O Abu Hasan! How is the health of Allah's Apostle this morning?" 'Ali said, "This morning he is better, with the grace of Allah." Al-'Abbas held Ali by the hand and said, "Don't you see him (about to die)? By Allah, within three days you will be the slave of the stick (i.e., under the command of another ruler). By Allah, I think that Allah's Apostle will die from his present ailment, for I know the signs of death on the faces of the offspring of 'Abdul Muttalib. So let us go to Allah's Apostle to ask him who will take over the Caliphate. If the authority is given to us, we will know it, and if it is given to somebody else we will request him to recommend us to him. " 'Ali said, "By Allah! If we ask Allah's Apostle for the rulership and he refuses, then the people will never give it to us. Besides, I will never ask Allah's Apostle for it." (See Hadith No 728, Vol 5)

Volume 8, Book 74, Number 283:

Narrated Muadh:

While I was a companion rider with the Prophet he said, "O Mu'adh!" I replied, "Labbaik wa Sa'daik." He repeated this call three times and then said, "Do you know what Allah's Right on His slaves is?" I replied, "No." He said, Allah's Right on His slaves is that they should worship Him (Alone) and should not join partners in worship with Him." He said, "O Mu'adh!" I replied, "Labbaik wa Sa'daik." He said, "Do you know what the right of (Allah's) salves on Allah is, if they do that (worship Him Alone and join none in His worship)? It is that He will not punish them."

Volume 8, Book 74, Number 284:

Narrated Mu'adh:

as above, No. 283.

Volume 8, Book 74, Number 285:

Narrated Abu Dhar:

While I was walking with the Prophet at the Hurra of Medina in the evening, the mountain of Uhud appeared before us. The Prophet said, "O Abu Dhar! I would not like to have gold equal to Uhud (mountain) for me, unless nothing of it, not even a single Dinar remains of it with me, for more than one day or three days, except that single Dinar which I will keep for repaying debts. I will spend all of it (the whole amount) among Allah's slaves like this and like this and like this." The Prophet pointed out with his hand to illustrate it and then said, "O Abu Dhar!" I replied, "Labbaik wa Sa'daik, O Allah's Apostle!" He said, "Those who have much wealth (in this world) will be the least rewarded (in the Hereafter) except those who do like this and like this (i.e., spend their money in charity)." Then he ordered me, "Remain at your place and do not leave it, O Abu Dhar, till I come back." He went away till he disappeared from me. Then I heard a voice and feared that something might have happened to Allah's Apostle, and I intended to go (to find out) but I remembered the statement of Allah's Apostle that I should not leave, my place, so I kept on waiting (and after a while the Prophet came), and I said to him, "O Allah's Apostle, I heard a voice and I was afraid that something might have happened to you, but then I remembered your statement and stayed (there). The Prophet said, "That was Gabriel who came to me and informed me that whoever among my followers died without joining others in worship with Allah, would enter Paradise." I said, "O Allah's Apostle! Even if he had committed illegal sexual intercourse and theft?" He said, "Even if he had committed illegal sexual intercourse and theft '

Volume 8, Book 74, Number 286:

Narrated Ibn 'Umar:

The Prophet said, "A man should not make another man get up from his (the latter's) seat (in a gathering) in order to sit there.

Volume 8, Book 74, Number 287:

Narrated Ibn 'Umar:

The Prophet forbade that a man should be made to get up from his seat so that another might sit on it, but one should make room and spread out. Ibn 'Umar disliked that a man should get up from his seat and then somebody else sit at his place.

Volume 8, Book 74, Number 288,

Narrated Anas bin Malik,

When Allah's Apostle married Zainab bint Jahsh, he invited the people who took their meals and then remained sitting and talking. The Prophet pretended to be ready to get up, but the people did not get up. When he noticed that, he got up, and when he had got up, some of those people got up along with him and there remained three (who kept on sitting). Then the Prophet came back and found those people still sitting. Later on those people got up and went away. So I went to the Prophet and informed him that they had left.

The Prophet came, and entered (his house). I wanted to enter(along with him) but he dropped a curtain between me and him. Allah then revealed, 'O you who believe! Do not enter the Prophet's Houses until leave is given... (to His statement)... Verily! That shall be an enormity, in Allah's sight.' (33.53)

Volume 8, Book 74, Number 289,

Narrated Ibn 'Umar,

I saw Allah's Apostle in the courtyard of the Ka'ba in the Ihtiba.' posture putting his hand round his legs like this.

Volume 8, Book 74, Number 290,

Narrated Abu Bakra,

Allah's Apostle said, "Shall I inform you of the biggest of the great sins?" They said, "Yes, O Allah's Apostle!" He said, "To join partners in worship with Allah, and to be undutiful to one's parents. "

Volume 8, Book 74, Number 291,

Narrated Bishr,

as above (No. 290) adding, The Prophet was reclining (leaning) and then he sat up saying, "And I warn you against giving a false statement." And he kept on saying that warning so much so that we said, "Would that he had stopped."

Volume 8, Book 74, Number 292,

Narrated 'Uqba bin Al-Harith,

Once the Prophet offered the 'Asr prayer and then he walked quickly and entered his house.

Volume 8, Book 74, Number 293:

Narrated 'Aisha:

Allah's Apostle used to offer his prayer (while standing) in the midst of the bed, and I used to lie in front of him between him and the Qibla It I had any necessity for getting up and I used to dislike to get up and face him (while he was in prayer), but I would gradually slip away from the bed.

Volume 8, Book 74, Number 294:

Narrated Abdullah bin 'Amr:

The news of my fasting was mentioned to the Prophet . So he entered upon me and I put for him a leather cushion stuffed with palm-fibres. The Prophet sat on the floor and the cushion was between me and him. He said to me, "Isn't it sufficient for you (that you fast) three days a month?" I said, "O Allah's Apostle! (I can fast more than this)." He said, "You may fast five days a month." I said, "O Allah's Apostle! (I can fast more than this)." He said, "(You may fast) seven days." I said, "O Allah's Apostle!" He said, "Nine." I said, "O Allah's Apostle!" He said, "Eleven." I said, "O Allah's Apostle!" He said, "No fasting is superior to the fasting of (the Prophet David) which was one half of a year, and he used, to fast on alternate days. (See Hadith No. 300, Vol 3)

Volume 8, Book 74, Number 295:

Narrated Ibrahim:

'Alaqama went to Sham and came to the mosque and offered a two-Rak'at prayer, and invoked Allah: "O Allah! Bless me with a (pious) good companion." So he sat beside Abu Ad-Darda' who asked, "From where are you?" He said, "From the people of Kufa." Abu Darda' said, "Wasn't there among you the person who keeps the secrets (of the Prophet) which nobody knew except him (i.e., Hudhaifa (bin Al-Yaman)). And isn't there among you the person whom Allah gave refuge from Satan through the request (tongue) of Allah's Apostle? (i.e., 'Ammar). Isn't there among you the one who used to carry the Siwak and the cushion (or pillows (of the Prophets)? (i.e., Ibn Mas'ud). How did Ibn Mas'ud use to recite 'By the night as it conceals (the light)?" (Sura 92). 'Alqama said, "Wadhdhakari Wal Untha' (And by male and female.") Abu Ad-Darda added. 'These people continued to argue with me regarding it till they were about to cause me to have doubts although I heard it from Allah's Apostle "

Volume 8, Book 74, Number 296:

Narrated Sahl bin Sad:

We used to have a midday nap and take our meals after the Jumua (prayer).

Volume 8, Book 74, Number 297:

Narrated Sahl bin Sad:

There was no name dearer to 'Ali than his nickname Abu Turab (the father of dust). He used to feel happy whenever he was called by this name. Once Allah's Apostle came to the house of Fatima but did not find 'Ali in the house. So he asked "Where is your cousin?" She replied, "There was something (a quarrel) between me and him whereupon he got angry with me and went out without having a midday nap in my house." Allah's Apostle asked a person to look for him. That person came, and said, "O Allah's Apostle! He (Ali) is sleeping in the mosque." So Allah's Apostle went there and found him lying. His upper body cover had fallen off to one side of his body, and so he was covered with dust. Allah's Apostle started cleaning the dust from him, saying, "Get up, O Abu Turab! Get up, Abu Turab!" (See Hadith No. 432, Vol 1)

Volume 8, Book 74, Number 298:

Narrated Thumama:

Anas said, "Um Sulaim used to spread a leather sheet for the Prophet and he used to take a midday nap on that leather sheet at her home." Anas added, "When the Prophet had slept, she would take some of his sweat and hair and collect it (the sweat) in a bottle and then mix it with Suk (a kind of perfume) while he was still sleeping. "When the death of Anas bin Malik approached, he advised that some of that Suk be mixed with his Hanut (perfume for embalming the dead body), and it was mixed with his Hanut.

Volume 8, Book 74, Number 299:

Narrated Anas bin Malik:

Whenever Allah's Apostle went to Quba, he used to visit Um Haram bint Milhan who would offer him meals; and she was the wife of 'Ubada bin As-samit. One day he went to her house and she offered him a meal, and after that he slept, and then woke up smiling. She (Um Haram) said, "I asked him, 'What makes you laugh, O Allah's Apostle?' He said, 'Some people of my followers were displayed before me as warriors fighting for Allah's Cause and sailing over this sea, kings on thrones,' or said, 'like kings on thrones.' (The narrator, Ishaq is in doubt about it.) I (Um Haram) said, 'O Allah's Apostle! Invoke Allah that He may make me one of them.' He invoked (Allah) for her and then lay his head and slept again and then woke up smiling. I asked, 'What makes you laugh, O Allah's Apostle?' He said, 'Some people of my followers were displayed before me as warriors fighting for Allah's Cause and sailing over this sea, kings on the thrones,' or said, 'like kings on the thrones.' I (Um Haram) said, 'O Allah's Apostle! Invoke Allah that He may make me one of them.' He said, You will be amongst the first ones." It is said that Um Haram sailed over the sea at the time of Muawiya, and on coming out of the sea, she fell down from her riding animal and died.

Volume 8, Book 74, Number 300:

Narrated Abu Sa'id Al-Khudri:

The Prophet forbade two kinds of dresses and two kinds of bargains; Ishtimal As-Samma and Al-Ihtiba in one garment with no part of it covering one's private parts. (The two kinds of bargains were:) Al-Mulamasa and Al-Munabadha.

Volume 8, Book 74, Number 301:

Narrated 'Aisha:

He added, 'But this year he reviewed it with me twice, and therefore I think that my time of death has approached. So, be afraid of Allah, and be patient, for I am the best predecessor for you (in the Hereafter).' " Fatima added, "So I wept as you ('Aisha) witnessed. And when the Prophet saw me in this sorrowful state, he confided the second secret to me saying, 'O Fatima! Will you not be pleased that you will be chief of all the believing women (or chief of the women of this nation i.e. my followers?")

Volume 8, Book 74, Number 302:

Narrated the uncle of 'Abbas bin Tamim:

I saw Allah's Apostle lying on his back in the mosque and putting one of his legs over the other.

Volume 8, Book 74, Number 303:

Narrated 'Abdullah:

the Prophet said "When three persons are together, then no two of them should hold secret counsel excluding the third person."

Volume 8, Book 74, Number 304:

Narrated Anas bin Malik:

The Prophet confided to me a secret which I did not disclose to anybody after him. And Um Sulaim asked me (about that secret) but I did not tell her.

Volume 8, Book 74, Number 305:

Narrated 'Abdullah:

The Prophet said, "When you are three persons sitting together, then no two of you should hold secret counsel excluding the third person until you are with some other people too, for that would grieve him."

Volume 8, Book 74, Number 306:

Narrated 'Abdullah:

One day the Prophet divided and distributed something amongst the people whereupon an Ansari man said, "In this division Allah's Countenance has not been sought." I said, "By Allah! I will go (and inform) the Prophet." So I went to him while he was with a group of people, and I secretly informed him of that, whereupon he became so angry that his face became red, and he then said, "May Allah bestow His Mercy on Moses (for) he was hurt more than that, yet he remained patient."

Volume 8, Book 74, Number 307:

Narrated Anas:

The Iqama for the prayer was announced while a man was talking to Allah's Apostle privately. He continued talking in that way till the Prophet's companions slept, and afterwards the Prophet got up and offered the prayer with them.

Volume 8, Book 74, Number 308:

Narrated Salim's father:

The Prophet said, "Do not keep the fire burning in your houses when you go to bed."

Volume 8, Book 74, Number 309:

Narrated Abu Musa:

One night a house in Medina was burnt with its occupants. The Prophet spoke about them, saying, "This fire is indeed your enemy, so whenever you go to bed, put it out to protect yourselves."

Volume 8, Book 74, Number 310:

Narrated Jabir bin 'Abdullah:

Allah's Apostle said, "(At bedtime) cover the utensils, close the doors, and put out the lights, lest the evil creature (the rat) should pull away the wick and thus burn the people of the house."

Volume 8, Book 74, Number 311:

Narrated Jabir:

Allah s Apostle said, "When you intend going to bed at night, put out the lights, close the doors, tie the mouths of the water skins, and cover your food and drinks." Hamrnam said, "I think he (the other narrator) added, 'even with piece of wood across the utensil.'

Volume 8, Book 74, Number 312:

Narrated Abu Huraira:

The Prophet said "Five things are in accordance with Al Fitra (i.e. the tradition of prophets): to be circumcised, to shave the pelvic region, to pull out the hair of the armpits, to cut short the moustaches, and to clip the nails.'

Volume 8, Book 74, Number 313:

Narrated Abu Huraira:

Allah's Apostle said "The Prophet) Abraham circumcised himself after he had passed the age of eighty years and he circumcised himself with an adze."

Narrated Said bin Jubair: Ibn 'Abbas was asked, "How old were you when the Prophet died?" He replied. "At that time I had been circumcised." At that time, people did not circumcise the boys till they attained the age of puberty. Sa'id bin Jubair said, "Ibn 'Abbas said, 'When the Prophet died, I had already been circumcised. "

Volume 8, Book 74, Number 314:

Narrated Abu Huraira:

Allah's Apostle said, "Whoever among you takes an oath wherein he says, 'By Al-Lat and Al-'Uzza,' names of two Idols worshipped by the Pagans, he should say, 'None has the right to be worshipped but Allah; And whoever says to his friend, 'Come, let me gamble with you ! He should give something in charity. " (See Hadith No. 645)

Volume 8, Book 74, Number 315:

Narrated Ibn 'Umar:

During the life-time of the Prophet I built a house with my own hands so that it might protect me from the rain and shade me from the sun; and none of Allah's creatures assisted me in building it.

Volume 8, Book 74, Number 316:

Narrated, 'Amr:

Ibn 'Umar said, "By Allah, I have not put a brick over a brick (i.e. constructed a building) or planted any date-palm tree since the death of the Prophet." Sufyan (the sub narrator) said, "I told this narration (of Ibn 'Umar) to one of his (Ibn 'Umar's) relatives, and he said, 'By Allah, he did build (something.' "Sufyan added, "I said, 'He must have said (the above narration) before he built."

Book 75: Invocations

Volume 8, Book 75, Number 317e:

Narrated Abu Huraira:

Allah's Apostle said, "For every prophet there is one (special invocation (that will not be rejected) with which he appeals (to Allah), and I want to keep such an invocation for interceding for my followers in the Hereafter."

Volume 8, Book 75, Number 317o:

Narrated Anas:

that the Prophet said, "For every prophet there is an invocation that surely will be responded by Allah," (or said), "For every prophet there was an invocation with which he appealed to Allah, and his invocation was accepted (in his lifetime), but I kept my (this special) invocation to intercede for my followers on the Day of Resurrection."

Volume 8, Book 75, Number 318:

Narrated Shaddad bin Aus:

The Prophet said "The most superior way of asking for forgiveness from Allah is: 'Allahumma anta Rabbi la ilaha illa anta, Anta Khalaqtani wa ana abduka, wa ana 'ala ahdika wa wa'dika mastata'tu, A'udhu bika min Sharri ma sana'tu, abu'u Laka bini'matika 'alaiya, wa Abu Laka bidhanbi faghfirli innahu la yaghfiru adhdhunuba illa anta." The Prophet added. "If somebody recites it during the day with firm faith in it, and dies on the same day before the evening, he will be from the people of Paradise; and if somebody recites it at night with firm faith in it, and dies before the morning, he will be from the people of Paradise."

Volume 8, Book 75, Number 319:

Narrated Abu Huraira:

I heard Allah's Apostle saying." By Allah! I ask for forgiveness from Allah and turn to Him in repentance more than seventy times a day."

Volume 8, Book 75, Number 320:

Narrated Al-Harith bin Suwaid:

'Abdullah bin Mas'ud related to us two narrations, One from the Prophet and the other from himself, saying, A believer sees his sins as if he were sitting under a mountain which, he is afraid, may fall on him; whereas the wicked person considers his sins as flies passing over his nose and he just drives them away like this." Abu Shihab (the sub-narrator) moved his hand over his nose in illustration. (Ibn Mas'ud added), Allah's Apostle said, "Allah is more pleased with the repentance of His slave than a man who encamps at a place where his life is jeopardized, but he has his riding beast carrying his food and water. He then rests his head and sleeps for a short while and wakes to find his riding beast gone. (He starts looking for it) and suffers from severe heat and thirst or what Allah wished (him to suffer from). He then says, 'I will go back to my place.' He returns and sleeps again, and then (getting up), he raises his head to find his riding beast standing beside him."

Volume 8, Book 75, Number 321,

Narrated Anas bin Malik,

Allah's Apostle said, "Allah is more pleased with the repentance of His slave than anyone of you is pleased with finding his camel which he had lost in the desert. "

Volume 8, Book 75, Number 322,

Narrated Aisha,

The Prophet used to pray eleven Rakat in the late part of the night, and when dawn appeared, he would offer two Rakat and then lie on his right side till the Muadhdhin came to inform him (that the morning prayer was due).

Volume 8, Book 75, Number 323,

Narrated Al-Bara bin 'Azib,

Allah's Apostle said to me, "When you want to go to bed, perform ablution as you do for prayer, then lie down on your right side and say, 'Allahumma aslamtu wajhi ilaika, wa fauwadtu Amri ilaika wa aljatu zahri ilaika, raghbatan wa rahbatan ilaika, lamalja'a wa la manna mink a ill a ilaika. Amantu bikitabi kalladhi anzalta wa bi nabiyyikal-ladhi arsalta'. If you should die then (after reciting this) you will die on the religion of Islam (i.e., as a Muslim); so let these words be the last you say (before going to bed)" While I was memorizing it, I said, "Wa birasiulikal-ladhi arsalta (in Your Apostle whom You have sent).' The Prophet said, "No, but say, Wa binabiyyi-kalladhi arsalta (in Your Prophet whom You have sent)."

Volume 8, Book 75, Number 324,

Narrated Hudhaifa,

When the Prophet went to bed, he would say: "Bismika amutu wa ahya." and when he got up he would say:" Al-hamdu lillahil-ladhi ahyana ba'da ma amatana wa ilaihin-nushur."

Volume 8, Book 75, Number 325:

Narrated Al-Bara bin 'Azib:

e then (after reciting this before going to bed) you will die on the r ???

Volume 8, Book 75, Number 326:

Narrated Hudhaifa:

When the Prophet went to bed at night, he would put his hand under his cheek and then say, "Al-lahumma bismika amutu wa ahya," and when he got up, he would say, "Al-Hamdu lil-lahi al-ladhi ahyana ba'da ma amatana, wa ilaihi an-nushur."

Volume 8, Book 75, Number 327:

Narrated Al-Bara' bin 'Azib:

When Allah's Apostle went to bed, he used to sleep on his right side and then say, "All-ahumma aslamtu nafsi ilaika, wa wajjahtu wajhi ilaika, wa fauwadtu Amri ilaika, wa alja'tu zahri ilaika, ragh-batan wa rahbatan ilaika. La Malja'a wa la manja minka illa ilaika. Amantu bikitabika al-ladhi anza-lta wa nabiyyika al-ladhi arsalta! Allah's Apostle said, "Whoever recites these words (before going to bed) and dies the same night, he will die on the Islamic religion (as a Muslim)."

Volume 8, Book 75, Number 328:

Narrated Ibn 'Abbas:

One night I slept at the house of Maimuna. The Prophet woke up, answered the call of nature, washed his face and hands, and then slept. He got up (late at night), went to a water skin, opened the mouth thereof and performed ablution not using much water, yet he washed al l the parts properly and then offered the prayer. I got up and straightened my back in order that the Prophet might not feel that I was watching him, and then I performed the ablution, and when he got up to offer the prayer, stood on his left. He caught hold of my ear and brought me over to his right side. He offered thirteen Rak'at in all and then lay down and slept till he started blowing out his breath as he used to do when he slept. In the meantime Bilal informed the Prophet of the approaching time for the (Fajr) prayer, and the Prophet offered the Fajr (Morning) prayer without performing new ablution. He used to say in his invocation, Allaihumma ij'al fi qalbi nuran wa fi basari nuran, wa fi sam'i nuran, wa'an yamini nuran, wa'an yasari nuran, wa fawqi nuran, wa tahti nuran, wa amami nuran, wa khalfi nuran, waj'al li nuran." Kuraib (a sub narrator) said, "I have forgotten seven other words, (which the Prophet mentioned in this invocation). I met a man from the offspring of Al-'Abbas and he narrated those seven things to me, mentioning, '(Let there be light in) my nerves, my flesh, my blood, my hair and my body,' and he also mentioned two other things."

Volume 8, Book 75, Number 329:

Narrated Ibn 'Abbas:

When the Prophet got up at night to offer the night prayer, he used to say: "Allahumma laka-l-hamdu; Anta nuras-samawati wal ardi wa man fihinna. Wa laka-l-hamdu; Anta qaiyim as-samawati wal ardi wa man flhinna. Wa lakaI-hamdu; Anta-l-,haqqun, wa wa'daka haqqun, wa qauluka haqqun, wa liqauka haqqun, wal-jannatu haqqun, wannaru haqqun, was-sa atu haqqun, wan-nabiyyuna huqqun, Mahammadun haqqun, Allahumma laka aslamtu, wa Alaika tawakkaltu, wa bika amantu, wa ilaika anabtu, wa bika Khasamtu, wa ilaika hakamtu, faghfirli ma qaddamtu wa ma akh-khartu, wa ma asrartu, wa ma a'lantu. Anta al-muqaddimu, wa anta al-mu-'akhkhiru. La il-aha il-la anta (or La ilaha ghairuka)"

Volume 8, Book 75, Number 330:

Narrated 'Ali:

Fatima complained about the blisters on her hand because of using a mill-stone. She went to ask the Prophet for servant, but she did not find him (at home) and had to inform 'Aisha of her need. When he came, 'Aisha informed him about it. Ali added: The Prophet came to us when we had gone to our beds. When I was going to get up, he said, "Stay in your places," and sat between us, till I felt the coolness of the feet on my chest. The Prophet then said, "Shall I not tell you of a thing which is better for you than a servant? When you (both) go to your beds, say 'Allahu Akbar' thirty-four times, and 'Subhan Allah' thirty-three times, 'Alhamdu 'illah' thirty-three times, for that is better for you than a servant." Ibn Sirin said, "Subhan Allah' (is to be said for) thirty-four times."

Volume 8, Book 75, Number 331:

Narrated 'Aisha:

Whenever Allah's Apostle went to bed, he used to blow on his hands while reciting the Mu'auwid-hat (i.e. Suratal-Falaq and Surat-an-Nas, 113 and 114) and then pass his hands over his body,

Volume 8, Book 75, Number 332:

Narrated Abu Huraira:

The Prophet said, "When anyone of you go to bed, he should shake out his bed with the inside of his waist sheet, for he does not know what has come on to it after him, and then he should say: 'Bismika Rabbi wada'tu Janbi wa bika arfa'uhu, In amsakta nafsi farhamha wa in arsaltaha fahfazha bima tahfazu bihi ibadakas-salihin."

Volume 8, Book 75, Number 333:

Narrated Abu Huraira:

Allah's Apostle said, "When it is the last third of the night, our Lord, the Blessed, the Superior, descends every night to the heaven of the world and says, 'Is there anyone who invokes Me (demand anything from Me), that I may respond to his invocation; Is there anyone who asks Me for something that I may give (it to) him; Is there anyone who asks My forgiveness that I may forgive him?' "

Volume 8, Book 75, Number 334:

Narrated Anas bin Malik:

Whenever the Prophet went to the lavatory, he used to say: "Allahumma Inni a'udhu bika mina-lkhubthi Wal khaba'ith."

Volume 8, Book 75, Number 335:

Narrated Shaddad bin 'Aus:

The Prophet said, "The most superior way of asking for forgiveness from Allah is: 'Allahumma anta Rabbi la ilaha illa anta. Khalaqtani wa ana 'abduka, wa ana 'ala 'ahdika wa Wa'dika mastata'tu abu'u Laka bi ni 'matika wa abu'u Laka bidhanbi; faghfirli fa'innahu la yaghfiru-dh-dhunuba ill a ant a. A'uidhu bika min sharri ma sana'tu.' If somebody recites this invocation during the night, and if he should die then, he will go to Paradise (or he will be from the people of Paradise). And if he recites it in the morning, and if he should die on the same day, he will have the same fate."

Volume 8, Book 75, Number 336:

Narrated Hudhaifa:

Whenever the Prophet intended to go to bed, he would recite: "Bismika Allahumma amutu wa ahya (With Your name, O Allah, I die and I live)." And when he woke up from his sleep, he would say: "Al-hamdu lil-lahil-ladhi ahyana ba'da ma amatana; wa ilaihi an-nushur (All the Praises are for Allah Who has made us alive after He made us die (sleep) and unto Him is the Resurrection). "

Volume 8, Book 75, Number 337:

Narrated Abu Dhar:

Whenever the Prophet lay on his bed, he used to say: "Allahumma bismika amutu wa ahya," and when he woke up he would say: "Al-hamdu lil-lahilladhi ahyana ba'da ma an atana, wa ilaihi an-nushur."

Volume 8, Book 75, Number 338:

Narrated 'Abdullah bin 'Amr:

Abu Bakr As-Siddiq said to the Prophet, "Teach me an invocation with which I may invoke (Allah) in my prayer." The Prophet said, "Say: Allahumma inni zalamtu nafsi zulman kathiran wala yagh-firudh-dhunuba illa anta, Faghfirli maghfiratan min indika war-hamni, innaka antalGhafur-Rahim."

Volume 8, Book 75, Number 339:

Narrated 'Aisha:

The Verse: 'Neither say your prayer aloud, nor say it in a low tone.' (17.110) was revealed as re-gards invocation.

Volume 8, Book 75, Number 340:

Narrated 'Abdullah:

We used to say in the prayer: 'AsSalam be on Allah, As-Salam be on so-and so.' So one day the Prophet said to us, "Allah Himself is As-Salam; when anyone of you sits during his prayer, he should say: 'At-tah, iyyatu-lillahi,' up to 'As-Salihin,' (All the compliments are for Allah ...righteous people) for when he recites this, then he says his Salam to all the righteous people present in the heavens and on the earth. Then he should say, 'I testify that none has the right to be worshipped except Allah, and that Muhammad is His slave and His Apostle,' and then he can select whatever he likes to celebrate (Allah's) Praises."

Volume 8, Book 75, Number 341:

Narrated Abu Huraira:

The people said, "O Allah's Apostle! The rich people have got the highest degrees of prestige and the permanent pleasures (in this life and the life to come in the Hereafter)." He said, "How is that?" They said, "The rich pray as we pray, and strive in Allah's Cause as we do, and spend from their sur-plus wealth in charity, while we have no wealth (to spend likewise)." He said, "Shall I not tell you a thing, by doing which, you will catch up with those who are ahead of you and supersede those who will come after you; and nobody will be able to do such a good deed as you do except the one who does the same (deed as you do). That deed is to recite 'Subhan Allah ten times, and 'Al-Hamdulillah ten times, and 'AllahuAkbar' ten times after every prayer."

Volume 8, Book 75, Number 342:

Narrated Warrad:

(the freed slave of Al-Mughira bin Shu'ba) Al-Mughira wrote to Muawiya bin Abu Sufyan that Allah's Apostle used to say at the end of every prayer after the Taslim, "La ilaha illa-l-lahu wahdahu la sharika lahu; lahu-l-mulk wa lahu-l-hamd, wahuwa 'ala kulli shai'n qadir. Allahumma la mani'a Lima a taita, wa la mu'ta Lima mana'ta, wa la yanfa'u dhal-jaddu minkal-jadd.

Volume 8, Book 75, Number 343:

Narrated Salama bin Al-Akwa':

We went out with the Prophet to Khaibar. A man among the people said, "O 'Amir! Will you please recite to us some of your poetic verses?" So 'Amir got down and started chanting among them, saying, "By Allah! Had it not been for Allah, we would not have been guided." 'Amir also said other poetic verses which I do not remember. Allah's Apostle said, "Who is this (camel) driver?" The people said, "He is 'Amir bin Al-Akwa'," He said, "May Allah bestow His Mercy on him." A man from the People said, "O Allah's Apostle! Would that you let us enjoy his company longer." When the people (Muslims) lined up, the battle started, and 'Amir was struck with his own sword (by chance) by himself and died. In the evening, the people made a large number of fires (for cooking meals). Allah's Apostle said, "What is this fire? What are you making the fire for?" They said, "For cooking the meat of donkeys." He said, "Throw away what is in the pots and break the pots!" A man said, "O Allah's Prophet! May we throw away what is in them and wash them?" He said, "Never mind, you may do so." (See Hadith No. 509, Vol. 5).

Volume 8, Book 75, Number 344:

Narrated Ibn Abi Aufa:

Whenever a man brought his alms to the Prophet, the Prophet would say, "O Allah! Bestow Your Blessing upon the family of so-and-so." When my father came to him (with his alms), he said, "O Allah! Bestow Your Blessings upon the family of Abi Aufa."

Volume 8, Book 75, Number 345:

Narrated Jarir:

Allah's Apostle said to me. "Will you relieve me from Dhi-al-Khalasa? " Dhi-al-Khalasa was an idol which the people used to worship and it was called Al-Ka'ba al Yamaniyya. I said, "O Allah's

Apostle I am a man who can't sit firm on horses." So he stroked my chest (with his hand) and said, "O Allah! Make him firm and make him a guiding and well-guided man." So I went out with fifty (men) from my tribe of Ahrnas. (The sub-narrator, Sufyan, quoting Jarir, perhaps said, "I went out with a group of men from my nation.") and came to Dhi-al-Khalasa and burnt it, and then came to the Prophet and said, "O Allah's Apostle! I have not come to you till I left it like a camel with a skin disease." The Prophet then invoked good upon Ahmas and their cavalry (fighters).

Volume 8, Book 75, Number 346:

Narrated Anas:

Um Sulaim said to the Prophet "Anas is your servant." The Prophet said, "O Allah! increase his wealth and offspring, and bless (for him) what ever you give him."

Volume 8, Book 75, Number 347:

Narrated 'Aisha:

The Prophet heard a man reciting (the Qur'an) in the mosque. He said," May Allah bestow His Mercy on him, as he made me remember such and-such Verse which I had missed in such-and-such Sura."

Volume 8, Book 75, Number 348:

Narrated 'Abdullah:

The Prophet divided something (among the Muslims) and distributed the shares (of the booty). A man said, "This division has not been made to please Allah." When I informed the Prophet about it, he became so furious that I noticed the signs of anger on his face and he then said, "May Allah bestow His Mercy on Moses, for he was hurt with more than this, yet he remained patient."

Volume 8, Book 75, Number 349:

Narrated 'Ikrima:

Ibn 'Abbas said, "Preach to the people once a week, and if you won't, then preach them twice, but if you want to preach more, then let it be three times (a week only), and do not make the people fed-up with this Qur'an. If you come to some people who are engaged in a talk, don't start interrupting their talk by preaching, lest you should cause them to be bored. You should rather keep quiet, and if they ask you, then preach to them at the time when they are eager to hear what you say. And avoid the use of rhymed prose in invocation for I noticed that Allah's Apostle and his companions always avoided it."

Volume 8, Book 75, Number 350:

Narrated Anas:

Allah's Apostle said, "When anyone of you appeal to Allah for something, he should ask with determination and should not say, 'O Allah, if You wish, give me.', for nobody can force Allah to do something against His Will.

Volume 8, Book 75, Number 351:

Narrated Abu Huraira:

Allah's Apostle said, "None of you should say: 'O Allah, forgive me if You wish; O Allah, be merciful to me if You wish,' but he should always appeal to Allah with determination, for nobody can force Allah to do something against His Will."

Volume 8, Book 75, Number 352:

Narrated Abu Huraira:

Allah's Apostle said, "The invocation of anyone of you is granted (by Allah) if he does not show impatience (by saying, "I invoked Allah but my request has not been granted.")

Volume 8, Book 75, Number 353:

Narrated Anas:

While the Prophet was delivering a sermon on a Friday, a man stood up and said, "O Allah's Apostle! Invoke Allah to bless us with rain." (The Prophet invoked Allah for rain.) So, the sky became overcast and it started raining till one could hardly reach one's home. It kept on raining till the next Friday when the same man or another man got up and said (to the Prophet), "Invoke Allah to withhold the rain from us, for we have been drowned (with heavy rain)." The Prophet said, "O Allah! Let it rain around us and not on us." Then the clouds started dispersing around Medina and rain ceased to fall on the people of Medina.

Volume 8, Book 75, Number 354:

Narrated 'Abdullah bin Zaid:

Allah's Apostle went out to this Musalla (praying place) to offer the prayer of Istisqa.' He invoked Allah for rain and then faced the Qibla and turned his Rida' (upper garment) inside out.

Volume 8, Book 75, Number 355,

Narrated Anas,

My mother said, "O Allah's Apostle! Please invoke Allah on behalf of your servant." He said, "O Allah! Increase his wealth and children, and bestow Your Blessing on whatever You give him." a time of distress.

Volume 8, Book 75, Number 356,

Narrated Ibn Abbas,

The Prophet used to invoke Allah at the time of distress, saying, "La ilaha illal-lahu al-'Azim, al-Halim, La ilaha illal-lahu Rabbu-s-samawati wal-ard wa Rabbu-1-arsh il-azim,"

Volume 8, Book 75, Number 357,

Narrated Ibn 'Abbas,

Allah's Apostle used to say at a time of distress, "La ilaha illal-lahu Rabbul-1-'arsh il-'azim, La ilaha illallahu Rabbu-s-samawati wa Rabbu-1-ard, Rabbu-1-'arsh-il-Karim."

Volume 8, Book 75, Number 358,

Narrated Abu Huraira,

Allah's Apostle used to seek refuge with Allah from the difficult moment of a calamity and from being overtaken by destruction and from being destined to an evil end, and from the malicious joy of enemies. Sufyan said, "This narration contained three items only, but I added one. I do not know which one that was."

Volume 8, Book 75, Number 359,

Narrated 'Aisha,

When Allah's Apostle was healthy, he used to say, "No prophet dies till he is shown his place in Paradise, and then he is given the option (to live or die)." So when death approached him(during his illness), and while his head was on my thigh, he became unconscious for a while, and when he recovered, he fixed his eyes on the ceiling and said, "O Allah! (Let me join) the Highest Companions (see Qur'an 4.69)," I said, "So, he does not choose us." Then I realized that it was the application of the statement he used to relate to us when he was healthy. So that was his last utterance (before he died), i.e. "O Allah! (Let me join) the Highest Companions."

Volume 8, Book 75, Number 360:

Narrated Qais:

I came to Khabbab who had been branded with seven brands(1) and he said, "Had Allah's Apostle not forbidden us to invoke (Allah) for death, I would have invoked (Allah) for it."

Volume 8, Book 75, Number 361:

Narrated Qais:

I came to Khabbab who had been branded with seven brands over his abdomen, and I heard him saying, "If the Prophet: had not forbidden us to invoke (Allah) for death, I would have invoked Allah for it."

Volume 8, Book 75, Number 362:

Narrated Anas:

Allah's Apostle said," None of you should long for death because of a calamity that had befallen him, and if he cannot, but long for death, then he should say, 'O Allah! Let me live as long as life is better for me, and take my life if death is better for me.' "

Volume 8, Book 75, Number 363:

Narrated As-Sa'ib bin Yazid:

My aunt took me to Allah's Apostle and said, "O Allah's Apostle! My sister's son is sick." So he passed his hand over my head and invoked for Allah's blessing upon me and then performed the ablution. I drank from the water of his ablution and I stood behind him and looked at his Khatam (the seal of Prophethood) between his shoulders (and its size was) like the button of a tent.

Volume 8, Book 75, Number 364:

Narrated Abu 'Aqil:

that his grandfather. 'Abdullah bin Hisham used to take him from the market or to the market (the narrator is in doubt) and used to buy grain and when Ibn Az-Zubair and Ibn 'Umar met him, they would say to him, "Let us be your partners (in trading) as the Prophet invoked for Allah's blessing upon you." He would then take them as partners and he would Sometimes gain a whole load carried by an animal which he would send home.

Volume 8, Book 75, Number 365:

Narrated Mahmud bin Ar-Rabi:

On whose face Allah's Apostle had thrown water from his mouth, the water having been taken from their well while he was still a young boy (who has not yet attained the age of puberty).

Volume 8, Book 75, Number 366:

Narrated 'Aisha:

The boys used to be brought to the Prophet and he used to invoke for Allah's blessing upon them. Once an infant was brought to him and it urinated on his clothes. He asked for water and poured it over the place of the urine and did not wash his clothes.

Volume 8, Book 75, Number 367:

Narrated 'Abdullah bin Tha'laba bin Su'air:

whose eye Allah's Apostle had touched, that he had seen Sa'd bin Abi Waqqas offering one Rak'a only for the Witr prayer.

Volume 8, Book 75, Number 368:

Narrated 'Abdur-Rahman bin Abi Laila:

Ka'b bin 'Ujra met me and said, "Shall I give you a present? Once the Prophet came to us and we said, 'O Allah's Apostle ! We know how to greet you; but how to send 'Salat' upon you? He said, 'Say: Allahumma Salli ala Muhammadin wa 'ala Ali Muhammadin, kama sal-laita 'ala ali Ibrahima innaka Hamidun Majid. Allahumma barik 'ala Muhammadin wa 'ala ali Muhammadin, kama barakta 'ala ali Ibrahima, innaka Hamidun Majid."

Volume 8, Book 75, Number 369:

Narrated Abu Sa'id Al-Khudri:

We said, "O Allah's Apostle This is (i.e. we know) the greeting to you; will you tell us how to send Salat on you?" He said, "Say: 'Allahumma Salli 'ala Muhammadin 'abdika wa rasulika kama sal-laita 'ala Ibrahima wa barik 'ala Muhammadin wa ali Muhammadin kama barakta 'ala Ibrahima wa Ali Ibrahim."

Volume 8, Book 75, Number 370:

Narrated Ibn Abi Aufa:

Whenever somebody brought alms to the Prophet the used to say, "Allahumma Salli 'Alaihi (O Allah! Send Your Salat (Grace and Honor) on him)." Once when my father brought his alms to him, he said, "O Allah! Send Your Salat (Grace and Honor) on the family of Abi Aufa."

Volume 8, Book 75, Number 371.

Narrated Abu Humaid As-Saidi.

The people said, "O Allah's Apostle ! How may we send Salat on you?" He said, "Say: Allahumma Salli 'ala- Muhammadin wa azwajihi wa dhurriyyatihi kama sal-laita 'ala ali Ibrahim; wa barik 'ala Muhammadin wa azwajihi wa dhurriyyatihi kamabarakta 'ala ali Ibrahim innaka hamidun majid."

Volume 8, Book 75, Number 372.

Narrated Abu Huraira.

that he heard the Prophet saying, "O Allah! If I should ever abuse a believer, please let that be a means of bringing him near to You on the Day of Resurrection."

Volume 8, Book 75, Number 373.

Narrated Anas.

Once the people started asking Allah's Apostle questions, and they asked so many questions that he became angry and ascended the pulpit and said, "I will answer whatever questions you may ask me today." I looked right and left and saw everyone covering his face with his garment and weeping. Behold ! There was a man who, on quarreling with the people, used to be called as a son of a person other than h is father. He said, "O Allah's Apostle! Who is my father?" The Prophet replied, "Your father is Hudhaifa." And then 'Umar got up and said, "We accept Allah as our Lord, and Islam as (our) religion, and Muhammad as (our) Apostle; and we seek refuge with Allah from the afflictions." Allah's Apostle said, " I have never seen a day like today in its good and its evil for Paradise and the Hell Fire were displayed in front of me, till I saw them just beyond this wall." Qatada, when relating this Hadith, used to mention the following Verse:--

'O you who believe! Ask not questions about things which, If made plain to you, May cause you trouble. (5.101)

Volume 8, Book 75, Number 374.

Narrated Anas bin Malik.

The Prophet said to Abu Talha, "Choose one of your boys to serve me." So Abu Talha took me (to serve the Prophet) by giving me a ride behind him (on his camel). So I used to serve Allah's Apostle whenever he stayed somewhere. I used to hear him saying, "O Allah! I seek refuge with you (Allah) from (worries) care and grief, from incapacity and laziness, from miserliness and cowardice, from being heavily in debt and from being overpowered by other men." I kept on serving him till he returned from (the battle of) Khaibar. He then brought Safiya, the daughter of Huyay whom he had got (from the booty). I saw him making a kind of cushion with a cloak or a garment for her. He then let her ride behind him. When we reached a place called As-Sahba', he prepared (a special meal called) Hais, and asked me to invite the men who (came and) ate, and that was the marriage banquet given on the consummation of his marriage to her. Then he proceeded till the mountain of Uhud appeared, whereupon he said, "This mountain loves us and we love it." When he approached Medina, he said, "O Allah! I make the land between its (i.e., Medina's) two mountains a sanctuary, as the prophet Abraham made Mecca a sanctuary. O Allah! Bless them (the people of Medina) in their Mudd and the Sa' (units of measuring)."

Volume 8, Book 75, Number 375:

Narrated Um Khalid bint Khalid:

I heard the Prophet seeking refuge with Allah from the punishment of the grave.

Volume 8, Book 75, Number 376:

Narrated Mus'ab:

Sa'd used to recommend five (statements) and mentioned that the Prophet I used to recommend it. (It was) "O Allah! I seek refuge with You from miserliness; and seek refuge with You from cowardice; and seek refuge with You from being sent back to geriatric old age; and I seek refuge with You from the affliction of this world (i.e., the affliction of Ad-Dajjal etc.); and seek refuge with You from the punishment of the grave."

Volume 8, Book 75, Number 377:

Narrated 'Aisha:

Two old ladies from among the Jewish ladies entered upon me and said' "The dead are punished in their graves," but I thought they were telling a lie and did not believe them in the beginning. When they went away and the Prophet entered upon me, I said, "O Allah's Apostle! Two old ladies.." and told him the whole story. He said, "They told the truth; the dead are really punished, to the extent that all the animals hear (the sound resulting from) their punishment." Since then I always saw him seeking refuge with Allah from the punishment of the grave in his prayers.

Volume 8, Book 75, Number 378:

Narrated Anas bin Malik:

Allah's Prophet used to say, "O Allah! I seek refuge with You from incapacity and laziness, from cowardice and geriatric old age, and seek refuge with You from the punishment of the grave, and I seek refuge with You from the afflictions of life and death."

Volume 8, Book 75, Number 379:

Narrated 'Aisha:

The Prophet used to say, "O Allah! I seek refuge with You from laziness and geriatric old age, from all kinds of sins and from being in debt; from the affliction of the Fire and from the punishment of the Fire and from the evil of the affliction of wealth; and I seek refuge with You from the affliction of poverty, and I seek refuge with You from the affliction of Al-Mesiah Ad-Dajjal. O Allah! Wash away my sins with the water of snow and hail, and cleanse my heart from all the sins as a white garment is cleansed from the filth, and let there be a long distance between me and my sins, as You made East and West far from each other."

Volume 8, Book 75, Number 380:

Narrated Anas bin Malik:

The Prophet used to say, "O Allah! I seek refuge with You from worry and grief, from incapacity and laziness, from cowardice and miserliness, from being heavily in debt and from being over-powered by (other) men." (See Hadith No. 374)

Volume 8, Book 75, Number 381:

Narrated Mus'ab bin Sa'd:

Sa'd bin Abi Waqqas used to recommend these five (statements) and say that the Prophet said so (and they are): "O Allah! I seek refuge with You from miserliness, and seek refuge with You from cowardice, and seek refuge with You from being brought back to geriatric old age, and seek refuge with You from the afflictions of the world, and seek refuge with You from the punishment of the grave."

Volume 8, Book 75, Number 382:

Narrated Anas bin Malik:

Allah's Apostle used to seek refuge with Allah saying, "O Allah! I seek refuge with You from laziness, and seek refuge with You from cowardice, and seek refuge with You from geriatric old age, and seek refuge with You from miserliness."

Volume 8, Book 75, Number 383:

Narrated 'Aisha:

The Prophet said, "O Allah! Make us love Medina as You made us love Mecca, or more, and trans-
fer the fever that is in it, to Al-Juhfa. O Allah! Bless our Mudd and our Sam' (kinds of measures)."

Volume 8, Book 75, Number 384:

Narrated 'Amir bin Sa'd:

that his father said, "In the year of Hajjatal-Wada', the Prophet paid me a visit while I was suffering from an ailment that had brought me to the verge of death. I said, 'O Allah's Apostle! My sickness
has reduced me to the (bad) state as you see, and I am a rich man, but have no heirs except one
daughter. Shall I give 2/3 of my property in charity?' He said, 'No.' I said, 'Then 1/2 of it?' He said,
'Even 1/3 is too much, for, to leave your inheritors wealthy is better than to leave them in poverty,
begging from people. And (know that) whatever you spend in Allah's Cause, you will get reward for
it, even for the morsel of food which you put in your wife's mouth.' I said, 'O Allah's Apostle! Will I be
left behind my companions (in Mecca)?' He said, 'If you remain behind, whatever good deed you will
do for Allah's Sake, will raise and upgrade you to a higher position (in Allah's Sight). May be you will
live longer so that some people may benefit by you, and some e others (pagans) may get harmed by
you. O Allah! Complete the migration of my companions and do not turn them on their heels; But
(we pity) the poor Sa'd bin Khaula (not the above mentioned Sa'd) (died in Mecca)" Allah's Apostle
lamented (or pitied) for him as he died in Mecca. (See Hadith No. 693, Vol. 5)

Volume 8, Book 75, Number 385:

Narrated Sa'd:

Seek refuge with Allah by saying the words which the Prophet used to say while seeking refuge
with Allah, "O Allah! I seek refuge with You from cowardice, and seek refuge with You from miserliness, and seek refuge with You from reaching a degraded geriatric old age, and seek refuge with You
from the afflictions of the world and from the punishment in the grave."

Volume 8, Book 75, Number 386:

Narrated 'Aisha:

The Prophet used to say, "O Allah! I seek refuge with You from laziness from geriatric old age,
from being in debt, and from committing sins. O Allah! I seek refuge with You from the punishment
of the Fire, the afflictions of the grave, the punishment in the grave, and the evil of the affliction of
poverty and from the evil of the affliction caused by Al-Masih Ad-Dajjal. O Allah! Wash away my

sins with the water of snow and hail, and cleanse my heart from the sins as a white garment is cleansed of filth, and let there be a far away distance between me and my sins as You have set far away the East and the West from each other."

Volume 8, Book 75, Number 387:

Narrated 'Aisha:

The Prophet used to seek refuge with Allah (by saying), "O Allah! I seek refuge with You from the affliction of the Fire and from the punishment in the Fire, and seek refuge with You from the affliction of the grave, and I seek refuge with You from the affliction of wealth, and I seek refuge with You from the affliction of poverty, and seek refuge with You from the affliction of Al-Masih Ad-Dajjal."

Volume 8, Book 75, Number 388:

Narrated 'Aisha:

The Prophet used to say, 'O Allah! I seek refuge with You from the affliction of the Fire, the punishment of the Fire, the affliction of the grave, the punishment of the grave, and the evil of the affliction of poverty. O Allah! I seek refuge with You from the evil of the affliction of Al-Masih Ad-Dajjal, O Allah! Cleanse my heart with the water of snow and hail, and cleanse my heart from all sins as a white garment is cleansed from filth, and let there be a far away distance between me and my sins as You made the East and West far away from each other. O Allah! I seek refuge with You from laziness, sins, and from being in debt."

Volume 8, Book 75, Number 389:

Narrated Um Sulaim:

that she said, "O Allah's Apostle! Anas is your servant, so please invoke for Allah's blessing for him." The Prophet said, "O Allah! Increase his wealth and offspring and bless (for him) whatever You give him."

Volume 8, Book 75, Number 390:

Narrated Anas:

Um Sulaim said (to the Prophet), "Anas is your servant; so please invoke for Allah's blessings for him." He said "O Allah! Increase his wealth and offspring, and Bless (for him) whatever You give him."

Volume 8, Book 75, Number 391.

Narrated Jabir.

The Prophet used to teach us the Istikhara for each and every matter as he used to teach us the Suras from the Holy Qur'an. (He used to say), "If anyone of you intends to do something, he should offer a two-Rak'at prayer other than the obligatory prayer, and then say. 'Allahumma inni as-takhiruka bi'ilmika, wa astaqdiruka biqudratika, wa as'aluka min fadlika-l-'azim, fa innaka taqdiru wala aqdiru, wa ta'lamu wala a'lamu, wa anta'allamu-l-ghuyub. Allahumma in kunta ta'lamu anna hadha-lamra khairun li fi dini wa ma'ashi wa 'aqibati amri (or said, fi 'ajili amri wa ajilihi) fa-qdurhu li, Wa in junta ta'lamu anna ha-dha-l-amra sharrun li fi dini wa ma'ashi wa 'aqibati amri (or said, fi ajili amri wa ajilihi) fasrifhu 'anni was-rifni 'anhu wa aqdur li alkhaira haithu kana, thumma Raddani bihi," Then he should mention his matter (need).

Volume 8, Book 75, Number 392.

Narrated Abu Musa.

The Prophet asked for some water and performed the ablution, and then raised his hands (towards the sky) and said, "O Allah! Forgive 'Ubaid Abi 'Amir." I saw the whiteness of his armpits (while he was raising his hands) and he added, "O Allah! Upgrade him over many of Your human creatures on the Day of Resurrection "

Volume 8, Book 75, Number 393.

Narrated Abu Musa.

We were in the company of the Prophet on a journey, and whenever we ascended a high place, we used to say Takbir (in a loud voice). The Prophet said, "O people! Be kind to yourselves, for you are not calling upon a deaf or an absent one, but You are calling an All-Hearer, and an All-Seer." Then he came to me as I was reciting silently, "La haul a wala quwwata illa bil-lah." He said, "O 'Abdullah bin Qais! Say. La haul a walaquwata illa bil-lah, for it is one of the treasures of Paradise." Or he said, "Shall I tell you a word which is one of the treasures of Paradise? It is. La haul a wala quwwata illa bil-lah."

Volume 8, Book 75, Number 394.

Narrated Ibn Umar.

Whenever Allah's Apostle returned from a Ghazwa or Hajj or 'Umra, he used to say, "Allahu Akbar," three times; whenever he went up a high place, he used to say, "La ilaha illal-lahu wahdahu la sharika lahu, lahu-l-mulk wa lahu-l-hamd, wa huwa'ala kulli Shai 'in qadir. Ayibuna ta'ibuna 'abiduna lirabbina hamidun. Sadaqa-l-lahu wa'dahu, wa nasara'abdahu wa hazama-l-ahzaba wah-dahu."

Volume 8, Book 75, Number 395:

Narrated Anas:

The Prophet seeing a yellow mark (of perfume) on the clothes of 'Abdur-Rahman bin 'Auf, said, "What about you?" 'Abdur-Rahman replied, "I have married a woman with a Mahr of gold equal to a date-stone." The Prophet said, "May Allah bestow His Blessing on you (in your marriage). Give a wedding banquet, (Walima) even with one sheep."

Volume 8, Book 75, Number 396:

Narrated Jabir:

My father died and left behind seven or nine daughters, and I married a woman. The Prophet said, "Did you get married, O Jabir?" I replied, "Yes." He asked, "Is she a virgin or a matron?" I replied, "She is a matron." He said, "Why didn't you marry a virgin girl so that you might play with her and she with you (or, you might make her laugh and she make you laugh)?" I said, "My father died, leaving seven or nine girls (orphans) and I did not like to bring a young girl like them, so I married a woman who can look after them." He said, "May Allah bestow His Blessing on you."

Volume 8, Book 75, Number 397:

Narrated Ibn 'Abbas:

The Prophet said, "If anyone of you, when intending to have a sexual intercourse with his wife, says: 'Bismillah, Allahumma jannibna-sh-shaitan, wa jannibi-sh-shaitan ma razaqtana,' and if the couple are destined to have a child (out of that very sexual relation), then Satan will never be able to harm that child."

Volume 8, Book 75, Number 398:

Narrated Anas:

The most frequent invocation of The Prophet was: "O Allah! Give to us in the world that which is good and in the Hereafter that which is good, and save us from the torment of the Fire." (2.201)

Volume 8, Book 75, Number 399:

Narrated Sa'd bin Abi Waqqas:

The Prophet used to teach us these words as he used to teach us the Book (Qur'an): "O Allah! seek refuge with You from miserliness, and seek refuge with You from cowardice, and seek refuge with You from being brought back to (senile) geriatric old age, and seek refuge with You from the affliction of the world and from the punishment in the Hereafter."

Volume 8, Book 75, Number 400:

Narrated 'Aisha:

that Allah's Apostle was affected by magic, so much that he used to think that he had done something which in fact, he did not do, and he invoked his Lord (for a remedy). Then (one day) he said, "O 'Aisha!) Do you know that Allah has advised me as to the problem I consulted Him about?" 'Aisha said, "O Allah's Apostle! What's that?" He said, "Two men came to me and one of them sat at my head and the other at my feet, and one of them asked his companion, 'What is wrong with this man?' The latter replied, 'He is under the effect of magic.' The former asked, 'Who has worked magic on him?' The latter replied, 'Labid bin Al-A'sam.' The former asked, 'With what did he work the magic?' The latter replied, 'With a comb and the hair, which are stuck to the comb, and the skin of pollen of a date-palm tree.' The former asked, 'Where is that?' The latter replied, 'It is in Dharwan.' Dharwan was a well in the dwelling place of the (tribe of) Bani Zuraiq. Allah's Apostle went to that well and returned to 'Aisha, saying, 'By Allah, the water (of the well) was as red as the infusion of Hinna, (1) and the date-palm trees look like the heads of devils.' 'Aisha added, Allah's Apostle came to me and informed me about the well. I asked the Prophet, 'O Allah's Apostle, why didn't you take out the skin of pollen?' He said, 'As for me, Allah has cured me and I hated to draw the attention of the people to such evil (which they might learn and harm others with).' "

Narrated Hisham's father: 'Aisha said, "Allah's Apostle was bewitched, so he invoked Allah repeatedly requesting Him to cure him from that magic)." Hisham then narrated the above narration. (See Hadith No. 658, Vol. 7)

Volume 8, Book 75, Number 401:

Narrated Ibn Abi Aufa:

Allah's Apostle asked for Allah's wrath upon the Ahzab (confederates), saying, "O Allah, the Revealer of the Holy Book, and the One swift at reckoning! Defeat the confederates; Defeat them and shake them."

Volume 8, Book 75, Number 402:

Narrated Abu Huraira:

When the Prophet said, "Sami' al-lahu Liman hamidah (Allah heard him who sent his praises to Him)" in the last Rak'a of the 'Isha' prayer, he used to invoke Allah, saying, "O Allah! Save 'Aiyash bin

Abi Rabi'a; O Allah! Save Al-Walid bin Al-Walid; O Allah! Save the weak people among the believers; O Allah! Be hard on the Tribe of Mudar; O Allah! Inflict years of drought upon them like the years (of drought) of the Prophet Joseph."

Volume 8, Book 75, Number 403:

Narrated Anas:

The Prophet sent a Sariya (an army detachment) consisting of men called Al-Qurra', and all of them were martyred. I had never seen the Prophet so sad over anything as he was over them. So he said Qunut (invocation in the prayer) for one month in the Fajr prayer, invoking for Allah's wrath upon the tribe of 'Usaiya, and he used to say, "The people of 'Usaiya have disobeyed Allah and His Apostle."

Volume 8, Book 75, Number 404:

Narrated 'Aisha:

The Jews used to greet the Prophet by saying, "As-Samu 'Alaika (i.e., death be upon you), so I understood what they said, and I said to them, "As-Samu 'alaikum wal-la'na (i.e. Death and Allah's Curse be upon you)." The Prophet said, "Be gentle and calm, O 'Aisha, as Allah likes gentleness in all affairs." I said, "O Allah's Prophet! Didn't you hear what they said?" He said, "Didn't you hear me answering them back by saying, 'Alaikum (i.e., the same be upon you)?"

Volume 8, Book 75, Number 405:

Narrated 'Ali bin Abi Talib:

We were in the company of the Prophet on the day (of the battle) of Al-Khandaq (the Trench). The Prophet said, "May Allah fill their (the infidels') graves and houses with fire, as they have kept us so busy that we could not offer the middle prayer till the sun had set; and that prayer was the 'Asr prayer."

Volume 8, Book 75, Number 406:

Narrated Abu Huraira:

At-Tufail bin 'Amr came to Allah's Apostle and said, "O Allah's Apostle! The tribe of Daus has disobeyed (Allah and His Apostle) and refused (to embrace Islam), therefore, invoke Allah's wrath for them." The people thought that the Prophet would invoke Allah's wrath for them, but he said, "O Allah! Guide the tribe Of Daus and let them come to us,"

Volume 8, Book 75, Number 407,

Narrated Abu Musa,

The Prophet used to invoke Allah with the following invocation, 'Rabbi-ghfir-li Khati 'ati wa jahli wa israfi fi amri kullihi, wa ma anta a'lamu bihi minni. Allahumma ighfirli khatayaya wa 'amdi, wa jahli wa jiddi, wa kullu dhalika'indi. Allahumma ighrifli ma qaddamtu wa ma akhartu wa ma as-rartu wa ma a'lantu. Anta-l-muqaddimu wa anta-l-mu'akh-khiru, wa anta 'ala kulli shai'in qadir.'

Volume 8, Book 75, Number 408,

Narrated Abu Musa Al-Ash'ari,

The Prophet used to invoke Allah, saying, "Allahumma ighfirli khati'ati wa jahli wa israfi fi amri, wa ma anta a-'lamu bihi minni. Allahumma ighfirli hazali wa jiddi wa khata'i wa amdi, wa kullu dhalika 'indi"

Volume 8, Book 75, Number 409,

Narrated Abu Huraira,

Abu-l-Qasim (the Prophet) said, "On Friday there is a particular time. If a Muslim happens to be praying and invoking Allah for something good during that time, Allah will surely fulfill his request." The Prophet pointed out with his hand. We thought that he wanted to illustrate how short that time was.

Volume 8, Book 75, Number 410,

Narrated Ibn Abi Mulaika,

'Aisha said, "The Jews came to the Prophet and said to him, "As-Samu 'Alaika (i.e., Death be upon you)." He replied, 'The same on you.' " 'Aisha said to them, "Death be upon you, and may Allah curse you and shower His wrath upon you!" Allah's Apostle I said, "Be gentle and calm, O 'Aisha! Be gentle and beware of being harsh and of saying evil things." She said, "Didn't you hear what they said?" He said, "Didn't you hear what I replied (to them)? have returned their statement to them, and my invocation against them will be accepted but theirs against me will not be accepted."

Volume 8, Book 75, Number 411,

Narrated Abu Huraira,

The Prophet said, "When the Imam says 'Amin', then you should all say 'Amin', for the angels say 'Amin' at that time, and he whose 'Amin' coincides with the 'Amin' of the angels, all his past sins will be forgiven."

Volume 8, Book 75, Number 412:

Narrated Abu Huraira:

Allah's Apostle said," Whoever says: "La ilaha illal-lah wahdahu la sharika lahu, lahu-l-mulk wa lahu-l-hamd wa huwa 'ala kulli shai'in qadir," one hundred times will get the same reward as given for manumitting ten slaves; and one hundred good deeds will be written in his accounts, and one hundred sins will be deducted from his accounts, and it (his saying) will be a shield for him from Satan on that day till night, and nobody will be able to do a better deed except the one who does more than he."

Volume 8, Book 75, Number 413:

Narrated 'Amr bin Maimun:

Whoever recites it (i.e., the invocation in the above Hadith (412) ten times will be as if he manumitted one of Ishmael's descendants. Abu Aiyub narrated the same Hadith from the Prophet saying, "(Whoever recites it ten times) will be as if he had manumitted one of Ishmael's descendants."

Volume 8, Book 75, Number 414:

Narrated Abu Huraira:

Allah's Apostle said, "Whoever says, 'Subhan Allah wa bihamdihi,' one hundred times a day, will be forgiven all his sins even if they were as much as the foam of the sea.

Volume 8, Book 75, Number 415:

Narrated Abu Huraira:

The Prophet said, "There are two expressions which are very easy for the tongue to say, but they are very heavy in the balance and are very dear to The Beneficent (Allah), and they are, 'Subhan Allah Al-'Azim and 'Subhan Allah wa bihamdihi.'"

Volume 8, Book 75, Number 416:

Narrated Abu Musa: The Prophet said, "The example of the one who celebrates the Praises of his Lord (Allah) in comparison to the one who does not celebrate the Praises of his Lord, is that of a living creature compared to a dead one."

Volume 8, Book 75, Number 417:

Narrated Abu Huraira:

Allah 's Apostle said, "Allah has some angels who look for those who celebrate the Praises of Allah on the roads and paths. And when they find some people celebrating the Praises of Allah, they call each other, saying, "Come to the object of your pursuit.' " He added, "Then the angels encircle them with their wings up to the sky of the world." He added. "(after those people celebrated the Praises of Allah, and the angels go back), their Lord, asks them (those angels)----though He knows better than them----'What do My slaves say?' The angels reply, 'They say: Subhan Allah, Allahu Akbar, and Al-ham-du-lillah, Allah then says 'Did they see Me?' The angels reply, 'No! By Allah, they didn't see You.'

Allah says, How it would have been if they saw Me?' The angels reply, 'If they saw You, they would worship You more devoutly and celebrate Your Glory more deeply, and declare Your freedom from any resemblance to anything more often.' Allah says (to the angels), 'What do they ask Me for?' The angels reply, 'They ask You for Paradise.' Allah says (to the angels), 'Did they see it?' The angels say, 'No! By Allah, O Lord! They did not see it.' Allah says, How it would have been if they saw it?' The angels say, 'If they saw it, they would have greater covetousness for it and would seek It with greater zeal and would have greater desire for it.' Allah says, 'From what do they seek refuge?' The angels reply, 'They seek refuge from the (Hell) Fire.' Allah says, 'Did they see it?' The angels say, 'No By Allah, O Lord! They did not see it.' Allah says, How it would have been if they saw it?' The angels say, 'If they saw it they would flee from it with the extreme fleeing and would have extreme fear from it.' Then Allah says, 'I make you witnesses that I have forgiven them.'" Allah's Apostle added, "One of the angels would say, 'There was so-and-so amongst them, and he was not one of them, but he had just come for some need.' Allah would say, 'These are those people whose companions will not be reduced to misery.' "

Volume 8, Book 75, Number 418:

Narrated Abu Musa Al-Ash'ari:

The Prophet started ascending a high place or hill. A man (amongst his companions) ascended it and shouted in a loud voice, "La ilaha illal-lahu wallahu Akbar." (At that time) Allah's Apostle was riding his mule. Allah's Apostle said, "You are not calling upon a deaf or an absent one." and added, "O Abu Musa (or, O 'Abdullah)! Shall I tell you a sentence from the treasure of Paradise?" I said, "Yes." He said, "La haul a wala quwwata illa billah,"

Volume 8, Book 75, Number 419:

Narrated Abu Huraira:

Allah has ninety-nine Names, i.e., one hundred minus one, and whoever believes in their meanings and acts accordingly, will enter Paradise; and Allah is Witr (one) and loves 'the Witr' (i.e., odd numbers).

Volume 8, Book 75, Number 420:

Narrated Shaqiq:

While we were waiting for 'Abdullah (bin Mas'ud). Yazid bin Muawiya came. I said (to him), "Will you sit down?" He said, "No, but I will go into the house (of Ibn Mas'ud) and let your companion (Ibn Mas'ud) come out to you; and if he should not (come out), I will come out and sit (with you)." Then 'Abdullah came out, holding the hand of Yazid, addressed us, saying, "I know that you are assembled here, but the reason that prevents me from coming out to you, is that Allah's Apostle used to preach to us at intervals during the days, lest we should become bored."

Book 76: To make the Heart Tender (Ar-Riqaq)

Volume 8, Book 76, Number 421:

Narrated Ibn 'Abbas:

The Prophet said, "There are two blessings which many people lose: (They are) Health and free time for doing good."

Volume 8, Book 76, Number 422:

Narrated Anas:

The Prophet said, "O Allah! There is no life worth living except the life of the Hereafter, so (please) make righteous the Ansar and the Emigrants."

Volume 8, Book 76, Number 423:

Narrated Sahl bin Sa'd As-Sa'idi:

We were in the company of Allah's Apostle in (the battle of) Al-Khandaq, and he was digging the trench while we were carrying the earth away. He looked at us and said, "O Allah! There is no life worth living except the life of the Hereafter, so (please) forgive the Ansar and the Emigrants."

Volume 8, Book 76, Number 424:

Narrated Sahl:

I heard the Prophet saying, "A (small) place equal to an area occupied by a whip in Paradise is better than the (whole) world and whatever is in it; and an undertaking (journey) in the forenoon or in the afternoon for Allah's Cause, is better than the whole world and whatever is in it."

Volume 8, Book 76, Number 425:

Narrated Mujahid:

'Abdullah bin 'Umar said, "Allah's Apostle took hold of my shoulder and said, 'Be in this world as if you were a stranger or a traveler." The sub-narrator added: Ibn 'Umar used to say, "If you survive till the evening, do not expect to be alive in the morning, and if you survive till the morning, do not expect to be alive in the evening, and take from your health for your sickness, and (take) from your life for your death."

Volume 8, Book 76, Number 426:

Narrated 'Abdullah:

The Prophet drew a square and then drew a line in the middle of it and let it extend outside the square and then drew several small lines attached to that central line, and said, "This is the human being, and this, (the square) in his lease of life, encircles him from all sides (or has encircled him), and this (line), which is outside (the square), is his hope, and these small lines are the calamities and troubles (which may befall him), and if one misses him, an-other will snap (i.e. overtake) him, and if the other misses him, a third will snap (i.e. overtake) him."

Volume 8, Book 76, Number 427:

Narrated Anas bin Malik:

The Prophet drew a few lines and said, "This is (man's) hope, and this is the instant of his death, and while he is in this state (of hope), the nearer line (death) comes to Him."

Volume 8, Book 76, Number 428:

Narrated Abu Huraira:

The Prophet said, "Allah will not accept the excuse of any person whose instant of death is delayed till he is sixty years of age."

Volume 8, Book 76, Number 429:

Narrated Abu Huraira:

I heard Allah's Apostle saying, "The heart of an old man remains young in two respects, i.e., his love for the world (its wealth, amusements and luxuries) and his incessant hope."

Volume 8, Book 76, Number 430:

Narrated Anas bin Malik:

Allah's Apostle said, "The son of Adam (i.e. man) grows old and so also two (desires) grow old with him, i.e., love for wealth and (a wish for) a long life."

Volume 8, Book 76, Number 431:

Narrated 'Utban bin Malik Al-Ansari:

who was one of the men of the tribe of Bani Salim: Allah's Apostle came to me and said, "If anybody comes on the Day of Resurrection who has said: La ilaha illal-lah, sincerely, with the intention to win Allah's Pleasure, Allah will make the Hell-Fire forbidden for him."

Volume 8, Book 76, Number 432:

Narrated Abu Huraira: Allah's Apostle said, "Allah says, 'I have nothing to give but Paradise as a reward to my believer slave, who, if I cause his dear friend (or relative) to die, remains patient (and hopes for Allah's Reward)."

Volume 8, Book 76, Number 433:

Narrated 'Amr bin 'Auf:

(an ally of the tribe of Bani 'Amir bin Lu'ai and one of those who had witnessed the battle of Badr with Allah's Apostle) Allah's Apostle sent Abu 'Ubaida bin AlJarrah to Bahrain to collect the Jizya tax. Allah's Apostle had concluded a peace treaty with the people of Bahrain and appointed Al 'Ala bin Al-Hadrami as their chief; Abu Ubaida arrived from Bahrain with the money. The Ansar heard of Abu 'Ubaida's arrival which coincided with the Fajr (morning) prayer led by Allah's Apostle. When the Prophet finished the prayer, they came to him. Allah's Apostle smiled when he saw them and said, "I think you have heard of the arrival of Abu 'Ubaida and that he has brought something." They replied, "Yes, O Allah's Apostle! " He said, "Have the good news, and hope for what will please you. By Allah, I am not afraid that you will become poor, but I am afraid that worldly wealth will be given to you in abundance as it was given to those (nations) before you, and you will start competing each other for it as the previous nations competed for it, and then it will divert you (from good) as it diverted them." '

Volume 8, Book 76, Number 434:

Narrated 'Uqba bin 'Amir:

The Prophet went out and offered the funeral prayer for the martyrs of the (battle of) Uhud and then ascended the pulpit and said, "I am your predecessor and I am a witness against you. By Allah, I am now looking at my Tank-lake (Al-Kauthar) and I have been given the keys of the treasures of the earth (or the keys of the earth). By Allah! I am not afraid that after me you will worship others besides Allah, but I am afraid that you will start competing for (the pleasures of) this world."

Volume 8, Book 76, Number 435:

Narrated Abu Sa'id Al-Khudri:

Allah's Apostle said, "The thing I am afraid of most for your sake, is the worldly blessings which Allah will bring forth to you." It was said, "What are the blessings of this world?" The Prophet said, "The pleasures of the world." A man said, "Can the good bring forth evil?" The Prophet kept quiet for a while till we thought that he was being inspired divinely. Then he started removing the sweat from his forehead and said," Where is the questioner?" That man said, "I (am present)." Abu Sa'id added: We thanked the man when the result (of his question) was such. The Prophet said, "Good never brings forth but good. This wealth (of the world) is (like) green and sweet (fruit), and all the vegetation which grows on the bank of a stream either kills or nearly kills the animal that eats too much of it, except the animal that eats the Khadira (a kind of vegetation). Such an animal eats till its stomach is full and then it faces the sun and starts ruminating and then it passes out dung and urine and goes to eat again. This worldly wealth is (like) sweet (fruit), and if a person earns it (the wealth) in a legal way and spends it properly, then it is an excellent helper, and whoever earns it in an illegal way, he will be like the one who eats but is never satisfied."

Volume 8, Book 76, Number 436:

Narrated Zahdam bin Mudarrib:

'Imran bin Husain said: The Prophet said, "The best people are my contemporaries (i.e., the present (my) generation) and then those who come after them (i.e., the next generation)." Imran added: I am not sure whether the Prophet repeated the statement twice after his first saying. The Prophet added, "And after them there will come people who will bear witness, though they will not be asked to give their witness; and they will be treacherous and nobody will trust them, and they will make vows, but will not fulfill them, and fatness will appear among them."

Volume 8, Book 76, Number 437:

Narrated 'Abdullah :

The Prophet said, "The best people are those of my generation, and then those who will come after them (the next generation), and then those who will come after them (i.e. the next generation), and then after them, there will come people whose witness will precede their oaths, and whose oaths will precede their witness."

Volume 8, Book 76, Number 438:

Narrated Qais:

I heard Khabbab, who had branded his abdomen with seven brands, saying, "Had Allah's Apostle not forbidden us to invoke Allah for death, I would have invoked Allah for death. The companions of Muhammad have left this world without taking anything of their reward in it (i.e., they will have perfect reward in the Hereafter), but we have collected of the worldly wealth what we cannot spend but on earth (i.e. on building houses)."

Volume 8, Book 76, Number 439:

Narrated Qais:

I came to Khabbab while he was building a wall, and he (Khabbab) said, "Our companions who have left this world, did not enjoy anything of their reward therein, while we have collected after them, much wealth that we cannot spend but on earth (i.e., on building)."

Volume 8, Book 76, Number 440:

Narrated Khabbab:

We migrated with the Prophet..(This narration is related in the chapter of migration).

Volume 8, Book 76, Number 441:

Narrated Ibn 'Abbas:

I brought water to Uthman bin 'Affan to perform the ablution while he was sitting on his seat. He performed the ablution in a perfect way and said, "I saw the Prophet performing the ablution in this place and he performed it in a perfect way and said, "Whoever performs the ablution as I have done this time and then proceeds to the mosque and offers a two-Rak'at prayer and then sits there (waiting for the compulsory congregational prayers), then all his past sins will be forgiven." The Prophet further added, "Do not be conceited (thinking that your sins will be forgiven because of your prayer)."

Volume 8, Book 76, Number 442:

Narrated Mirdas Al-Aslami:

The Prophet said, "The righteous (pious people will depart (die) in succession one after the other, and there will remain (on the earth) useless people like the useless husk of barley seeds or bad dates, and Allah will not

Volume 8, Book 76, Number 443:

Narrated Abu Huraira:

The Prophet said, "Perish the slave of Dinar, Dirham, Qatifa (thick soft cloth), and Khamisa (a garment), for if he is given, he is pleased; otherwise he is dissatisfied."

Volume 8, Book 76, Number 444:

Narrated Ibn 'Abbas:

I heard the Prophet saying, "If the son of Adam (the human being) had two valley of money, he would wish for a third, for nothing can fill the belly of Adam's son except dust, and Allah forgives him who repents to Him."

Volume 8, Book 76, Number 445:

Narrated Ibn 'Abbas:

I heard Allah's Apostle saying, "If the son of Adam had money equal to a valley, then he will wish for another similar to it, for nothing can satisfy the eye of Adam's son except dust. And Allah forgives him who repents to Him." Ibn 'Abbas said: I do not know whether this saying was quoted from the Qur'an or not. 'Ata' said, "I heard Ibn AzZubair saying this narration while he was on the pulpit."

Volume 8, Book 76, Number 446:

Narrated Sahl bin Sa'd:

I heard Ibn Az-Zubair who was on the pulpit at Mecca, delivering a sermon, saying, "O men! The Prophet used to say, "If the son of Adam were given a valley full of gold, he would love to have a second one; and if he were given the second one, he would love to have a third, for nothing fills the belly of Adam's son except dust. And Allah forgives he who repents to Him." Ubai said, "We considered this as a saying from the Qur'an till the Sura (beginning with) 'The mutual rivalry for piling up of worldly things diverts you..' (102.1) was revealed."

Volume 8, Book 76, Number 447:

Narrated Anas bin Malik:

Allah's Apostle said, "If Adam's son had a valley full of gold, he would like to have two valleys, for nothing fills his mouth except dust. And Allah forgives him who repents to Him."

Volume 8, Book 76, Number 448:

Narrated Hakim bin Hizam:

I asked the Prophet (for some money) and he gave me, and then again I asked him and he gave me, and then again I asked him and he gave me and he then said, "This wealth is (like) green and sweet (fruit), and whoever takes it without greed, Allah will bless it for him, but whoever takes it with greed, Allah will not bless it for him, and he will be like the one who eats but is never satisfied. And the upper (giving) hand is better than the lower (taking) hand."

Volume 8, Book 76, Number 449:

Narrated 'Abdullah:

The Prophet said, "Who among you considers the wealth of his heirs dearer to him than his own wealth?" They replied, "O Allah's Apostle! There is none among us but loves his own wealth more." The Prophet said, "So his wealth is whatever he spends (in Allah's Cause) during his life (on good deeds) while the wealth of his heirs is whatever he leaves after his death."

Volume 8, Book 76, Number 450:

Narrated Abu Dhar:

Once I went out at night and found Allah's Apostle walking all alone accompanied by nobody, and I thought that perhaps he disliked that someone should accompany him. So I walked in the shade, away from the moonlight, but the Prophet looked behind and saw me and said, "Who is that?" I replied, "Abu Dhar, let Allah get me sacrificed for you!" He said, "O Abu Dhar, come here!" So I accompanied him for a while and then he said, "The rich are in fact the poor (little rewarded) on the Day of Resurrection except him whom Allah gives wealth which he gives (in charity) to his right, left, front and back, and does good deeds with it. I walked with him a little longer. Then he said to me, "Sit down here." So he made me sit in an open space surrounded by rocks, and said to me, "Sit here till I come back to you." He went towards Al-Harra till I could not see him, and he stayed away for a long period, and then I heard him saying, while he was coming, "Even if he had committed theft, and even if he had committed illegal sexual intercourse?" When he came, I could not remain patient and asked him, "O Allah's Prophet! Let Allah get me sacrificed for you! Whom were you speaking to by the side of Al-Harra? I did not hear anybody responding to your talk." He said, "It was Gabriel who appeared to me beside Al-Harra and said, 'Give the good news to your followers that whoever dies without having worshipped anything besides Allah, will enter Paradise.' I said, 'O Gabriel! Even if he had committed theft or committed illegal sexual intercourse?' He said, 'Yes.' I said, 'Even if he has committed theft or committed illegal sexual intercourse?' He said, 'Yes.' I said, 'Even if he has committed theft or committed illegal sexual intercourse?' He said, 'Yes.' "

Volume 8, Book 76, Number 451:

Narrated Abu Dhar:

While I was walking with the Prophet in the Harra of Medina, Uhud came in sight. The Prophet said, "O Abu Dhar!" I said, "Labbaik, O Allah's Apostle!" He said, "I would not like to have gold equal to this mountain of Uhud, unless nothing of it, not even a single Dinar of it remains with me for more than three days, except something which I will keep for repaying debts. I would have spent all of it (distributed it) amongst Allah's Slaves like this, and like this, and like this." The Prophet pointed out with his hand towards his right, his left and his back (while illustrating it). He proceeded with his walk and said, "The rich are in fact the poor (little rewarded) on the Day of Resurrection except those who spend their wealth like this, and like this, and like this, to their right, left and back, but such people are few in number." Then he said to me, "Stay at your place and do not leave it till I come back." Then he proceeded in the darkness of the night till he went out of sight, and then I heard a loud voice, and was afraid that something might have happened to the Prophet .1 intended to go to him, but I remembered what he had said to me, i.e. 'Don't leave your place till I come back to you,' so I remained at my place till he came back to me. I said, "O Allah's Apostle! I heard a voice and I was afraid." So I mentioned the whole story to him. He said, "Did you hear it?" I replied, "Yes." He said, "It was Gabriel who came to me and said, 'Whoever died without joining others in worship with Allah, will enter Paradise.' I asked (Gabriel), 'Even if he had committed theft or committed illegal sexual intercourse? Gabriel said, 'Yes, even if he had committed theft or committed illegal sexual intercourse."

Volume 8, Book 76, Number 452:

Narrated Abu Huraira:

Allah Apostle said, "If I had gold equal to the mountain of Uhud, it would not please me that anything of it should remain with me after three nights (i.e., I would spend all of it in Allah's Cause) except what I would keep for repaying debts."

Volume 8, Book 76, Number 453:

Narrated Abu Huraira:

The Prophet said, "Riches does not mean, having a great amount of property, but riches is self-contentment."

Volume 8, Book 76, Number 454:

Narrated Sahl bin Sa'd As-Sa'id:

A man passed by Allah's Apostle and the Prophet asked a man sitting beside him, "What is your opinion about this (passer-by)?" He replied, "This (passer-by) is from the noble class of people. By Allah, if he should ask for a lady's hand in marriage, he ought to be given her in marriage, and if he intercedes for somebody, his intercession will be accepted. Allah's Apostle kept quiet, and then another man passed by and Allah's Apostle asked the same man (his companion) again, "What is your opinion about this (second) one?" He said, "O Allah's Apostle! This person is one of the poor Muslims. If he should ask a lady's hand in marriage, no-one will accept him, and if he intercedes for somebody, no one will accept his intercession, and if he talks, no-one will listen to his talk." Then Allah's Apostle said, "This (poor man) is better than such a large number of the first type (i.e. rich men) as to fill the earth."

Volume 8, Book 76, Number 455:

Narrated Abu Wail:

We paid a visit to Khabbab who was sick, and he said, "We migrated with the Prophet for Allah's Sake and our wages became due on Allah. Some of us died without having received anything of the wages, and one of them was Mus'ab bin 'Umar, who was martyred on the day of the battle of Uhud, leaving only one sheet (to shroud him in). If we covered his head with it, his feet became uncovered, and if we covered his feet with it, his head became uncovered. So the Prophet ordered us to cover his head with it and put some Idhkhir (a kind of grass) over his feet. On the other hand, some of us have had the fruits (of our good deed) and are plucking them (in this world)."

Volume 8, Book 76, Number 456:

Narrated 'Imran bin Husain:

The Prophet said, "I looked into Paradise and found that the majority of its dwellers were the poor people, and I looked into the (Hell) Fire and found that the majority of its dwellers were women."

Volume 8, Book 76, Number 457:

Narrated Anas:

The Prophet did not eat at a table till he died, and he did not eat a thin nicely baked wheat bread till he died.

Volume 8, Book 76, Number 458:

Narrated 'Aisha:

When the Prophet died, nothing which can be eaten by a living creature was left on my shelf except some barley grain. I ate of it for a period and when I measured it, it finished.

Volume 8, Book 76, Number 459:

Narrated Abu Huraira:

By Allah except Whom none has the right to- be worshipped, (sometimes) I used to lay (sleep) on the ground on my liver (abdomen) because of hunger, and (sometimes) I used to bind a stone over my belly because of hunger. One day I sat by the way from where they (the Prophet and h is companions) used to come out. When Abu Bakr passed by, I asked him about a Verse from Allah's Book and I asked him only that he might satisfy my hunger, but he passed by and did not do so. Then Umar passed by me and I asked him about a Verse from Allah's Book, and I asked him only that he might satisfy my hunger, but he passed by without doing so. Finally Abu-l-Qasim (the Prophet) passed by me and he smiled when he saw me, for he knew what was in my heart and on my face. He said, "O Aba Hirr (Abu Huraira)!" I replied, "Labbaik, O Allah's Apostle!" He said to me, "Follow me." He left and I followed him.

Then he entered the house and I asked permission to enter and was admitted. He found milk in a bowl and said, "From where is this milk?" They said, "It has been presented to you by such-and-such man (or by such and such woman)." He said, "O Aba Hirr!" I said, "Labbaik, O Allah's Apostle!" He said, "Go and call the people of Suffa to me." These people of Suffa were the guests of Islam who had no families, nor money, nor anybody to depend upon, and whenever an object of charity was brought to the Prophet , he would send it to them and would not take anything from it, and whenever any present was given to him, he used to send some for them and take some of it for himself. The order off the Prophet upset me, and I said to myself, "How will this little milk be enough for the people of As-Suffa?" thought I was more entitled to drink from that milk in order to strengthen myself, but behold! The Prophet came to order me to give that milk to them. I wondered what will remain of that milk for me, but anyway, I could not but obey Allah and His Apostle so I went to the people of As-Suffa and called them, and they came and asked the Prophet's permission to enter. They were admitted and took their seats in the house.

The Prophet said, "O Aba-Hirr!" I said, "Labbaik, O Allah's Apostle!" He said, "Take it and give it to them." So I took the bowl (of Milk) and started giving it to one man who would drink his fill and return it to me, whereupon I would give it to another man who, in his turn, would drink his fill and return it to me, and I would then offer it to another man who would drink his fill and return it to me. Finally, after the whole group had drunk their fill, I reached the Prophet who took the bowl and put it on his hand, looked at me and smiled and said. "O Aba Hirr!" I replied, "Labbaik, O Allah's Apostle!" He said, "There remain you and I." I said, "You have said the truth, O Allah's Apostle!" He said, "Sit down and drink." I sat down and drank. He said, "Drink," and I drank. He kept on telling me repeatedly to drink, till I said, "No. by Allah Who sent you with the Truth, I have no space for it (in my stomach)." He said, "Hand it over to me." When I gave him the bowl, he praised Allah and pronounced Allah's Name on it and drank the remaining milk.

Volume 8, Book 76, Number 460:

Narrated Sa'd:

I was the first man among the Arabs to throw an arrow for Allah's Cause. We used to fight in Allah's Cause while we had nothing to eat except the leaves of the Hubla and the Sumur trees (desert trees) so that we discharged excrement like that of sheep (i.e. unmixed droppings). Today the (people of the) tribe of Bani Asad teach me the laws of Islam. If so, then I am lost, and all my efforts of that hard time had gone in vain.

Volume 8, Book 76, Number 461:

Narrated 'Aisha:

The family of Muhammad had never eaten their fill of wheat bread for three successive days since they had migrated to Medina till the death of the Prophet.

Volume 8, Book 76, Number 462:

Narrated 'Aisha:

The family of Muhammad did not eat two meals on one day, but one of the two was of dates.

Volume 8, Book 76, Number 463:

Narrated 'Aisha:

The bed mattress of the Prophet was made of a leather case stuffed with palm fibres.

Volume 8, Book 76, Number 464:

Narrated Qatada:

We used to go to Anas bin Malik and see his baker standing (preparing the bread). Anas said, "Eat. I have not known that the Prophet ever saw a thin well-baked loaf of bread till he died, and he never saw a roasted sheep with his eyes."

Volume 8, Book 76, Number 465:

Narrated 'Aisha:

A complete month would pass by during which we would not make a fire (for cooking), and our food used to be only dates and water unless we were given a present of some meat.

Volume 8, Book 76, Number 466:

Narrated 'Aisha:

that she said to Urwa, "O, the son of my sister! We used to see three crescents in two months, and no fire used to be made in the houses of Allah's Apostle (i.e. nothing used to be cooked)." 'Urwa said, "What used to sustain you?" 'Aisha said, "The two black things i.e. dates and water, except that Allah's

Apostle had neighbors from the Ansar who had some milch she-camels, and they used to give the Prophet some milk from their house, and he used to make us drink it."

Volume 8, Book 76, Number 467:

Narrated Abu Huraira:

Allah's Apostle said, "O Allah! Give food to the family of Muhammad."

Volume 8, Book 76, Number 468:

Narrated Masruq:

I asked 'Aisha "What deed was the most beloved to the Prophet?" She said, "The regular constant one." I said, "At what time did he use to get up at night (for the Tahajjud night prayer)?' She said, "He used to get up on hearing (the crowing of) the cock (the last third of the night)."

Volume 8, Book 76, Number 469:

Narrated 'Aisha:

The most beloved action to Allah's Apostle was that whose doer did it continuously and regularly.

Volume 8, Book 76, Number 470:

Narrated Abu Huraira:

Allah's Apostle said, "The deeds of anyone of you will not save you (from the (Hell) Fire)." They said, "Even you (will not be saved by your deeds), O Allah's Apostle?" He said, "No, even I (will not be saved) unless and until Allah bestows His Mercy on me. Therefore, do good deeds properly, sincerely and moderately, and worship Allah in the forenoon and in the afternoon and during a part of the night, and always adopt a middle, moderate, regular course whereby you will reach your target (Paradise)."

Volume 8, Book 76, Number 471:

Narrated 'Aisha:

Allah's Apostle said, "Do good deeds properly, sincerely and moderately and know that your deeds will not make you enter Paradise, and that the most beloved deed to Allah's is the most regular and constant even though it were little."

Volume 8, Book 76, Number 472:

Narrated 'Aisha:

The Prophet was asked, "What deeds are loved most by Allah?" He said, "The most regular constant deeds even though they may be few." He added, 'Don't take upon yourselves, except the deeds which are within your ability."

Volume 8, Book 76, Number 473:

Narrated 'Alqama:

I asked 'Aisha, mother of the believers, "O mother of the believers! How were the deeds of the Prophet? Did he use to do extra deeds of worship on special days?" She said, "No, but his deeds were regular and constant, and who among you is able to do what the Prophet was able to do (i.e. in worshipping Allah)?"

Volume 8, Book 76, Number 474:

Narrated 'Aisha:

The Prophet said, "Do good deeds properly, sincerely and moderately, and receive good news because one's good deeds will not make him enter Paradise." They asked, "Even you, O Allah's Apostle?" He said, "Even I, unless and until Allah bestows His pardon and Mercy on me."

Volume 8, Book 76, Number 475:

Narrated Anas bin Malik:

Once Allah's Apostle led us in prayer and then (after finishing it) ascended the pulpit and pointed with his hand towards the Qibla of the mosque and said, "While I was leading you in prayer, both Paradise and Hell were displayed in front of me in the direction of this wall. I had never seen a better thing (than Paradise) and a worse thing (than Hell) as I have seen today, I had never seen a better thing and a worse thing as I have seen today."

Volume 8, Book 76, Number 476:

Narrated Abu Huraira:

I heard Allah's Apostle saying, Verily Allah created Mercy. The day He created it, He made it into one hundred parts. He withheld with Him ninety-nine parts, and sent its one part to all His creatures. Had the non-believer known of all the Mercy which is in the Hands of Allah, he would not lose hope of entering Paradise, and had the believer known of all the punishment which is present with Allah, he would not consider himself safe from the Hell-Fire."

Volume 8, Book 76, Number 477:

Narrated Abu Said:

Some people from the Ansar asked Allah's Apostle (to give them something) and he gave to every-one of them, who asked him, until all that he had was finished. When everything was finished and he had spent all that was in his hand, he said to them, "(Know) that if I have any wealth, I will not withhold it from you (to keep for somebody else); And (know) that he who refrains from begging others (or doing prohibited deeds), Allah will make him contented and not in need of others; and he who remains patient, Allah will bestow patience upon him, and he who is satisfied with what he has, Allah will make him self-sufficient. And there is no gift better and vast (you may be given) than pa-tience."

Volume 8, Book 76, Number 478:

Narrated Al-Mughira bin Shu'ba:

The Prophet used to pray so much that his feet used to become edematous or swollen, and when he was asked as to why he prays so much, he would say, "Shall I not be a thankful slave (to Allah)?"

Volume 8, Book 76, Number 479:

Narrated Ibn Abbas:

Allah's Apostle said, "Seventy thousand people of my followers will enter Paradise without ac-counts, and they are those who do not practice Ar-Ruqya and do not see an evil omen in things, and put their trust in their Lord.

Volume 8, Book 76, Number 480:

Narrated Warrad:

(the clerk of Al-Mughira bin Shu'ba) Muawiya wrote to Al-Mughira: "Write to me a narration you have heard from Allah's Apostle." So Al-Mughira wrote to him, "I heard him saying the following after each prayer: 'La ilaha illal-lahu wahdahu la sharika lahu, lahu-l-mulk wa lahul-hamd, wa huwa 'ala kulli Shai-in qadir.' He also used to forbid idle talk, asking too many questions (in religion), wasting money, preventing what should be given, and asking others for something (except in great need), being undutiful to mothers, and burying one's little daughters (alive)."

Volume 8, Book 76, Number 481:

Narrated Sahl bin Sa'd:

Allah's Apostle said, "Whoever can guarantee (the chastity of) what is between his two jaw-bones and what is between his two legs (i.e. his tongue and his private parts), I guarantee Paradise for him."

Volume 8, Book 76, Number 482:

Narrated Abu Huraira:

Allah's Apostle said, "Whoever believes in Allah and the Last Day should talk what is good or keep quiet, and whoever believes in Allah and the Last Day should not hurt (or insult) his neighbor; and whoever believes in Allah and the Last Day, should entertain his guest generously."

Volume 8, Book 76, Number 483:

Narrated Abu Shuraih Al-Khuza'i:

My ears heard and my heart grasped (the statement which) the Prophet said, "The period for keeping one's guest is three days (and don't forget) his reward." It was asked, "What is his reward?" He said, "In the first night and the day he should be given a high class quality of meals; and whoever believes in Allah and the Last Day, should entertain his guest generously; and whoever believes in Allah and the Last Day should talk what is good (sense) or keep quiet."

Volume 8, Book 76, Number 484:

Narrated Abu Huraira:

That he heard Allah's Apostle saying, "A slave of Allah may utter a word without thinking whether it is right or wrong, he may slip down in the Fire as far away a distance equal to that between the east."

Volume 8, Book 76, Number 485:

Narrated Abu Huraira:

The Prophet; said, "A slave (of Allah) may utter a word which pleases Allah without giving it much importance, and because of that Allah will raise him to degrees (of reward); a slave (of Allah) may utter a word (carelessly) which displeases Allah without thinking of its gravity and because of that he will be thrown into the Hell-Fire."

Volume 8, Book 76, Number 486:

Narrated Abu Huraira:

The Prophet said Allah will give shade to seven (types of people) under His Shade (on the Day of Resurrection). (one of them will be) a person who remembers Allah and his eyes are then flooded with tears.

Volume 8, Book 76, Number 487:

Narrated Hudhaifa:

The Prophet said, "There was a man amongst the people who had suspicion as to the righteousness of his deeds. Therefore he said to his family, 'If I die, take me and burn my corpse and throw my ashes into the sea on a hot (or windy) day.' They did so, but Allah, collected his particles and asked (him), What made you do what you did?' He replied, 'The only thing that made me do it, was that I was afraid of You.' So Allah forgave him."

Volume 8, Book 76, Number 488:

Narrated Abu Said :

The Prophet mentioned a man from the previous generation or from the people preceding your age whom Allah had given both wealth and children. The Prophet said, "When the time of his death approached, he asked his children, 'What type of father have I been to you?' They replied: You have been a good father. He said, 'But he (i.e. your father) has not stored any good deeds with Allah (for the Hereafter): if he should face Allah, Allah will punish him. So listen, (O my children), when I die, burn my body till I become mere coal and then grind it into powder, and when there is a stormy wind, throw me (my ashes) in it.' So he took a firm promise from his children (to follow his instructions). And by Allah they (his sons) did accordingly(fulfilled their promise.) Then Allah said, "Be" and behold! That man was standing there! Allah then said. "O my slave! What made you do what you did?" That man said, "Fear of You." So Allah forgave him.

Volume 8, Book 76, Number 489:

Narrated Abu Musa:

Allah's Apostle said. "My example and the example of the message with which Allah has sent me is like that of a man who came to some people and said, "I have seen with my own eyes the enemy forces, and I am a naked warner (to you) so save yourself, save yourself! A group of them obeyed him and went out at night, slowly and stealthily and were safe, while another group did not believe him and thus the army took them in the morning and destroyed them."

Volume 8, Book 76, Number 490:

Narrated Abu Huraira:

I heard Allah's Apostle saying, "My example and the example of the people is that of a man who made a fire, and when it lighted what was around it, Moths and other insects started falling into the fire. The man tried (his best) to prevent them, (from falling in the fire) but they overpowered him and rushed into the fire. The Prophet added, Now, similarly, I take hold of the knots at your waist (belts) to prevent you from falling into the Fire, but you insist on falling into it."

Volume 8, Book 76, Number 491:

Narrated 'Abdullah bin 'Amr:

The Prophet said, "A Muslim is the one who avoids harming Muslims with his tongue or his hands. And a Muhajir (an emigrant) is the one who gives up (abandons) all what Allah has forbidden."

Volume 8, Book 76, Number 492:

Narrated Abu Huraira:

Allah's Apostle said, "If you knew that which I know you would laugh little and weep much."

Volume 8, Book 76, Number 493:

Narrated Anas:

The Prophet said, "If you knew that which I know, you would laugh little and weep much."

Volume 8, Book 76, Number 494:

Narrated Abu Huraira:

Allah's Apostle said, "The (Hell) Fire is surrounded by all kinds of desires and passions, while Paradise is surrounded by all kinds of disliked undesirable things."

Volume 8, Book 76, Number 495:

Narrated 'Abdullah:

The Prophet said, "Paradise is nearer to any of you than the Shirak (leather strap) of his shoe, and so is the (Hell) Fire.

Volume 8, Book 76, Number 496:

Narrated Abu Huraira:

The Prophet said, "The truest poetic verse ever said by a poet, is, Indeed! Everything except Allah, is perishable."

Volume 8, Book 76, Number 497:

Narrated Abu Huraira:

Allah's Apostle said, "If anyone of you looked at a person who was made superior to him in property and (in good) appearance, then he should also look at the one who is inferior to him, and to whom he has been made superior."

Volume 8, Book 76, Number 498:

Narrated Ibn 'Abbas:

The Prophet narrating about his Lord I'm and said, "Allah ordered (the appointed angels over you) that the good and the bad deeds be written, and He then showed (the way) how (to write). If somebody intends to do a good deed and he does not do it, then Allah will write for him a full good deed (in his account with Him); and if he intends to do a good deed and actually did it, then Allah will write for him (in his account) with Him (its reward equal) from ten to seven hundred times to many more times: and if somebody intended to do a bad deed and he does not do it, then Allah will write a full good deed (in his account) with Him, and if he intended to do it (a bad deed) and actually did it, then Allah will write one bad deed (in his account)."

Volume 8, Book 76, Number 499:

Narrated Ghailan:

Anas said "You people do (bad) deeds (commit sins) which seem in your eyes as tiny (minute) than hair while we used to consider those (very deeds) during the life-time of the Prophet as destructive sins."

Volume 8, Book 76, Number 500:

Narrated Sa'd bin Sahl As-Sa'idi:

The Prophet looked at a man fighting against the pagans and he was one of the most competent persons fighting on behalf of the Muslims. The Prophet said, "Let him who wants to look at a man from the dwellers of the (Hell) Fire, look at this (man)." Another man followed him and kept on following him till he (the fighter) was injured and, seeking to die quickly, he placed the blade tip of his sword between his breasts and leaned over it till it passed through his shoulders (i.e., committed suicide)." The Prophet added, "A person may do deeds that seem to the people as the deeds of the people of Paradise while in fact, he is from the dwellers of the (Hell) Fire: and similarly a person may do deeds that seem to the people as the deeds of the people of the (Hell) Fire while in fact, he is from the dwellers of Paradise. Verily, the (results of) deeds done, depend upon the last actions."

Volume 8, Book 76, Number 501:

Narrated Abu Sa'id Al-Khudri:

A bedouin came to the Prophet and said, "O Allah's Apostle! Who is the best of mankind!" The Prophet said, "A man who strives for Allah's Cause with his life and property, and also a man who lives (all alone) in a mountain path among the mountain paths to worship his Lord and save the people from his evil."

Volume 8, Book 76, Number 502:

Narrated Abu Said:

???

Volume 8, Book 76, Number 503:

Narrated Abu Huraira:

Allah's Apostle said, "When honesty is lost, then wait for the Hour." It was asked, "How will honesty be lost, O Allah's Apostle?" He said, "When authority is given to those who do not deserve it, then wait for the Hour."

Volume 8, Book 76, Number 504:

Narrated Hudhaifa:

Allah's Apostle narrated to us two narrations, one of which I have seen (happening) and I am waiting for the other. He narrated that honesty was preserved in the roots of the hearts of men (in the beginning) and then they learnt it (honesty) from the Qur'an, and then they learnt it from the (Prophet's) Sunna (tradition). He also told us about its disappearance, saying, "A man will go to sleep whereupon honesty will be taken away from his heart, and only its trace will remain, resembling the traces of fire. He then will sleep whereupon the remainder of the honesty will also be taken away (from his heart) and its trace will resemble a blister which is raised over the surface of skin, when an ember touches one's foot; and in fact, this blister does not contain anything. So there will come a day when people will deal in business with each other but there will hardly be any trustworthy persons among them. Then it will be said that in such-and-such a tribe there is such-and-such person who is honest, and a man will be admired for his intelligence, good manners and strength, though indeed he will not have belief equal to a mustard seed in his heart." The narrator added: There came upon me a time when I did not mind dealing with anyone of you, for if he was a Muslim, his religion would prevent him from cheating; and if he was a Christian, his Muslim ruler would prevent him from cheating; but today I cannot deal except with so-and-so and so-and-so. (See Hadith No. 208, Vol. 9)

Volume 8, Book 76, Number 505:

Narrated 'Abdullah bin 'Umar:

I heard Allah's Apostle saying, "People are just like camels, out of one hundred, one can hardly find a single camel suitable to ride."

Volume 8, Book 76, Number 506:

Narrated Jundub:

The Prophet said, "He who lets the people hear of his good deeds intentionally, to win their praise, Allah will let the people know his real intention (on the Day of Resurrection), and he who does good things in public to show off and win the praise of the people, Allah will disclose his real intention (and humiliate him).

Volume 8, Book 76, Number 507:

Narrated Mu'adh bin Jabal:

While I was riding behind the Prophet as a companion rider and there was nothing between me and him except the back of the saddle, he said, "O Mu'adh!" I replied, "Labbaik O Allah's Apostle! And Sa'diak!" He proceeded for a while and then said, "O Mu'adh!" I said, "Labbaik and Sa'daik, O Allah's Apostle!" He then proceeded for another while and said, "O Mu'adh bin Jabal!" I replied, "Labbaik, O Allah's Apostle, and Sa'daik!" He said, "Do you know what is Allah's right on His slaves?" I replied, "Allah and His Apostle know better." He said, "Allah's right on his slaves is that they should worship Him and not worship anything besides Him." He then proceeded for a while, and again said, "O Mu'adh bin Jabal!" I replied. "Labbaik, O Allah's Apostle, and Sa'daik." He said, "Do you know what is (Allah's) slaves' (people's) right on Allah if they did that?" I replied, "Allah and His Apostle know better." He said, "The right of (Allah's) slaves on Allah is that He should not punish them (if they did that)."

Volume 8, Book 76, Number 508:

Narrated Anas:

The Prophet had a she-camel called Al'Adba' and it was too fast to surpass in speed. There came a bedouin riding a camel of his, and that camel outstripped it (i.e. Al-Aqba'). That result was hard on the Muslims who said sorrowfully, "Al- Adba has been outstripped." Allah's Apostle said, "It is due from Allah that nothing would be raised high in this world except that He lowers or puts it down."

Volume 8, Book 76, Number 509:

Narrated Abu Huraira:

Allah's Apostle said, "Allah said, 'I will declare war against him who shows hostility to a pious worshipper of Mine. And the most beloved things with which My slave comes nearer to Me, is what I have enjoined upon him; and My slave keeps on coming closer to Me through performing Nawafil (praying or doing extra deeds besides what is obligatory) till I love him, so I become his sense of hearing with which he hears, and his sense of sight with which he sees, and his hand with which he grips, and his leg with which he walks; and if he asks Me, I will give him, and if he asks My protection (Refuge), I will protect him; (i.e. give him My Refuge) and I do not hesitate to do anything as I hesitate to take the soul of the believer, for he hates death, and I hate to disappoint him."

Volume 8, Book 76, Number 510:

Narrated Sahl:

Allah's Apostle said, "I have been sent and the Hour (is at hand) as these two," showing his two fingers and sticking (separating) them out.

Volume 8, Book 76, Number 511:

Narrated Anas:

Allah's Apostle said, "I have been sent and the Hour (is at hand) as these two (fingers)."

Volume 8, Book 76, Number 512:

Narrated Abu Huraira:

The Prophet said, "I have been sent and the Hour (is at hand) as these two (fingers)."

Volume 8, Book 76, Number 513:

Narrated Abu Huraira:

Allah's Apostle said, "The Hour will not be established till the sun rises from the west, and when it rises (from the west) and the people see it, then all of them will believe (in Allah). But that will be the time when 'No good it will do to a soul to believe then. If it believed not before..'" (6.158)

The Hour will be established (so suddenly) that two persons spreading a garment between them will not be able to finish their bargain, nor will they be able to fold it up. The Hour will be established while a man is carrying the milk of his she-camel, but cannot drink it; and the Hour will be established when someone is not able to prepare the tank to water his livestock from it; and the Hour will be established when some of you has raised his food to his mouth but cannot eat it."

Volume 8, Book 76, Number 514:

Narrated 'Ubada bin As-Samit:

The Prophet said, "Who-ever loves to meet Allah, Allah (too) loves to meet him and who-ever hates to meet Allah, Allah (too) hates to meet him". 'Aisha, or some of the wives of the Prophet said, "But we dislike death." He said: It is not like this, but it is meant that when the time of the death of a believer approaches, he receives the good news of Allah's pleasure with him and His blessings upon him, and so at that time nothing is dearer to him than what is in front of him. He therefore loves the meeting with Allah, and Allah (too) loves the meeting with him. But when the time of the death of a disbeliever approaches, he receives the evil news of Allah's torment and His Requital, whereupon nothing is more hateful to him than what is before him. Therefore, he hates the meeting with Allah, and Allah too, hates the meeting with him."

Volume 8, Book 76, Number 515:

Narrated Abu Musa:

The Prophet said, "Whoever loves the meeting with Allah, Allah too, loves the meeting with him; and whoever hates the meeting with Allah, Allah too, hates the meeting with him."

Volume 8, Book 76, Number 516:

Narrated 'Aisha:

(the wife of the Prophet) When Allah's Apostle was in good health, he used to say, "No prophet's soul is ever captured unless he is shown his place in Paradise and given the option (to die or survive)." So when the death of the Prophet approached and his head was on my thigh, he became unconscious for a while and then he came to his senses and fixed his eyes on the ceiling and said, "O Allah (with) the highest companions." (See Qur'an 4.69). I said' "Hence he is not going to choose us." And I came to know that it was the application of the narration which he (the Prophet) used to narrate to us. And that was the last statement of the Prophet (before his death) i.e., "O Allah! With the highest companions." (See Qur'an 4.69)

Volume 8, Book 76, Number 517:

Narrated 'Aisha:

There was a leather or wood container full of water in front of Allah's Apostle (at the time of his death). He would put his hand into the water and rub his face with it, saying, "None has the right to be worshipped but Allah! No doubt, death has its stupors." Then he raised his hand and started saying, "(O Allah!) with the highest companions." (See Qur'an 4.69) (and kept on saying it) till he expired and his hand dropped."

Volume 8, Book 76, Number 518:

Narrated 'Aisha:

Some rough bedouins used to visit the Prophet and ask him, "When will the Hour be?" He would look at the youngest of all of them and say, "If this should live till he is very old, your Hour (the death of the people addressed) will take place." Hisham said that he meant (by the Hour), their death.

Volume 8, Book 76, Number 519:

Narrated Abu Qatada bin Rib'i Al-Ansari:

A funeral procession passed by Allah's Apostle who said, "Relieved or relieving?" The people asked, "O Allah's Apostle! What is relieved and relieving?" He said, "A believer is relieved (by death) from the troubles and hardships of the world and leaves for the Mercy of Allah, while (the death of) a wicked person relieves the people, the land, the trees, (and) the animals from him."

Volume 8, Book 76, Number 520:

Narrated Abu Qatada:

The Prophet said, "Relieved or relieving. And a believer is relieved (by death)."

Volume 8, Book 76, Number 521:

Narrated Anas bin Malik:

Allah's Apostle said, "When carried to his grave, a dead person is followed by three, two of which return (after his burial) and one remains with him: his relative, his property, and his deeds follow him; relatives and his property go back while his deeds remain with him."

Volume 8, Book 76, Number 522:

Narrated Ibn 'Umar:

Allah's Apostle said, "When anyone of you dies, his destination is displayed before him in the forenoon and in the afternoon, either in the (Hell) Fire or in Paradise, and it is said to him, "That is your place till you are resurrected and sent to it."

Volume 8, Book 76, Number 523:

Narrated 'Aisha:

The Prophet said, "Do not abuse the dead, for they have reached the result of what they have done."

Volume 8, Book 76, Number 524:

Narrated Abu Huraira:

Two men, a Muslim and a Jew, abused each other. The Muslim said, "By Him Who gave superiority to Muhammad over all the people." On that, the Jew said, "By Him Who gave superiority to Moses over all the people." The Muslim became furious at that and slapped the Jew in the face. The Jew went to Allah's Apostle and informed him of what had happened between him and the Muslim. Allah's Apostle said, "Don't give me superiority over Moses, for the people will fall unconscious on the Day of Resurrection and I will be the first to gain consciousness, and behold ! Moses will be there holding the side of Allah's Throne. I will not know whether Moses has been among those people who have become unconscious and then has regained consciousness before me, or has been among those exempted by Allah from falling unconscious."

Volume 8, Book 76, Number 525:

Narrated Abu Huraira:

The Prophet said, "The people will fall down unconscious at the time when they should fall down (i.e., on the Day of Resurrection), and then I will be the first man to get up, and behold, Moses will be there holding (Allah's) Throne. I will not know whether he has been amongst those who have fallen unconscious."

Volume 8, Book 76, Number 526:

Narrated Abu Huraira:

The Prophet said, "Allah will take the whole earth (in His Hand) and will roll up the Heaven in His right Hand, and then He will say, "I am King! Where are the kings of the earth ? "

Volume 8, Book 76, Number 527:

Narrated Abu Said Al-Khudri:

The Prophet said, "The (planet of) earth will be a bread on the Day of Resurrection, and The resistible (Allah) will topple turn it with His Hand like anyone of you topple turns a bread with his hands while (preparing the bread) for a journey, and that bread will be the entertainment for the people of Paradise." A man from the Jews came (to the Prophet) and said, "May The Beneficent (Allah) bless you, O Abul Qasim! Shall I tell you of the entertainment of the people of Paradise on the Day of Resurrection?" The Prophet said, "Yes." The Jew said, "The earth will be a bread," as the Prophet had said. Thereupon the Prophet looked at us and smiled till his premolar tooth became visible. Then the Jew further said, "Shall I tell you of the udm (additional food taken with bread) they will have with the bread?" He added, "That will be Balam and Nun." The people asked, "What is that?" He said, "It is an ox and a fish, and seventy thousand people will eat of the caudate lobe (i.e. extra lobe) of their livers."

Volume 8, Book 76, Number 528:

Narrated Sahl bin Sa'd:

I heard the Prophet saying, "The people will be gathered on the Day of Resurrection on reddish white land like a pure loaf of bread (made of pure fine flour)." Sahl added: That land will have no landmarks for anybody (to make use of).

Volume 8, Book 76, Number 529:

Narrated Abu Huraira:

The Prophet said, "The people will be gathered in three ways: (The first way will be of) those who will wish or have a hope (for Paradise) and will have a fear (of punishment), (The second batch will be those who will gather) riding two on a camel or three on a camel or ten on a camel. (The third batch) the rest of the people will be urged to gather by the Fire which will accompany them at the time of their afternoon nap and stay with them where they will spend the night, and will be with them in the morning wherever they may be then, and will be with them in the afternoon wherever they may be then."

Volume 8, Book 76, Number 530:

Narrated Anas bin Malik:

A man said, "O Allah's Prophet! Will a Kafir (disbeliever) be gathered (driven prone) on his face?" The Prophet said, "Is not He Who made him walk with his legs in this world, able to make him walk on his face on the Day of Resurrection?" (Qatada, a sub-narrator said: Yes, (He can), by the Power of Our Lord!")

Volume 8, Book 76, Number 531:

Narrated Ibn Abbas:

The Prophet said, "You will meet Allah barefooted, naked, walking on feet, and uncircumcised."

Volume 8, Book 76, Number 532:

Narrated Ibn 'Abbas:

I heard Allah's Apostle while he was delivering a sermon on a pulpit, saying, "You will meet Allah barefooted, naked, and uncircumcised."

Volume 8, Book 76, Number 533:

Narrated Ibn 'Abbas:

The Prophet stood up among us and addressed (saying) "You will be gathered, barefooted, naked, and uncircumcised (as Allah says): 'As We began the first creation, We shall repeat it..' (21.104) And the first human being to be dressed on the Day of Resurrection will be (the Prophet) Abraham Al-Khalil. Then will be brought some men of my followers who will be taken towards the left (i.e., to the Fire), and I will say, 'O Lord! My companions whereupon Allah will say: You do not know what they did after you left them. I will then say as the pious slave, Jesus said, And I was witness over them while I dwelt amongst them..........(up to) ...the All-Wise.' (5.117-118). The narrator added: Then it will be said that those people (relegated from Islam, that is) kept on turning on their heels (deserted Islam).

Volume 8, Book 76, Number 534:

Narrated 'Aisha:

Allah's Apostle said, "The people will be gathered barefooted, naked, and uncircumcised." I said, "O Allah's Apostle! Will the men and the women look at each other?" He said, "The situation will be too hard for them to pay attention to that."

Volume 8, Book 76, Number 535:

Narrated 'Abdullah:

While we were in the company of the Prophet in a tent he said, "Would it please you to be one fourth of the people of Paradise?" We said, "Yes." He said, "Would It please you to be one-third of the people of Paradise?" We said, "Yes." He said, "Would it please you to be half of the people of Paradise?" We said, "Yes." Thereupon he said, "I hope that you will be one half of the people of Paradise, for none will enter Paradise but a Muslim soul, and you people, in comparison to the people who associate others in worship with Allah, are like a white hair on the skin of a black ox, or a black hair on the skin of a red ox."

Volume 8, Book 76, Number 536:

Narrated Abu Huraira:

The Prophet said, "The first man to be called on the Day of Resurrection will be Adam who will be shown his offspring, and it will be said to them, 'This is your father, Adam.' Adam will say (responding to the call), 'Labbaik and Sa'daik' Then Allah will say (to Adam), 'Take out of your offspring, the people of Hell.' Adam will say, 'O Lord, how many should I take out?' Allah will say, 'Take out ninety-nine out of every hundred." They (the Prophet's companions) said, "O Allah's Apostle! If ninety-nine out of every one hundred of us are taken away, what will remain out of us?" He said, "My followers in comparison to the other nations are like a white hair on a black ox."

Volume 8, Book 76, Number 537:

Narrated Abu Said:

The Prophet said, "Allah will say, 'O Adam!. Adam will reply, 'Labbaik and Sa'daik (I respond to Your Calls, I am obedient to Your orders), wal Khair fi Yadaik (and all the good is in Your Hands)!' Then Allah will say (to Adam), Bring out the people of the Fire.' Adam will say, 'What (how many) are the people of the Fire?' Allah will say, 'Out of every thousand (take out) nine-hundred and ninety-nine (persons).' At that time children will become hoary-headed and every pregnant female will drop her load (have an abortion) and you will see the people as if they were drunk, yet not drunk; But Allah's punishment will be very severe."

That news distressed the companions of the Prophet too much, and they said, "O Allah's Apostle! Who amongst us will be that man (the lucky one out of one-thousand who will be saved from the Fire)?" He said, "Have the good news that one-thousand will be from Gog and Magog, and the one (to be saved will be) from you." The Prophet added, "By Him in Whose Hand my soul is, I Hope that you (Muslims) will be one third of the people of Paradise." On that, we glorified and praised Allah and said, "Allahu Akbar." The Prophet then said, "By Him in Whose Hand my soul is, I hope that you will be one half of the people of Paradise, as your (Muslims) example in comparison to the other people (non-Muslims), is like that of a white hair on the skin of a black ox, or a round hairless spot on the foreleg of a donkey."

Volume 8, Book 76, Number 538:

Narrated Ibn 'Umar:

The Prophet said (regarding the Verse), "A Day when all mankind will stand before the Lord of the Worlds,' (that day) they will stand, drowned in their sweat up to the middle of their ears."

Volume 8, Book 76, Number 539:

Narrated Abu Huraira :

Allah's Apostle said, "The people will sweat so profusely on the Day of Resurrection that their sweat will sink seventy cubits deep into the earth, and it will rise up till it reaches the people's mouths and ears."

Volume 8, Book 76, Number 540:

Narrated 'Abdullah:

The Prophet said, "The cases which will be decided first (on the Day of Resurrection) will be the cases of blood-shedding. "

Volume 8, Book 76, Number 541:

Narrated Abu Huraira:

Allah's Apostle said, "Whoever has wronged his brother, should ask for his pardon (before his death), as (in the Hereafter) there will be neither a Dinar nor a Dirham. (He should secure pardon in this life) before some of his good deeds are taken and paid to his brother, or, if he has done no good deeds, some of the bad deeds of his brother are taken to be loaded on him (in the Hereafter)."

Volume 8, Book 76, Number 542:

Narrated Abu Said Al-Khudri:

Allah's Apostle said, "The believers, after being saved from the (Hell) Fire, will be stopped at a bridge between Paradise and Hell and mutual retaliation will be established among them regarding wrongs they have committed in the world against one another. After they are cleansed and purified (through the retaliation), they will be admitted into Paradise; and by Him in Whose Hand Muhammad's soul is, everyone of them will know his dwelling in Paradise better than he knew his dwelling in this world."

Volume 8, Book 76, Number 543:

Narrated Ibn Abi Mulaika:

'Aisha said, "The Prophet said, 'Anybody whose account (record) is questioned will surely be punished.' I said, 'Doesn't Allah say: 'He surely will receive an easy reckoning?' (84.8) The Prophet replied. 'This means only the presentation of the account.'"

Volume 8, Book 76, Number 544:

Narrated 'Aisha:

The Prophet said (as above, 543).

Volume 8, Book 76, Number 545:

Narrated 'Aisha:

Allah's Apostle, said, "None will be called to account on the Day of Resurrection, but will be ruined." I said "O Allah's Apostle! Hasn't Allah said: 'Then as for him who will be given his record in his right hand, he surely will receive an easy reckoning? (84.7-8) -- Allah's Apostle said, "That

(Verse) means only the presentation of the accounts, but anybody whose account (record) is questioned on the Day of Resurrection, will surely be punished."

Volume 8, Book 76, Number 546:

Narrated Anas bin Malik:

Allah's Prophet used to say, "A disbeliever will be brought on the Day of Resurrection and will be asked. "Suppose you had as much gold as to fill the earth, would you offer it to ransom yourself?" He will reply, "Yes." Then it will be said to him, "You were asked for something easier than that (to join none in worship with Allah (i.e. to accept Islam, but you refused)."

Volume 8, Book 76, Number 547:

Narrated 'Adi bin Hatim:

The Prophet said, "There will be none among you but will be talked to by Allah on the Day of Resurrection, without there being an interpreter between him and Him (Allah). He will look and see nothing ahead of him, and then he will look (again for the second time) in front of him, and the (Hell) Fire will confront him. So, whoever among you can save himself from the Fire, should do so even with one half of a date (to give in charity)."

Volume 8, Book 76, Number 548:

Narrated 'Adi bin Hatim:

The Prophet said, "Protect yourself from the Fire." He then turned his face aside (as if he were looking at it) and said again, "Protect yourself from the Fire," and then turned his face aside (as if he were looking at it), and he said so for the third time till we thought he was looking at it. He then said, "Protect yourselves from the Fire, even if with one half of a date and he who hasn't got even this, (should do so) by (saying) a good, pleasant word.'

Volume 8, Book 76, Number 549:

Narrated Ibn 'Abbas:

The Prophet said, "The people were displayed in front of me and I saw one prophet passing by with a large group of his followers, and another prophet passing by with only a small group of people, and another prophet passing by with only ten (persons), and another prophet passing by with only five (persons), and another prophet passed by alone. And then I looked and saw a large multitude of people, so I asked Gabriel, "Are these people my followers?' He said, 'No, but look towards the horizon.' I looked and saw a very large multitude of people. Gabriel said. 'Those are your followers, and those are seventy thousand (persons) in front of them who will neither have any reckoning of their accounts nor will receive any punishment.' I asked, 'Why?' He said, 'For they used not to treat them-selves with branding (cauterization) nor with Ruqya (get oneself treated by the recitation of some Verses of the Qur'an) and not to see evil omen in things, and they used to put their trust (only) in their Lord." On hearing that, 'Ukasha bin Mihsan got up and said (to the Prophet), "Invoke Allah to make me one of them." The Prophet said, "O Allah, make him one of them." Then another man got up and said (to the Prophet), "Invoke Allah to make me one of them." The Prophet said, 'Ukasha has pre-ceded you."

Volume 8, Book 76, Number 550:

Narrated Abu Huraira:

I heard Allah's Apostle saying, "From my followers there will enter Paradise a crowd, seventy thou-sand in number whose faces will glitter as the moon does when it is full." On hearing that, 'Ukasha bin Mihsan Al-Asdi got up, lifting his covering sheet, and said, "O Allah's Apostle! Invoke Allah that He may make me one of them." The Prophet said, "O Allah, make him one of them." Another man from the Ansar got up and said, "O Allah's Apostle! Invoke Allah to make me one of them. "The Prophet said (to him), ""Ukasha has preceded you."

Volume 8, Book 76, Number 551:

Narrated Sahl bin Sa'd:

The Prophet said, "Seventy-thousand or seven-hundred thousand of my followers (the narrator is in doubt as to the correct number) will enter Paradise holding each other till the first and the last of them enter Paradise at the same time, and their faces will have a glitter like that of the moon at night when it is full."

Volume 8, Book 76, Number 552:

Narrated Ibn 'Umar:

The Prophet; said, "The people of Paradise will enter Paradise, and the people of the (Hell) Fire will enter the (Hell) Fire; then a call-maker will get up (and make an announcement) among them, 'O the people of the (Hell) Fire! No death anymore ! And O people of Paradise! No death (anymore) but Eternity."

Volume 8, Book 76, Number 553:

Narrated Abu Huraira:

The Prophet said, " It will be said to the people of Paradise, 'O people of Paradise! Eternity (for you) and no death,' and to the people of the Fire, 'O people of the Fire, eternity (for you) and no death!"

Volume 8, Book 76, Number 554,

Narrated 'Imran,

The Prophet said, "I looked into paradise and saw that the majority of its people were the poor, and I looked into the Fire and found that the majority of its people were women."

Volume 8, Book 76, Number 555,

Narrated Usama,

The Prophet said, "I stood at the gate of Paradise and saw that the majority of the people who had entered it were poor people, while the rich were forbidden (to enter along with the poor, because they were waiting the reckoning of their accounts), but the people of the Fire had been ordered to be driven to the Fire. And I stood at the gate of the Fire and found that the majority of the people entering it were women."

Volume 8, Book 76, Number 556,

Narrated Ibn 'Umar,

Allah's Apostle said, "When the people of Paradise have entered Paradise and the people of the Fire have entered the Fire, death will be brought and will be placed between the Fire and Paradise, and then it will be slaughtered, and a call will be made (that), 'O people of Paradise, no more death ! O people of the Fire, no more death ! ' So the people of Paradise will have happiness added to their previous happiness, and the people of the Fire will have sorrow added to their previous sorrow."

Volume 8, Book 76, Number 557,

Narrated Abu Said Al-Khudri,

Allah's Apostle said, "Allah will say to the people of Paradise, 'O the people of Paradise!' They will say, 'Labbaik, O our Lord, and Sa'daik!' Allah will say, 'Are you pleased?" They will say, 'Why should we not be pleased since You have given us what You have not given to anyone of Your creation?' Allah will say, 'I will give you something better than that.' They will reply, 'O our Lord! And what is better than that?' Allah will say, 'I will bestow My pleasure and contentment upon you so that I will never be angry with you after for-ever.' "

Volume 8, Book 76, Number 558,

Narrated Anas,

Haritha was martyred on the day (of the battle) of Badr while he was young. His mother came to the Prophet saying, "O Allah's Apostle! You know the relation of Haritha to me (how fond of him I was); so, if he is in Paradise, I will remain patient and wish for Allah's reward, but if he is not there, then you will see what I will do." The Prophet replied, "May Allah be merciful upon you! Have you gone mad? (Do you think) it is one Paradise? There are many Paradises and he is in the (most superior) Paradise of Al-Firdaus."

Volume 8, Book 76, Number 559:

Narrated Abu Huraira:

The Prophet said, "The width between the two shoulders of a Kafir (disbeliever) will be equal to the distance covered by a fast rider in three days."

Volume 8, Book 76, Number 559t:

Narrated Sahl bin Sa'd:

Allah's Apostle said, "In Paradise there is a tree so big that in its shade a rider may travel for one hundred years without being able to cross it."

Volume 8, Book 76, Number 559e:

Narrated Abu Sa'id:

The Prophet said, There is a tree in Paradise (so huge) that a fast (or a trained) rider may travel, for one hundred years without being able to cross it.

Volume 8, Book 76, Number 560:

Narrated Sahl bin Sa'd:

Allah's Apostle said, "Seventy thousand or seven hundred thousand of my followers will enter Paradise. (Abu Hazim, the sub-narrator, is not sure as to which of the two numbers is correct.) And they will be holding on to one another, and the first of them will not enter till the last of them has entered, and their faces will be like the moon on a full moon night."

Volume 8, Book 76, Number 561:

Narrated Sahl:

The Prophet said, "The people of Paradise will see the Ghuraf (special abodes) in Paradise as you see a star in the sky." Abu Said added: "As you see a glittering star remaining in the eastern horizon and the western horizon."

Volume 8, Book 76, Number 562:

Narrated Anas bin Malik:

The Prophet said, "Allah will say to the person who will have the minimum punishment in the Fire on the Day of Resurrection, 'If you had things equal to whatever is on the earth, would you ransom yourself (from the punishment) with it?' He will reply, Yes. Allah will say, 'I asked you a much easier thing than this while you were in the backbone of Adam, that is, not to worship others besides Me, but you refused and insisted to worship others besides Me.'"

Volume 8, Book 76, Number 563:

Narrated Hammad from 'Amr from Jabir:

The Prophet said, "Some people will come out of the Fire through intercession looking like The Thaarir." I asked 'Amr, "What is the Thaarir?" He said, Ad Daghabis, and at that time he was toothless. Hammad added: I said to 'Amr bin Dinar, "O Abu Muhammad! Did you hear Jabir bin 'Abdullah saying, 'I heard the Prophet saying: 'Some people will come out of the Fire through intercession?" He said, "Yes. "

Volume 8, Book 76, Number 564:

Narrated Anas bin Malik:

The Prophet said, "Some people will come out of the Fire after they have received a touch of the Fire, changing their color, and they will enter Paradise, and the people of Paradise will name them 'Al-Jahannamiyin' the (Hell) Fire people."

Volume 8, Book 76, Number 565:

Narrated Abu Said Al-Khudri:

Allah's Apostle said, "When the people of Paradise have entered Paradise, and the people of the Fire have entered the Fire, Allah will say. 'Take out (of the Fire) whoever has got faith equal to a mustard seed in his heart.' They will come out, and by that time they would have burnt and became like coal, and then they will be thrown into the river of Al-Hayyat (life) and they will spring up just as a seed grows on the bank of a rainwater stream." The Prophet said, "Don't you see that the germinating seed comes out yellow and twisted?"

Volume 8, Book 76, Number 566:

Narrated An-Nu'man:

I heard the Prophet saying, "The person who will have the least punishment from amongst the Hell Fire people on the Day of Resurrection, will be a man under whose arch of the feet a smoldering ember will be placed so that his brain will boil because of it."

Volume 8, Book 76, Number 567:

Narrated An-Nu'man bin Bashir:

I heard the Prophet saying, "The least punished person of the (Hell) Fire people on the Day of Resurrection will be a man under whose arch of the feet two smoldering embers will be placed, because of which his brain will boil just like Al-Mirjal (copper vessel) or a Qum-qum (narrow-necked vessel) is boiling with water."

Volume 8, Book 76, Number 568:

Narrated 'Adi bin Hatim:

The Prophet mentioned the Fire and turned his face aside and asked for Allah's protection from it, and then again he mentioned the Fire and turned his face aside and asked for Allah's protection from it and said, "Protect yourselves from the Hell-Fire, even if with one half of a date, and he who cannot afford that, then (let him do so) by (saying) a good, pleasant word."

Volume 8, Book 76, Number 569:

Narrated Abu Said Al-Khudri:

I heard Allah's Apostles when his uncle, Abu Talib had been mentioned in his presence, saying, "May be my intercession will help him (Abu Talib) on the Day of Resurrection so that he may be put in a shallow place in the Fire, with fire reaching his ankles and causing his brain to boil."

Volume 8, Book 76, Number 570:

Narrated Anas:

Allah's Apostle said, "Allah will gather all the people on the Day of Resurrection and they will say, 'Let us request someone to intercede for us with our Lord so that He may relieve us from this place of ours.' Then they will go to Adam and say, 'You are the one whom Allah created with His Own Hands, and breathed in you of His soul, and ordered the angels to prostrate to you; so please intercede for us with our Lord.' Adam will reply, 'I am not fit for this undertaking, and will remember his sin, and will say, 'Go to Noah, the first Apostle sent by Allah' They will go to him and he will say, 'I am not fit for this undertaking', and will remember his sin and say, 'Go to Abraham whom Allah took as a Khalil. They will go to him (and request similarly). He will reply, 'I am not fit for this undertaking,' and will remember his sin and say, 'Go to Moses to whom Allah spoke directly.' They will go to Moses and he will say, 'I am not fit for this undertaking,' and will remember his sin and say, 'Go to Jesus.' They will go to him, and he will say, 'I am not fit for this undertaking, go to Muhammad as Allah has forgiven his past and future sins.' They will come to me and I will ask my Lord's permission, and when I see Him, I will fall down in prostration to Him, and He will leave me in that state as long as (He) Allah will, and then I will be addressed. 'Raise up your head (O Muhammad)! Ask, and your request will be granted, and say, and your saying will be listened to; intercede, and your intercession will be accepted.' Then I will raise my head, and I will glorify and praise my Lord with a saying(i.e. invocation) He will teach me, and then I will intercede, Allah will fix a limit for me (i.e., certain type of people for whom I may intercede), and I will take them out of the (Hell) Fire and let them enter Paradise. Then I will come back (to Allah) and fall in prostration, and will do the same for the third and fourth times till no-one remains in the (Hell) Fire except those whom the Qur'an has imprisoned therein." (The sub-narrator, Qatada used to say at that point, "...those upon whom eternity (in Hell) has been imposed.") (See Hadith No. 3, Vol 6).

Volume 8, Book 76, Number 571.

Narrated 'Imran bin Husain.

The Prophet said, "Some people will be taken out of the Fire through the intercession of Muhammad they will enter Paradise and will be called Al-Jahannamiyin (the Hell Fire people)."

Volume 8, Book 76, Number 572.

Narrated Anas.

Um (the mother of) Haritha came to Allah's Apostle after Haritha had been martyred on the Day (of the battle) of Badr by an arrow thrown by an unknown person. She said, "O Allah's Apostle! You know the position of Haritha in my heart (i.e. how dear to me he was), so if he is in Paradise, I will not weep for him, or otherwise, you will see what I will do." The Prophet said, "Are you mad? Is there only one Paradise? There are many Paradises, and he is in the highest Paradise of Firdaus." The Prophet added, "A forenoon journey or an after noon journey in Allah's Cause is better than the whole world and whatever is in it; and a place equal to an arrow bow of anyone of you, or a place equal to a foot in Paradise is better than the whole world and whatever is in it; and if one of the women of Paradise looked at the earth, she would fill the whole space between them (the earth and the heaven) with light, and would fill whatever is in between them, with perfume, and the veil of her face is better than the whole world and whatever is in it."

Volume 8, Book 76, Number 573.

Narrated Abu Huraira.

The Prophet said, "None will enter Paradise but will be shown the place he would have occupied in the (Hell) Fire if he had rejected faith, so that he may be more thankful; and none will enter the (Hell) Fire but will be shown the place he would have occupied in Paradise if he had faith, so that may be a cause of sorrow for him."

Volume 8, Book 76, Number 574:

Narrated Abu Huraira:

I said, "O Allah's Apostle! Who will be the luckiest person who will gain your intercession on the Day of Resurrection?" The Prophet said, "O Abu Huraira! I have thought that none will ask me about this Hadith before you, as I know your longing for the (learning of) Hadiths. The luckiest person who will have my intercession on the Day of Resurrection will be the one who said, 'None has the right to be worshipped but Allah,' sincerely from the bottom of his heart."

Volume 8, Book 76, Number 575:

Narrated 'Abdullah:

The Prophet said, "I know the person who will be the last to come out of the (Hell) Fire, and the last to enter Paradise. He will be a man who will come out of the (Hell) Fire crawling, and Allah will say to him, 'Go and enter Paradise.' He will go to it, but he will imagine that it had been filled, and then he will return and say, 'O Lord, I have found it full.' Allah will say, 'Go and enter Paradise, and you will have what equals the world and ten times as much (or, you will have as much as ten times the like of the world).' On that, the man will say, 'Do you mock at me (or laugh at me) though You are the King?" I saw Allah's Apostle (while saying that) smiling that his premolar teeth became visible. It is said that will be the lowest in degree amongst the people of Paradise.

Volume 8, Book 76, Number 576:

Narrated 'Abbas:

that he said to the Prophet "Did you benefit Abu Talib with anything?"

Volume 8, Book 76, Number 577:

Narrated Abu Huraira:

Some people said, "O Allah's Apostle! Shall we see our Lord on the Day of Resurrection?" He said, "Do you crowd and squeeze each other on looking at the sun when it is not hidden by clouds?" They replied, "No, Allah's Apostle." He said, "Do you crowd and squeeze each other on looking at the moon when it is full and not hidden by clouds?" They replied, No, O Allah's Apostle!" He said, "So you will see Him (your Lord) on the Day of Resurrection similarly Allah will gather all the people and say,

'Whoever used to worship anything should follow that thing. 'So, he who used to worship the sun, will follow it, and he who used to worship the moon will follow it, and he who used to worship false deities will follow them; and then only this nation (i.e., Muslims) will remain, including their hypocrites. Allah will come to them in a shape other than they know and will say, 'I am your Lord.' They will say, 'We seek refuge with Allah from you. This is our place; (we will not follow you) till our Lord comes to us, and when our Lord comes to us, we will recognize Him.

Then Allah will come to then in a shape they know and will say, "I am your Lord.' They will say, '(No doubt) You are our Lord,' and they will follow Him. Then a bridge will be laid over the (Hell) Fire." Allah's Apostle added, "I will be the first to cross it. And the invocation of the Apostles on that Day, will be 'Allahukka Sallim, Sallim (O Allah, save us, save us!),' and over that bridge there will be hooks Similar to the thorns of As Sa'dan (a thorny tree). Didn't you see the thorns of As-Sa'dan?" The companions said, "Yes, O Allah's Apostle." He added, "So the hooks over that bridge will be like the thorns of As-Sa-dan except that their greatness in size is only known to Allah. These hooks will snatch the people according to their deeds. Some people will be ruined because of their evil deeds, and some will be cut into pieces and fall down in Hell, but will be saved afterwards, when Allah has finished the judgments among His slaves, and intends to take out of the Fire whoever He wishes to take out from among those who used to testify that none had the right to be worshipped but Allah.

We will order the angels to take them out and the angels will know them by the mark of the traces of prostration (on their foreheads) for Allah banned the f ire to consume the traces of prostration on the body of Adam's son. So they will take them out, and by then they would have burnt (as coal), and then water, called Maul Hayat (water of life) will be poured on them, and they will spring out like a seed springs out on the bank of a rainwater stream, and there will remain one man who will be facing the (Hell) Fire and will say, 'O Lord! It's (Hell's) vapor has Poisoned and smoked me and its flame has burnt me; please turn my face away from the Fire.' He will keep on invoking Allah till Allah says, 'Perhaps, if I give you what you want), you will ask for another thing?' The man will say, 'No, by Your Power, I will not ask You for anything else.'

Then Allah will turn his face away from the Fire. The man will say after that, 'O Lord, bring me near the gate of Paradise.' Allah will say (to him), 'Didn't you promise not to ask for anything else? Woe to you, O son of Adam ! How treacherous you are!' The man will keep on invoking Allah till Allah will say, 'But if I give you that, you may ask me for something else.' The man will say, 'No, by Your Power. I will not ask for anything else.' He will give Allah his covenant and promise not to ask for anything else after that. So Allah will bring him near to the gate of Paradise, and when he sees what is in it, he will remain silent as long as Allah will, and then he will say, 'O Lord! Let me enter Paradise.' Allah will say, 'Didn't you promise that you would not ask Me for anything other than that? Woe to you, O son of Adam ! How treacherous you are!' On that, the man will say, 'O Lord! Do not make me the most wretched of Your creation,' and will keep on invoking Allah till Allah will smile and when Allah will smile because of him, then He will allow him to enter Paradise, and when he will enter Paradise, he will be addressed, 'Wish from so-and-so.' He will wish till all his wishes will be fulfilled, then Allah will say, All this (i.e. what you have wished for) and as much again therewith are for you.' "

Abu Huraira added: That man will be the last of the people of Paradise to enter (Paradise).

Narrated 'Ata (while Abu Huraira was narrating): Abu Said was sitting in the company of Abu Huraira and he did not deny anything of his narration till he reached his saying: "All this and as much again therewith are for you." Then Abu Sa'id said, "I heard Allah's Apostle saying, 'This is for you and ten times as much.' " Abu Huraira said, "In my memory it is 'as much again therewith.' "

Volume 8, Book 76, Number 578:

Narrated 'Abdullah:

The Prophet said, "I am your predecessor at the Lake-Fount." 'Abdullah added: The Prophet said, "I am your predecessor at the Lake-Fount, and some of you will be brought in front of me till I will see them and then they will be taken away from me and I will say, 'O Lord, my companions!' It will be said, 'You do not know what they did after you had left.'

Volume 8, Book 76, Number 579:

Narrated Ibn 'Umar:

The Prophet said, "There will be a tank (Lake-Fount) in front of you as large as the distance between Jarba and Adhruh (two towns in Sham)."

Volume 8, Book 76, Number 580:

Narrated Ibn 'Abbas:

The word 'Al-Kauthar' means the abundant good which Allah gave to him (the Prophet Muhammad). Abu Bishr said: I said to Said, "Some people claim that it (Al-Kauthar) is a river in Paradise." Said replied, "The river which is in Paradise is one item of that good which Allah has bestowed upon him (Muhammad)."

Volume 8, Book 76, Number 581:

Narrated 'Abdullah bin 'Amr:

The Prophet said, "My Lake-Fount is (so large that it takes) a month's journey to cross it. Its water is whiter than milk, and its smell is nicer than musk (a kind of Perfume), and its drinking cups are (as numerous) as the (number of) stars of the sky; and whoever drinks from it, will never be thirsty."

Volume 8, Book 76, Number 582:

Narrated Anas bin Malik:

Allah's Apostle said, "The width of my Lake-Fount is equal to the distance between Aila (a town in Sham) and Sana' (the capital of Yemen) and it has as many (numerous) jugs as the number of stars of the sky."

Volume 8, Book 76, Number 583:

Narrated Anas bin Malik:

The Prophet said: "While I was walking in Paradise (on the night of Mi'raj), I saw a river, on the two banks of which there were tents made of hollow pearls. I asked, "What is this, O Gabriel?' He said, 'That is the Kauthar which Your Lord has given to you.' Behold! Its scent or its mud was sharp smelling musk!" (The sub-narrator, Hudba is in doubt as to the correct expression.)

Volume 8, Book 76, Number 584:

Narrated Anas:

The Prophet said, "Some of my companions will come to me at my Lake Fount, and after I recognize them, they will then be taken away from me, whereupon I will say, 'My companions!' Then it will be said, 'You do not know what they innovated (new things) in the religion after you."

Volume 8, Book 76, Number 585:

Narrated Abu Hazim from Sahl bin Sa'd:

The Prophet said, "I am your predecessor (forerunner) at the Lake-Fount, and whoever will pass by there, he will drink from it and whoever will drink from it, he will never be thirsty. There will come to me some people whom I will recognize, and they will recognize me, but a barrier will be placed between me and them." Abu Hazim added: An-Nu'man bin Abi 'Aiyash, on hearing me, said. "Did you hear this from Sahl?" I said, "Yes." He said, " I bear witness that I heard Abu Said Al-Khudri saying the same, adding that the Prophet said: 'I will say: They are of me (i.e. my followers). It will be said, 'You do not know what they innovated (new things) in the religion after you left'. I will say, 'Far removed, far removed (from mercy), those who changed (their religion) after me." Abu Huraira narrated that the Prophet said, "On the Day of Resurrection a group of companions will come to me, but will be driven away from the Lake-Fount, and I will say, 'O Lord (those are) my companions!' It will be said, 'You have no knowledge as to what they innovated after you left; they turned apostate as renegades (reverted from Islam)."

Volume 8, Book 76, Number 586:

Narrated Ibn Al-Musaiyab:

The companions of the Prophet said, "Some men from my companions will come to my Lake-Fount and they will be driven away from it, and I will say, 'O Lord, my companions!' It will be said, 'You have no knowledge of what they innovated after you left: they turned apostate as renegades (reverted from Islam).

Volume 8, Book 76, Number 587:

Narrated Abu Huraira:

The Prophet said, "While I was sleeping, a group (of my followers were brought close to me), and when I recognized them, a man (an angel) came out from amongst (us) me and them, he said (to them), 'Come along.' I asked, 'Where?' He said, 'To the (Hell) Fire, by Allah' I asked, 'what is wrong with them' He said, 'They turned apostate as renegades after you left.' Then behold! (Another) group (of my followers) were brought close to me, and when I recognized them, a man (an angel) came out from (me and them) he said (to them); Come along.' I asked, "Where?' He said, 'To the (Hell) Fire, by Allah.' I asked, What is wrong with them?' He said, 'They turned apostate as renegades after you left. So I did not see anyone of them escaping except a few who were like camels without a shepherd."

Volume 8, Book 76, Number 588:

Narrated Abu Huraira:

Allah's Apostle said, "Between my house and my pulpit there is a garden from amongst the gardens of Paradise, and my pulpit is over my Lake-Fount."

Volume 8, Book 76, Number 589:

Narrated Jundab:

I heard the Prophet, saying, "I am your predecessor at the Lake-Fount. (Al-Kauthar) .

Volume 8, Book 76, Number 590:

Narrated 'Uqba bin 'Amir:

Once the Prophet went out and offered the funeral prayers for the martyrs of Uhud, and then went to the pulpit and said, "I am a predecessor for you and I am a witness for you: and by Allah, I am looking at my Fount just now, and the keys of the treasures of the earth (or the keys of the earth) have been given to me: and by Allah, I am not afraid that you will worship others besides Allah after me, but I am afraid that you will strive and struggle against each other over these treasures of the world."

Volume 8, Book 76, Number 591:

Narrated Haritha bin Wahb:

I heard the Prophet mentioning the Lake-Fount (Al-Kauthar), saying, "(The width of the Lake-Fount) is equal to the distance between Medina and Sana' (capital of Yemen)." Haritha said that he heard the Prophet saying that his Lake-Fount would be as large as the distance between Sana' and Medina. Al-Mustaurid said to Haritha, "Didn't you hear him talking about the vessels?" He said, "No." Al-Mustaurid said, "The vessels are seen in it as (numberless as) the stars."

Volume 8, Book 76, Number 592:

Narrated Asma 'bint Abu Bakr:

The Prophet said, "I will be standing at the Lake-Fount so that I will see whom among you will come to me; and some people will be taken away from me, and I will say, 'O Lord, (they are) from me and from my followers.' Then it will be said, 'Did you notice what they did after you? By Allah, they kept on turning on their heels (turned as renegades).' " The sub-narrator, Ibn Abi Mulaika said, "O Allah, we seek refuge with You from turning on our heels, or being put to trial in our religion."

Book 77: Divine Will (Al-Qadar)

Volume 8, Book 77, Number 593:

Narrated 'Abdullah:

Allah's Apostle, the truthful and truly-inspired, said, "Each one of you collected in the womb of his mother for forty days, and then turns into a clot for an equal period (of forty days) and turns into a piece of flesh for a similar period (of forty days) and then Allah sends an angel and orders him to write four things, i.e., his provision, his age, and whether he will be of the wretched or the blessed (in the Hereafter). Then the soul is breathed into him. And by Allah, a person among you (or a man) may do deeds of the people of the Fire till there is only a cubit or an arm-breadth distance between him and the Fire, but then that writing (which Allah has ordered the angel to write) precedes, and he does the deeds of the people of Paradise and enters it; and a man may do the deeds of the people of Paradise till there is only a cubit or two between him and Paradise, and then that writing precedes and he does the deeds of the people of the Fire and enters it."

Volume 8, Book 77, Number 594:

Narrated Anas bin Malik:

The Prophet said, "Allah puts an angel in charge of the uterus and the angel says, 'O Lord, (it is) semen! O Lord, (it is now) a clot! O Lord, (it is now) a piece of flesh.' And then, if Allah wishes to complete its creation, the angel asks, 'O Lord, (will it be) a male or a female? A wretched (an evil doer) or a blessed (doer of good)? How much will his provisions be? What will his age be?' So all that is written while the creature is still in the mother's womb."

Volume 8, Book 77, Number 595:

Narrated Imran bin Husain:

A man said, "O Allah's Apostle! Can the people of Paradise be known (differentiated) from the people of the Fire; The Prophet replied, "Yes." The man said, "Why do people (try to) do (good) deeds?" The Prophet said, "Everyone will do the deeds for which he has been created to do or he will do those deeds which will be made easy for him to do." (i.e. everybody will find easy to do such deeds as will lead him to his destined place for which he has been created).

Volume 8, Book 77, Number 596:

Narrated Ibn 'Abbas:

The Prophet ; was asked about the offspring of the pagans. He said, "Allah knows what they would have done (were they to live)."

Volume 8, Book 77, Number 597:

Narrated Abu Huraira:

Allah's Apostle was asked about the offspring of the pagans. He said, "Allah knows what they would have done (were they to live)."

Narrated Abu Huraira: Allah's Apostle said, "No child is born but has the Islamic Faith, but its parents turn it into a Jew or a Christian. It is as you help the animals give birth. Do you find among their offspring a mutilated one before you mutilate them yourself?" The people said, "O Allah's Apostle! What do you think about those (of them) who die young?" The Prophet said, "Allah knows what they would have done (were they to live)."

Volume 8, Book 77, Number 598:

Narrated Abu Huraira:

Allah's Apostle said, "No woman should ask for the divorce of her sister (Muslim) so as to take her place, but she should marry the man (without compelling him to divorce his other wife), for she will have nothing but what Allah has written for her."

Volume 8, Book 77, Number 599:

Narrated Usama:

Once while I was with the Prophet and Sa'd, Ubai bin Ka'b and Mu'adh were also sitting with him, there came to him a messenger from one of his daughters, telling him that her child was on the verge of death. The Prophet told the messenger to tell her, "It is for Allah what He takes, and it is for Allah what He gives, and everything has its fixed time (limit). So (she should) be patient and look for Allah's reward."

Volume 8, Book 77, Number 600:

Narrated Abu Said Al-Khudri:

That while he was sitting with the Prophet a man from the Ansar came and said, "O Allah's Apostle! We get slave girls from the war captives and we love property; what do you think about co-itus interruptus?" Allah's Apostle said, "Do you do that? It is better for you not to do it, for there is no soul which Allah has ordained to come into existence but will be created."

Volume 8, Book 77, Number 601:

Narrated Hudhaifa:

The Prophet once delivered a speech in front of us wherein he left nothing but mentioned (about) everything that would happen till the Hour. Some of us stored that our minds and some forgot it. (After that speech) I used to see events taking place (which had been referred to in that speech) but I had forgotten them (before their occurrence). Then I would recognize such events as a man recognizes another man who has been absent and then sees and recognizes him.

Volume 8, Book 77, Number 602:

Narrated 'Ali:

While we were sitting with the Prophet who had a stick with which he was scraping the earth, he lowered his head and said, "There is none of you but has his place assigned either in the Fire or in Paradise." Thereupon a man from the people said, "Shall we not depend upon this, O Allah's Apostle?" The Prophet said, "No, but carry on and do your deeds, for everybody finds it easy to do such deeds (as will lead him to his place)." The Prophet then recited the Verse: 'As for him who gives (in charity) and keeps his duty to Allah..' (92.5)

Volume 8, Book 77, Number 603:

Narrated Abu Huraira:

We witnessed along with Allah's Apostle the Khaibar (campaign). Allah's Apostle told his companions about a man who claimed to be a Muslim, "This man is from the people of the Fire." When the battle started, the man fought very bravely and received a great number of wounds and got crippled. On that, a man from among the companions of the Prophet came and said, "O Allah's Apostle! Do you know what the man you described as of the people of the Fire has done? He has fought very bravely for Allah's Cause and he has received many wounds." The Prophet said, "But he is indeed one of the people of the Fire." Some of the Muslims were about to have some doubt about that statement. So while the man was in that state, the pain caused by the wounds troubled him so much that he put his hand into his quiver and took out an arrow and committed suicide with it. Off went some men from among the Muslims to Allah's Apostle and said, "O Allah's Apostle! Allah has made your statement true. So-and-so has committed suicide." Allah's Apostle said, "O Bilal! Get up and announce in public: None will enter Paradise but a believer, and Allah may support this religion (Islam) with a wicked man."

Volume 8, Book 77, Number 604:

Narrated Sahl bin Sa'd:

There was a man who fought most bravely of all the Muslims on behalf of the Muslims in a battle (Ghazwa) in the company of the Prophet. The Prophet looked at him and said. "If anyone would like to see a man from the people of the Fire, let him look at this (brave man)." On that, a man from the People (Muslims) followed him, and he was in that state i.e., fighting fiercely against the pagans till he was wounded, and then he hastened to end his life by placing his sword between his breasts (and pressed it with great force) till it came out between his shoulders. Then the man (who was watching that person) went quickly to the Prophet and said, "I testify that you are Allah's Apostle!" The Prophet asked him, "Why do you say that?" He said, "You said about so-and-so, 'If anyone would like to see a man from the people of the Fire, he should look at him.' He fought most bravely of all of us on behalf of the Muslims and I knew that he would not die as a Muslim (Martyr). So when he got wounded, he hastened to die and committed suicide." There-upon the Prophet said, "A man may do the deeds of the people of the Fire while in fact he is one of the people of Paradise, and he may do the deeds of the people of Paradise while in fact he belongs to the people of Fire, and verily, (the rewards of) the deeds are decided by the last actions (deeds)".

Volume 8, Book 77, Number 605:

Narrated Ibn 'Umar.

The Prophet forbade vowing and said, "In fact, vowing does not prevent anything, but it makes a miser to spend his property."

Volume 8, Book 77, Number 606:

Narrated Abu Huraira.

The Prophet said (that Allah said), "Vowing does not bring to the son of Adam anything I have not already written in his fate, but vowing is imposed on him by way of fore ordainment. Through vowing I make a miser spend of his wealth."

Volume 8, Book 77, Number 607:

Narrated Abu Musa.

While we were with Allah's Apostle in a holy battle, we never went up a hill or reached its peak or went down a valley but raised our voices with Takbir. Allah's Apostle came close to us and said, "O people! Don't exert yourselves, for you do not call a deaf or an absent one, but you call the All-Listener, the All-Seer." The Prophet then said, "O 'Abdullah bin Qais! Shall I teach you a sentence which is from the treasures of Paradise? (It is), 'La haula wala quwata illa billah. (There is neither might nor power except with Allah)."

Volume 8, Book 77, Number 608:

Narrated Abu Said Al-Khudri:

That the Prophet said, "No Caliph is appointed but has two groups of advisors: One group advises him to do good and urges him to adopt it, and the other group advises him to do bad and urges him to adopt it; and the protected is the one whom Allah protects."

Volume 8, Book 77, Number 609:

Narrated Ibn 'Abbas:

I did not see anything so resembling minor sins as what Abu Huraira said from the Prophet, who said, "Allah has written for the son of Adam his inevitable share of adultery whether he is aware of it or not: The adultery of the eye is the looking (at something which is sinful to look at), and the adultery of the tongue is to utter (what it is unlawful to utter), and the innerself wishes and longs for (adultery) and the private parts turn that into reality or refrain from submitting to the temptation."

Volume 8, Book 77, Number 610:

Narrated Ibn 'Abbas:

(regarding the Verse) "And We granted the vision (Ascension to the heavens "Miraj") which We showed you (O Muhammad as an actual eye witness) but as a trial for mankind.' (17.60): Allah's Apostle actually saw with his own eyes the vision (all the things which were shown to him) on the night of his Night Journey to Jerusalem (and then to the heavens). The cursed tree which is mentioned in the Qur'an is the tree of Az-Zaqqum.

Volume 8, Book 77, Number 611:

Narrated Abu Huraira:

The Prophet said, "Adam and Moses argued with each other. Moses said to Adam. 'O Adam! You are our father who disappointed us and turned us out of Paradise.' Then Adam said to him, 'O Moses! Allah favored you with His talk (talked to you directly) and He wrote (the Torah) for you with His Own Hand. Do you blame me for action which Allah had written in my fate forty years before my creation?' So Adam confuted Moses, Adam confuted Moses," the Prophet added, repeating the Statement three times.

Volume 8, Book 77, Number 612:

Narrated Warrad:

(the freed slave of Al-Mughira bin Shu'ba) Muawiya wrote to Mughira. 'Write to me what you heard the Prophet saying after his prayer.' So Al-Mughira dictated to me and said, "I heard the Prophet saying after the prayer, 'None has the right to be worshipped but Allah Alone Who has no partner. O Allah! No-one can withhold what You give, and none can give what You withhold, and the fortune of a man of means is useless before You (i.e., only good deeds are of value)."

Volume 8, Book 77, Number 613:

Narrated Abu Huraira:

The Prophet said, "Take refuge with Allah from the difficulties of severe calamities, from having an evil end and a bad fate and from the malicious joy of your enemies."

Volume 8, Book 77, Number 614:

Narrated 'Abdullah:

When taking an oath, the Prophet very often used to say, "No, by Him Who turns the hearts."

Volume 8, Book 77, Number 615:

Narrated Ibn 'Umar:

The Prophet said to Ibn Saiyad, "I have kept for you a secret." Ibn Saiyad said, "Ad-Dukh." The Prophet said, "Keep quiet, for you cannot go beyond your limits (or you cannot exceed what has been foreordained for you)." On that, 'Umar said (to the Prophet), "Allow me to chop off his neck!" The Prophet said, "Leave him, for if he is he (i.e., Ad-Dajjal), then you will not be able to overcome him, and if he is not, then you gain no good by killing him."

Volume 8, Book 77, Number 616:

Narrated 'Aisha:

I asked Allah's Apostle about the plague. He said, "That was a means of torture which Allah used to send upon whom-so-ever He wished, but He made it a source of mercy for the believers, for anyone who is residing in a town in which this disease is present, and remains there and does not leave that town, but has patience and hopes for Allah's reward, and knows that nothing will befall him except what Allah has written for him, then he will get such reward as that of a martyr."

Volume 8, Book 77, Number 617:

Narrated Al-Bara' bin 'Azib:

I saw the Prophet on the Day of (the battle of) Al-Khandaq, carrying earth with us and saying, "By Allah, without Allah we would not have been guided, neither would we have fasted, nor would we have prayed. O Allah! Send down Sakina (calmness) upon us and make our feet firm when we meet (the enemy). The pagans have rebelled against us, but if they want to put us in affliction (i.e., fight us) we refuse (to flee)." (See Hadith No. 430, Vol. 5).

Book 78: Oaths and Vows

Volume 8, Book 78, Number 618:

Narrated 'Aisha:

Abu Bakr As-Siddiq had never broken his oaths till Allah revealed the expiation for the oaths. Then he said, "If I take an oath to do something and later on I find something else better than the first one, then I do what is better and make expiation for my oath."

Volume 8, Book 78, Number 619:

Narrated 'Abdur-Rahman bin Samura:

The Prophet said, "O 'Abdur-Rahman bin Samura! Do not seek to be a ruler, because if you are given authority for it, then you will be held responsible for it, but if you are given it without asking for it, then you will be helped in it (by Allah), and whenever you take an oath to do something and later you find that something else is better than the first, then do the better one and make expiation for your oath."

Volume 8, Book 78, Number 620:

Narrated Abu Musa:

I went to the Prophet along with a group of Al-Ash'ariyin in order to request him to provide us with mounts. He said, "By Allah, I will not provide you with mounts and I haven't got anything to mount you on." Then we stayed there as long as Allah wished us to stay, and then three very nice looking she-camels were brought to him and he made us ride them. When we left, we, or some of us, said, "By Allah, we will not be blessed, as we came to the Prophet asking him for mounts, and he swore that he would not give us any mounts but then he did give us. So let us go back to the Prophet and remind him (of his oath)." When we returned to him (and reminded him of the fact), he said, "I did not give you mounts, but it is Allah Who gave you. By Allah, Allah willing, if I ever take an oath to do something and then I find something else than the first, I will make expiation for my oath and do the thing which is better (or do something which is better and give the expiation for my oath)."

Volume 8, Book 78, Number 621:

Narrated Abu Huraira:

The Prophet said, "We (Muslims) are the last in the world, but will be foremost on the Day of Resurrection." Allah's Apostle also said, "By Allah, if anyone of you insists on fulfilling an oath by which he may harm his family, he commits a greater sin in Allah's sight than that of dissolving his oath and making expiation for it."

Volume 8, Book 78, Number 622:

Narrated Abu Huraira:

Allah's Apostle said, "Anyone who takes an oath through which his family may be harmed, and insists on keeping it, he surely commits a sin greater (than that of dissolving his oath). He should rather compensate for that oath by making expiation."

Volume 8, Book 78, Number 623:

Narrated Ibn 'Umar:

Allah's Apostle sent an army detachment and made Usama bin Zaid its commander. Some people criticized (spoke badly of) Usama's leadership. So Allah's Apostle got up saying, "If you people are criticizing Usama's leadership, you have already criticized the leadership of his father before. But Wa-aimullah (i.e., By Allah), he (i.e. Zaid) deserved the leadership, and he was one of the most beloved persons to me; and now this (his son Usama) is one of the dearest persons to me after him." (See Hadith No. 745, Vol. 5)

Volume 8, Book 78, Number 624:

Narrated Ibn 'Umar:

The oath of the Prophet used to be: "No, by Him who turns the hearts."

Volume 8, Book 78, Number 625:

Narrated Jabir bin Samura:

The Prophet said, "If Caesar is ruined, there will be no Caesar after him; and if Khosrau is ruined, there will be no Khosrau, after him; and, by Him in Whose Hand my soul is, surely you will spend their treasures in Allah's Cause."

Volume 8, Book 78, Number 626:

Narrated Abu Huraira:

Allah's Apostle said, "If Khosrau is ruined, there will be no Khosrau after him; and if Caesar is ruined, there will be no Caesar after him. By Him in Whose Hand Muhammad's soul is, surely you will spend their treasures in Allah's Cause."

Volume 8, Book 78, Number 627:

Narrated 'Aisha:

The Prophet said, "O followers of Muhammad! By Allah, if you knew what I know, you would weep much and laugh little."

Volume 8, Book 78, Number 628:

Narrated 'Abdullah bin Hisham:

We were with the Prophet and he was holding the hand of 'Umar bin Al-Khattab. 'Umar said to Him, "O Allah's Apostle! You are dearer to me than everything except my own self." The Prophet said, "No, by Him in Whose Hand my soul is, (you will not have complete faith) till I am dearer to you than your own self." Then 'Umar said to him, "However, now, by Allah, you are dearer to me than my own self." The Prophet said, "Now, O 'Umar, (now you are a believer)."

Volume 8, Book 78, Number 629:

Narrated Abu Huraira and Zaid bin Khalid:

Two men had a dispute in the presence of Allah's Apostle. One of them said, "O Allah's Apostle! Judge between us according to Allah's Laws." The other who was wiser, said, "Yes, O Allah's Apostle! Judge between us according to Allah's Laws and allow me to speak. The Prophet said, "Speak." He said, "My son was a laborer serving this (person) and he committed illegal sexual intercourse with his wife, The people said that my son is to be stoned to death, but I ransomed him with one-hundred sheep and a slave girl. Then I asked the learned people, who informed me that my son should receive one hundred lashes and will be exiled for one year, and stoning will be the lot for the man's wife." Allah's Apostle said, "Indeed, by Him in Whose Hand my soul is, I will judge between you according to Allah's Laws: As for your sheep and slave girl, they are to be returned to you." Then he scourged his son one hundred lashes and exiled him for one year. Then Unais Al-Aslami was ordered to go to the wife of the second man, and if she confessed (the crime), then stone her to death. She did confess, so he stoned her to death.

Volume 8, Book 78, Number 630:

Narrated Abu Bakra:

The Prophet said, "Do you think if the tribes of Aslam, Ghifar, Muzaina and Juhaina are better than the tribes of Tamim, 'Amir bin Sa'sa'a, Ghatfan and Asad, they (the second group) are despairing and losing?" They (the Prophet's companions) said, "Yes, (they are)." He said, "By Him in Whose Hand my soul is, they (the first group) are better than them (the second group)."

Volume 8, Book 78, Number 631:

Narrated Abu Humaid As-Sa'idi:

Allah's Apostle employed an employee (to collect Zakat). The employee returned after completing his job and said, "O Allah's Apostle! This (amount of Zakat) is for you, and this (other amount) was given to me as a present." The Prophet said to him, "Why didn't you stay at your father's or mother's house and see if you would be given presents or not?" Then Allah's Apostle got up in the evening after the prayer, and having testified that none has the right to be worshipped but Allah and praised and glorified Allah as He deserved, he said, "Now then ! What about an employee whom we employ and then he comes and says, 'This amount (of Zakat) is for you, and this (amount) was given to me as a present'? Why didn't he stay at the house of his father and mother to see if he would be given presents or not? By Him in Whose Hand Muhammad's soul is, none of you will steal anything of it (i.e. Zakat) but will bring it by carrying it over his neck on the Day of Resurrection. If it has been a camel, he will bring it (over his neck) while it will be grunting, and if it has been a cow, he will bring it (over his neck), while it will be mooing; and if it has been a sheep, he will bring it (over his neck) while it will be bleeding." The Prophet added, "I have preached you (Allah's Message)." Abu Humaid said, "Then Allah's Apostle raised his hands so high that we saw the whiteness of his armpits."

Volume 8, Book 78, Number 632:

Narrated Abu Huraira:

Abu-l-Qasim (the Prophet) said, "By Him in Whose Hand Muhammad's soul is, if you know that which I know, you would weep much and laugh little."

Volume 8, Book 78, Number 633:

Narrated Abu Dhar:

I reached him (the Prophet) while in the shade of the Ka'ba; he was saying, "They are the losers, by the Lord of the Ka'ba! They are the losers, by the Lord of the Ka'ba!" I said (to myself), "What is wrong with me? Is anything improper detected in me? What is wrong with me? Then I sat beside him and he kept on saying his statement. I could not remain quiet, and Allah knows in what sorrowful state I was at that time. So I said, ' Who are they (the losers)? Let My father and mother be sacrificed for you, O Allah's Apostle!" He said, "They are the wealthy people, except the one who does like this and like this and like this (i.e., spends of his wealth in Allah's Cause)."

Volume 8, Book 78, Number 634:

Narrated Abu Huraira:

Allah's Apostle said, "(The Prophet) Solomon once said, 'Tonight I will sleep with ninety women, each of whom will bring forth a (would-be) cavalier who will fight in Allah's Cause." On this, his companion said to him, "Say: Allah willing!" But he did not say Allah willing. Solomon then slept with all the women, but none of them became pregnant but one woman who later delivered a half-man. By Him in Whose Hand Muhammad's soul is, if he (Solomon) had said, 'Allah willing' (all his wives would have brought forth boys) and they would have fought in Allah's Cause as cavaliers. "

Volume 8, Book 78, Number 635:

Narrated Al-Bara 'bin 'Azib:

A piece of silken cloth was given to the Prophet as a present and the people handed it over amongst themselves and were astonished at its beauty and softness. Allah's Apostle said, "Are you astonished at it?" They said, "Yes, O Allah's Apostle!" He said, "By Him in Whose Hand my soul is, the handkerchiefs of Sa'd in Paradise are better than it."

Volume 8, Book 78, Number 636:

Narrated 'Aisha:

Hind bint 'Utba bin Rabi 'a said, "O Allah 's Apostle! (Before I embraced Islam), there was no family on the surface of the earth, I wish to have degraded more than I did your family. But today there is no family whom I wish to have honored more than I did yours." Allah's Apostle said, "I thought similarly, by Him in Whose Hand Muhammad's soul is!" Hind said, "O Allah's Apostle! (My husband) Abu Sufyan is a miser. Is it sinful of me to feed my children from his property?" The Prophet said, "No, unless you take it for your needs what is just and reasonable."

Volume 8, Book 78, Number 637:

Narrated Abdullah bin Masud:

While Allah's Apostle was sitting, reclining his back against a Yemenite leather tent he said to his companions, "Will you be pleased to be one-fourth of the people of Paradise?" They said, 'Yes.' He said "Won't you be pleased to be one-third of the people of Paradise" They said, "Yes." He said, "By Him in Whose Hand Muhammad's soul is, I hope that you will be one-half of the people of Paradise."

Volume 8, Book 78, Number 638:

Narrated Abu Sa'id Al-Khudri:

A man heard another man reciting: Surat-ul-Ikhlas (The Unity) 'Say: He is Allah, the One (112) and he was repeating it. The next morning he came to Allah's Apostle and mentioned the whole story to him as if he regarded the recitation of that Sura as insufficient On that, Allah's Apostle said, "By Him in Whose Hand my soul is! That (Sura No. 112) equals one-third of the Qur'an."

Volume 8, Book 78, Number 639:

Narrated Anas bin Malik:

I heard the Prophet saying, "Perform the bowing and the prostration properly (with peace of mind), for, by Him in Whose Hand my soul is, I see you from behind my back when you bow and when you prostrate."

Volume 8, Book 78, Number 640:

Narrated Anas bin Malik:

An Ansari woman came to the Prophet in the company of her children, and the Prophet said to her, "By Him in Whose Hand my soul is, you are the most beloved people to me!" And he repeated the statement thrice.

Volume 8, Book 78, Number 641:

Narrated Ibn 'Umar:

Allah's Apostle met 'Umar bin Al-Khattab while the latter was going with a group of camel-riders, and he was swearing by his father. The Prophet said, "Lo! Allah forbids you to swear by your fathers, so whoever has to take an oath, he should swear by Allah or keep quiet."

Volume 8, Book 78, Number 642:

Narrated Ibn 'Umar:

???

Volume 8, Book 78, Number 643:

Narrated 'Abdullah bin 'Umar:

Allah's Apostle said, "Do not swear by your fathers."

Volume 8, Book 78, Number 644:

Narrated Zahdam:

There was a relation of love and brotherhood between this tribe of Jarm and Al-Ash'ariyin. Once we were with Abu Musa Al-Ash'ari, and then a meal containing chicken was brought to Abu Musa, and there was present, a man from the tribe of Taimillah who was of red complexion as if he were from non-Arab freed slaves. Abu Musa invited him to the meal. He said, "I have seen chickens eating dirty things, so I deemed it filthy and took an oath that I would never eat chicken." On that, Abu Musa said, "Get up, I will narrate to you about that. Once a group of the Ash'ariyin and I went to Allah's Apostle and asked him to provide us with mounts; he said, 'By Allah, I will never give you any mounts nor do I have anything to mount you on.' Then a few camels of war booty were brought to Allah's Apostle , and he asked about us, saying, 'Where are the Ash-'ariyin?' He then ordered five nice camels to be given to us, and when we had departed, we said, 'What have we done? Allah's Apostle had taken the oath not to give us any mounts, and that he had nothing to mount us on, and later he gave us that we might ride? Did we take advantage of the fact that Allah's Apostle had forgotten his oath? By Allah, we will never succeed.' So we went back to him and said to him, 'We came to you to give us mounts, and you took an oath that you would not give us any mounts and that you had nothing to mount us on.' On that he said, 'I did not provide you with mounts, but Allah did. By Allah, if I take an oath to do something, and then find something else better than it, I do that which is better and make expiation for the dissolution of the oath.' "

Volume 8, Book 78, Number 645:

Narrated Abu Huraira:

The Prophet said, "Whoever swears saying in his oath. 'By Al-Lat and Al'Uzza,' should say, 'None has the right to be worshipped but Allah; and whoever says to his friend, 'Come, let me gamble with you,' should give something in charity."

Volume 8, Book 78, Number 646:

Narrated Ibn 'Umar:

Allah's Apostle had a gold ring made for himself, and he used to wear it with the stone towards the inner part of his hand. Consequently, the people had similar rings made for themselves. Afterwards the Prophet; sat on the pulpit and took it off, saying, "I used to wear this ring and keep its stone towards the palm of my hand." He then threw it away and said, "By Allah, I will never wear it." Therefore all the people threw away their rings as well.

Volume 8, Book 78, Number 647:

Narrated Thabit bin Ad-Dahhak:

The Prophet said, "Whoever swears by a religion other than Islam, is, as he says; and whoever commits suicide with something, will be punished with the same thing in the (Hell) Fire; and cursing a believer is like murdering him; and whoever accuses a believer of disbelief, then it is as if he had killed him."

Volume 8, Book 78, Number 648:

Narrated Al-Bara:

The Prophet ordered us to help others to fulfill the oaths.

Volume 8, Book 78, Number 649:

Narrated Usama:

Once a daughter of Allah's Apostle sent a message to Allah's Apostle while Usama, Sa'd, and my father or Ubai were (sitting there) with him. She said, (in the message); My child is going to die; please come to us." Allah's Apostle returned the messenger and told him to convey his greetings to her, and say, "Whatever Allah takes, is for Him and whatever He gives is for Him, and everything with Him has a limited fixed term (in this world): so she should be patient and hope for Allah's reward." Then she again sent for him swearing that he should come; so The Prophet got up, and so did we. When he sat there (at the house of his daughter), the child was brought to him, and he took him into his lap while the child's breath was disturbed in his chest. The eyes of Allah's Apostle started shedding tears. Sa'd said, "What is this, O Allah's Apostle?" The Prophet said, "This is the mercy which Allah has lodged in the hearts of whoever He wants of His slaves, and verily Allah is merciful only to those of His slaves who are merciful (to others).'

Volume 8, Book 78, Number 650:

Narrated Abu Huraira:

Allah's Apostle said, "Any Muslim who has lost three of his children will not be touched by the Fire except that which will render Allah's oath fulfilled."

Volume 8, Book 78, Number 651:

Narrated Haritha bin Wahb:

I heard the Prophet saying, "Shall I tell you of the people of Paradise? They comprise every poor humble person, and if he swears by Allah to do something, Allah will fulfill it; while the people of the fire comprise every violent, cruel arrogant person."

Volume 8, Book 78, Number 652:

Narrated 'Abdullah:

The Prophet was asked, "Who are the best people?" He replied: The people of my generation, and then those who will follow (come after) them, and then those who will come after the later; after that there will come some people whose witness will precede their oaths and their oaths will go ahead of their witness." Ibrahim (a sub-narrator) said, "When we were young, our elder friends used to prohibit us from taking oaths by saying, 'I bear witness swearing by Allah, or by Allah's Covenant.'"

Volume 8, Book 78, Number 653:

Narrated 'Abdullah:

The Prophet said, "Whoever swears falsely in order to grab the property of a Muslim (or of his brother), Allah will be angry with him when he meets Him." Allah then revealed in confirmation of the above statement.--'Verily those who purchase a small gain at the cost of Allah's Covenant and their own oaths.' (3.77) Al-Ash'ath said, "This Verse was revealed regarding me and a companion of mine when we had a dispute about a well."

Volume 8, Book 78, Number 654:

Narrated Anas bin Malik:

The Prophet said, "The Hell Fire will keep on saying: 'Are there anymore (people to come)?' Till the Lord of Power and Honor will put His Foot over it and then it will say, 'Qat! Qat! (sufficient! sufficient!) by Your Power and Honor. And its various sides will come close to each other (i.e., it will contract). "

Volume 8, Book 78, Number 655:

Narrated Az-Zuhri:

I heard 'Urwa bin Az-Zubair, Said bin Al-Musaiyab, 'Alqama bin Waqqas and 'Ubaidullah bin 'Abdullah narrating from 'Aisha, the wife of the Prophet, the story about the liars who said what they said about her and how Allah revealed her innocence afterwards. Each one of the above four narrators narrated to me a portion of her narration. (It was said in it), "The Prophet stood up, saying, 'Is there anyone who can relieve me from 'Abdullah bin Ubai?' On that, Usaid bin Hudair got up and said to Sa'd bin 'Ubada, La'amrullahi (By the Eternity of Allah), we will kill him!' "

Volume 8, Book 78, Number 656:

Narrated 'Aisha:

regarding: 'Allah will not call you to account for that which is unintentional in your oaths...' (2.225) This Verse was revealed concerning such oath formulas as: 'No, by Allah!' and 'Yes, by Allah!' something against his oath due to forgetfulness should he make expiation?). And the Statement of Allah: 'And there is no blame on you if you make a mistake therein.' (33.5) And Allah said.-- '(Moses said to Khadir): Call me not to account for what I forgot.' (18.73)

Volume 8, Book 78, Number 657:

Narrated Abu Huraira:

The Prophet said, "Allah forgives my followers those (evil deeds) the

Volume 8, Book 78, Number 658:

Narrated 'Abdullah bin 'Amr bin Al-As:

While the Prophet was delivering a sermon on the Day of Nahr (i.e., 10th Dhul-Hijja-Day of slaughtering the sacrifice), a man got up saying, "I thought, O Allah's Apostle, such-and-such a thing was to be done before such-and-such a thing." Another man got up, saying, "O Allah's Apostle! As regards these three (acts of Hajj), thought so-and-so." The Prophet said, "Do, and there is no harm," concerning all those matters on that day. And so, on that day, whatever question he was asked, he said, "Do it, do it, and there is no harm therein."

Volume 8, Book 78, Number 659:

Narrated Ibn 'Abbas:

A man said to the Prophet (while he was delivering a sermon on the Day of Nahr), "I have performed the Tawaf round the Ka'ba before the Rami (throwing pebbles) at the Jamra." The Prophet said, "There is no harm (therein)." Another man said, "I had my head shaved before slaughtering (the sacrifice)." The Prophet said, "There is no harm." A third said, "I have slaughtered (the sacrifice) before the Rami (throwing pebbles) at the Jamra." The Prophet said, "There is no harm."

Volume 8, Book 78, Number 660:

Narrated Abu Huraira:

A man entered the mosque and started praying while Allah's Apostle was sitting somewhere in the mosque. Then (after finishing the prayer) the man came to the Prophet and greeted him. The Prophet said to him, "Go back and pray, for you have not prayed. The man went back, and having prayed, he came and greeted the Prophet. The Prophet after returning his greetings said, "Go back and pray, for you did not pray." On the third time the man said, "(O Allah's Apostle!) teach me (how to pray)." The Prophet said, "When you get up for the prayer, perform the ablution properly and then face the Qibla and say Takbir (Allahu Akbar), and then recite of what you know of the Quran, and then bow, and remain in this state till you feel at rest in bowing, and then raise your head and stand straight; and then prostrate till you feel at rest in prostration, and then sit up till you feel at rest while sitting; and then prostrate again till you feel at rest in prostration; and then get up and stand straight, and do all this in all your prayers."

Volume 8, Book 78, Number 661:

Narrated 'Aisha:

When the pagans were defeated during the (first stage) of the battle of Uhud, Satan shouted, "O Allah's slaves! Beware of what is behind you!" So the front files of the Muslims attacked their own back files. Hudhaifa bin Al-Yaman looked and on seeing his father he shouted: "My father! My father!" By Allah! The people did not stop till they killed his father. Hudhaifa then said, "May Allah forgive you." 'Urwa (the sub-narrator) added, "Hudhaifa continued asking Allah forgiveness for the killers of his father till he met Allah (till he died)."

Volume 8, Book 78, Number 662:

Narrated Abu Huraira:

The Prophet said, "If somebody eats something forgetfully while he is fasting, then he should complete his fast, for Allah has made him eat and drink."

Volume 8, Book 78, Number 663:

Narrated 'Abdullah bin Buhaina:

Once Allah's Apostle led us in prayer, and after finishing the first two Rakat, got up (instead of sitting for At-Tahiyyat) and then carried on with the prayer. When he had finished his prayer, the people were waiting for him to say Taslim, but before saying Tasiim, he said Takbir and prostrated; then he raised his head, and saying Takbir, he prostrated (SAHU) and then raised his head and finished his prayer with Taslim.

Volume 8, Book 78, Number 664:

Narrated Ibn Mas'ud:

that Allah's Prophet led them in the Zuhr prayer and he offered either more or less Rakat, and it was said to him, "O Allah's Apostle ! Has the prayer been reduced, or have you forgotten?" He asked, "What is that?" They said, "You have prayed so many Rak'at." So he performed with them two more prostrations and said, "These two prostrations are to be performed by the person who does not know whether he has prayed more or less (Rakat) in which case he should seek to follow what is right. And then complete the rest (of the prayer) and perform two extra prostrations."

Volume 8, Book 78, Number 665:

Narrated Ubai bin Ka'b:

that he heard Allah's Apostle saying, "(Moses) said, 'Call me not to account for what I forget and be not hard upon me for my affair (with you)' (18.73) the first excuse of Moses was his forgetfulness."

Narrated Al-Bara bin Azib that once he had a guest, so he told his family (on the Day of Id-ul-Adha) that they should slaughter the animal for sacrifice before he returned from the ('Id) prayer in order that their guest could take his meal. So his family slaughtered (the animal) before the prayer. Then they mentioned that event to the Prophet who ordered Al-Bara to slaughter another sacrifice. Al-Bara' said to the Prophet , "I have a young milch she-goat which is better than two sheep for slaughtering." (The sub-narrator, Ibn 'Aun used to say, "I don't know whether the permission (to slaughter a she-goat as a sacrifice) was especially given to Al-Bara' or if it was in general for all the Muslims.") (See Hadith No. 99, Vol. 2.)

Volume 8, Book 78, Number 666:

Narrated Jundub:

I witnessed the Prophet offering the 'Id prayer (and after finishing it) he delivered a sermon and said, "Whoever has slaughtered his sacrifice (before the prayer) should make up for it (i.e. slaughter another animal) and whoever has not slaughtered his sacrifice yet, should slaughter it by mentioning Allah's Name over it."

Volume 8, Book 78, Number 667:

Narrated 'Abdullah bin 'Amr:

The Prophet said, "The biggest sins are: To join others in worship with Allah; to be undutiful to one's parents; to kill somebody unlawfully; and to take an oath Al-Ghamus.

Volume 8, Book 78, Number 668:

Narrated 'Abdullah:

Allah's Apostle said, "If somebody is ordered (by the ruler or the judge) to take an oath, and he takes a false oath in order to grab the property of a Muslim, then he will incur Allah's Wrath when he will meet Him." And Allah revealed in its confirmation: 'Verily! Those who purchase a small gain at the cost of Allah's covenants and their own oaths.' (3.77) (The sub-narrator added:) Al-Ash'ath bin Qais entered, saying, "What did Abu 'Abdur-Rahman narrate to you?" They said, "So-and-so," Al-Ash'ath said, "This verse was revealed in my connection. I had a well on the land of my cousin (and we had a dispute about it). I reported him to Allah 's Apostle who said (to me). "You should give evidence (i.e. witness) otherwise the oath of your opponent will render your claim invalid." I said, "Then he (my opponent) will take the oath, O Allah's Apostle." Allah's Apostle said, "Whoever is ordered (by the ruler or the judge) to give an oath, and he takes a false oath in order to grab the property of a Muslim, then he will incur Allah's Wrath when he meets Him on the Day of Resurrection."

Volume 8, Book 78, Number 669.

Narrated Abu Musa.

My companions sent me to the Prophet to ask him for some mounts. He said, "By Allah! I will not mount you on anything!" When I met him, he was in an angry mood, but when I met him (again), he said, "Tell your companions that Allah or Allah's Apostle will provide you with mounts."

Volume 8, Book 78, Number 670.

Narrated Az-Zuhri.

I heard 'Urwa bin Az-Zubair, Said bin Al-Musaiyab, 'Alqama bin Waqqas and 'Ubaidullah bin 'Abdullah bin 'Uqba relating from 'Aisha, the wife of the Prophet the narration of the people (i.e. the liars) who spread the slander against her and they said what they said, and how Allah revealed her innocence. Each of them related to me a portion of that narration. (They said that 'Aisha said), "Then Allah revealed the ten Verses starting with.--'Verily! Those who spread the slander..' (24.11-21)

All these verses were in proof of my innocence. Abu Bakr As-Siddiq who used to provide for Mistah some financial aid because of his relation to him, said, "By Allah, I will never give anything (in charity) to Mistah, after what he has said about 'Aisha" Then Allah revealed.-- 'And let not those among you who are good and are wealthy swear not to give (any sort of help) to their kins men....' (24.22) On that, Abu Bakr said, "Yes, by Allah, I like that Allah should forgive me." and then resumed giving Mistah the aid he used to give him and said, "By Allah! I will never withhold it from him."

Volume 8, Book 78, Number 671.

Narrated Abu Musa Al-Ash'ari.

I went along with some men from the Ash-ariyin to Allah's Apostle and it happened that I met him while he was in an angry mood. We asked him to provide us with mounts, but he swore that he would not give us any. Later on he said, "By Allah, Allah willing, if ever I take an oath (to do something) and later on I find something else better than the first, then I do the better one and give expiation for the dissolution of my oath."

Volume 8, Book 78, Number 672.

Narrated Al-Musaiyab.

When the death of Abu Talib approached, Allah's Apostle came to him and said, "Say. La ilaha illallah, a word with which I will be able to defend you before Allah."

Volume 8, Book 78, Number 673:

Narrated Abu Huraira:

Allah's Apostle said, "(Following are) two words (sentences or utterances that are very easy for the tongue to say, and very heavy in the balance (of reward,) and the must beloved to the Gracious Almighty (And they are): Subhan Allah wa bi-hamdihi; Subhan Allahi-l-'Azim,"

Volume 8, Book 78, Number 674:

Narrated 'Abdullah:

Allah's Apostle said a sentence and I said another. He said, "Whoever dies while he is setting up rivals along with Allah (i.e. worshipping others along with Allah) shall be admitted into the (Hell) Fire." And I said the other: "W

Volume 8, Book 78, Number 675:

Narrated Anas:

Allah's Apostle took an oath for abstention from h is wives (for one month), and during those days he had a sprain in his foot. He stayed in a Mashrubah (an upper room) for twenty-nine nights and then came down. Then the people said, "O Allah's Apostle! You took an oath for abstention (from your wives) for one month." On that he said, A month can be of twenty-nine days '

Volume 8, Book 78, Number 676:

Narrated Abu Hazim:

Sahl bin Sa'd said, "Abu Usaid, the companion of the Prophet, got married, so he invited the Prophet to his wedding party, and the bride herself served them. Sahl said to the People, 'Do you know what drink she served him with? She infused some dates in a pot at night and the next morning she served him with the infusion."

Volume 8, Book 78, Number 677:

Narrated Sauda:

(the wife of the Prophet) One of our sheep died and we tanned its skin and kept on infusing dates in it till it was a worn out water skin.

Volume 8, Book 78, Number 678:

Narrated 'Aisha:

The family of (the Prophet) Muhammad never ate wheat-bread with meat for three consecutive days to their fill, till he met Allah.

Volume 8, Book 78, Number 679:

Narrated Anas bin Malik:

Abu Talha said to Um Sulaim, "I heard the voice of Allah's Apostle rather weak, and I knew that it was because of hunger. Have you anything (to present to the Prophet)?" She said, "Yes." Then she took out a few loaves of barley bread and took a veil of hers and wrapped the bread with a part of it and sent me to Allah's Apostle. I went and found Allah's Apostle sitting in the mosque with some people. I stood up before him. Allah's Apostle said to me, "Has Abu Talha sent you?" I said, ' Yes. Then Allah's Apostle said to those who were with him. "Get up and proceed." I went ahead of them (as their fore-runner) and came to Abu Talha and informed him about it. Abu Talha said, "O Um Sulaim! Allah's Apostle has come and we have no food to feed them." Um Sulaim said, "Allah and His Apostle know best." So Abu Talha went out (to receive them) till he met Allah's Apostle.

Allah's Apostle came in company with Abu Talha and they entered the house. Allah's Apostle said, "O Um Sulaim! Bring whatever you have." So she brought that (barley) bread and Allah's Apostle ordered that bread to be broken into small pieces, and then Um Sulaim poured over it some butter from a leather butter container, and then Allah's Apostle said what Allah wanted him to say, (i.e. blessing the food). Allah's Apostle then said, "Admit ten men." Abu Talha admitted them and they ate to their fill and went out. He again said, "Admit ten men." He admitted them, and in this way all the people ate to their fill, and they were seventy or eighty men."

Volume 8, Book 78, Number 680:

Narrated 'Umar bin Al-Khattab:

I heard Allah's Apostle saying, "The (reward of) deeds, depend upon the intentions and every person will get the reward according to what he has intended. So whoever emigrated for the sake of Allah and His Apostle, then his emigration will be considered to be for Allah and His Apostle, and whoever emigrated for the sake of worldly gain or for a woman to marry, then his emigration will be considered to be for what he emigrated for."

Volume 8, Book 78, Number 681:

Narrated Ka'b bin Malik:

In the last part of his narration about the three who remained behind (from the battle of Tabuk). (I said) "As a proof of my true repentance (for not joining the Holy battle of Tabuk), I shall give up all my property for the sake of Allah and His Apostle (as an expiation for that sin)." The Prophet said (to me), "Keep some of your wealth, for that is better for you."

Volume 8, Book 78, Number 682:

Narrated 'Aisha:

The Prophet used to stay (for a period) in the house of Zainab bint Jahsh (one of the wives of the Prophet) and he used to drink honey in her house. Hafsa and I decided that when the Prophet entered upon either of us, she would say, "I smell in you the bad smell of Maghafir (a bad smelling raisin). Have you eaten Maghafir?" When he entered upon one of us, she said that to him. He replied (to her), "No, but I have drunk honey in the house of Zainab bint Jahsh, and I will never drink it again." Then the following verse was revealed: 'O Prophet ! Why do you ban (for you) that which Allah has made lawful for you?. ..(up to) If you two (wives of the Prophet turn in repentance to Allah.' (66.1-4) The two were 'Aisha and Hafsa And also the Statement of Allah: 'And (Remember) when the Prophet disclosed a matter in confidence to one of his wives!' (66.3) i.e., his saying, "But I have drunk honey." Hisham said: It also meant his saying, "I will not drink anymore, and I have taken an oath, so do not inform anybody of that '

Volume 8, Book 78, Number 683:

Narrated Sa'id bin Al-Harith:

that he heard Ibn 'Umar saying, "Weren't people forbidden to make vows?" The Prophet said, 'A vow neither hastens nor delays anything, but by the making of vows, some of the wealth of a miser is taken out."

Volume 8, Book 78, Number 684:

Narrated 'Abdullah bin 'Umar:

The Prophet forbade the making of vows and said, "It (a vow) does not prevent anything (that has to take place), but the property of a miser is spent (taken out) with it."

Volume 8, Book 78, Number 685:

Narrated Abu Huraira:

The Prophet said, "Allah says, 'The vow, does not bring about for the son of Adam anything I have not decreed for him, but his vow may coincide with what has been decided for him, and by this way I cause a miser to spend of his wealth. So he gives Me (spends in charity) for the fulfillment of what has been decreed for him what he would not give Me before but for his vow."

Volume 8, Book 78, Number 686:

Narrated Zahdam bin Mudarrab:

'Imran bin Hussain said, "The Prophet said, 'The best of you (people) are my generation, and the second best will be those who will follow them, and then those who will follow the second generation." Imran added, "I do not remember whether he mentioned two or three (generations) after his generation. He added, 'Then will come some people who will make vows but will not fulfill them; and they will be dishonest and will not be trustworthy, and they will give their witness without being asked to give their witness, and fatness will appear among them.' "

Volume 8, Book 78, Number 687:

Narrated 'Aisha:

The Prophet said, "Whoever vows that he will be obedient to Allah, should remain obedient to Him; and whoever made a vow that he will disobey Allah, should not disobey Him."

Volume 8, Book 78, Number 688:

Narrated Ibn 'Umar:

'Umar said "O Allah's Apostle! I vowed to perform I'tikaf for one night in Al-Masjid-al-Haram, during the Pre-Islamic Period of ignorance (before embracing Islam). "The Prophet said, "Fulfill your vow." Ibn 'Umar said to the lady, "Pray on her behalf." Ibn 'Abbas said the same.

Volume 8, Book 78, Number 689:

Narrated Sa'id bin 'Ubada Al-Ansari:

that he consulted the Prophet about a vow that had been made by his mother who died without fulfilling it. The Prophet gave his verdict that he should fulfill it on her behalf. The verdict became Sunna (i.e. the Prophet's tradition).

Volume 8, Book 78, Number 690:

Narrated Ibn 'Abbas:

A man came to the Prophet and said to him, "My sister vowed to perform the Hajj, but she died (before fulfilling it)." The Prophet said, "Would you not have paid her debts if she had any?" The man said, "Yes." The Prophet said, "So pay Allah's Rights, as He is more entitled to receive His rights."

Volume 8, Book 78, Number 691:

Narrated 'Aisha:

The Prophet said, "Whoever vowed to be obedient to Allah, must be obedient to Him; and whoever vowed to be disobedient to Allah, should not be disobedient to Him."

Volume 8, Book 78, Number 692:

Narrated Anas:

The Prophet said, "Allah is not in need of this man) torturing himself," when he saw the man walking between his two sons (who were supporting him).

Volume 8, Book 78, Number 693:

Narrated Ibn 'Abbas:

The Prophet saw a man performing Tawaf around the Ka'ba, tied with a rope or something else (while another person was holding him). The Prophet cut that rope off.

Volume 8, Book 78, Number 694:

Narrated Ibn 'Abbas:

While performing the Tawaf around the Ka'ba, the Prophet passed by a person leading another person by a hair-rope nose-ring in his nose. The Prophet cut the hair-rope nose-ring off with his hand and ordered the man to lead him by the hand.

Volume 8, Book 78, Number 695:

Narrated Ibn 'Abbas:

While the Prophet was delivering a sermon, he saw a man standing, so he asked about that man. They (the people) said, "It is Abu Israil who has vowed that he will stand and never sit down, and he will never come in the shade, nor speak to anybody, and will fast." The Prophet said, "Order him to speak and let him come in the shade, and make him sit down, but let him complete his fast."

Volume 8, Book 78, Number 696:

Narrated 'Abdullah bin 'Umar:

that he was asked about a man who had vowed that he would fast all the days of his life then the day of 'Id al Adha or 'Id-al-Fitr came. 'Abdullah bin 'Umar said: You have indeed a good example in Allah's Apostle. He did not fast on the day of 'Id al Adha or the day of 'Id-al-Fitr, and we do not intend fasting on these two days.

Volume 8, Book 78, Number 697:

Narrated Ziyad bin Jubair:

I was with Ibn 'Umar when a man asked him, "I have vowed to fast every Tuesday or Wednesday throughout my life and if the day of my fasting coincided with the day of Nahr (the first day of 'Id-al-Adha), (What shall I do?)" Ibn 'Umar said, "Allah has ordered the vows to be fulfilled, and we are forbidden to fast on the day of Nahr." The man repeated his question and Ibn 'Umar repeated his former answer, adding nothing more.

Volume 8, Book 78, Number 698:

Narrated Abu Huraira:

We went out in the company of Allah's Apostle on the day of (the battle of) Khaibar, and we did not get any gold or silver as war booty, but we got property in the form of things and clothes. Then a man called Rifa'a bin Zaid, from the tribe of Bani Ad-Dubaib, presented a slave named Mid'am to Allah's Apostle. Allah's Apostle headed towards the valley of Al-Qura, and when he was in the valley of Al-Qura an arrow was thrown by an unidentified person, struck and killed Mid'am who was making a she-camel of Allah's Apostle kneel down. The people said, "Congratulations to him (the slave) for gaining Paradise." Allah's Apostle said, "No! By Him in Whose Hand my soul is, for the sheet which he stole from the war booty before its distribution on the day of Khaibar, is now burning over him." When the people heard that, a man brought one or two Shiraks (leather straps of shoes) to the Prophet. The Prophet said, "A Shirak of fire, or two Shiraks of fire."

Book 79: Expiation for Unfulfilled Oaths

Volume 8, Book 79, Number 699:

Narrated Ka'b bin 'Ujra:

I came to the Prophet and he said to me, "Come near." So I went near to him and he said, "Are your lice troubling you?" I replied, "Yes." He said, "(Shave your head and) make expiation in the form of fasting, Sadaqa (giving in charity), or offering a sacrifice." (The sub-narrator) Aiyub said, "Fasting should be for three days, and the Nusuk (sacrifice) is to be a sheep, and the Sadaqa is to be given to six poor persons."

Volume 8, Book 79, Number 700:

Narrated Abu Huraira:

A man came to the Prophet and said, "I am ruined!" The Prophet said, "What is the matter with you?" He said, "I had sexual relation with my wife (while I was fasting) in Ramadan." The Prophet said, "Have you got enough to manumit a slave?" He said, "No." The Prophet said, "Can you fast for two successive months?" The man said, "No." The Prophet said, "Can you feed sixty poor persons?" The man said, "No." Then the Prophet said to him, "Sit down," and he sat down. Afterwards an 'Irq, i.e., a big basket containing dates was brought to the Prophet and the Prophet said to him, "Take this and give it in charity." The man said, "To poorer people than we?" On that, the Prophet smiled till his premolar teeth became visible, and then told him, "Feed your family with it." (See Hadith No. 157, Vol 3)

Volume 8, Book 79, Number 701:

Narrated Abu Huraira:

A man came to Allah's Apostle and said, "I am ruined!" The Prophet said to him, "What is the matter?" He said, "I have done a sexual relation with my wife (while fasting) in Ramadan." The Prophet said to him?" "Can you afford to manumit a slave?" He said, "No." The Prophet said, "Can you fast for two successive months?" He said, "No." The Prophet said, "Can you feed sixty poor persons?" He said, "No." Then an Ansari man came with an Irq (a big basket full of dates). The Prophet said (to the man), "Take this (basket) and give it in charity." That man said, "To poorer people than we, O Allah's Apostle? By Him Who has sent you with the Truth! There is no house in between the two mountains (of the city of Medina) poorer than we." So the Prophet said (to him), "Go and feed it to your family."

Volume 8, Book 79, Number 702:

Narrated Abu Huraira :

A man came to the Prophets and said, "I am ruined!" The Prophet said, "What is the matter with you?" He said, "I have done a sexual relation with my wife (while fasting) in Ramadan" The Prophet said to him, "Can you afford to manumit a slave?" He said, "No." The Prophet said, "Can you fast for two successive months?" He said, "No." The Prophet said, "Can you feed sixty poor persons?" He said, "I have nothing." Later on an Irq (big basket) containing dates was given to the Prophet, and the Prophet said (to him), "Take this basket and give it in charity." The man said, "To poorer people than we? Indeed, there is nobody between its (i.e., Medina's) two mountains who is poorer than we." The Prophet then said, "Take it and feed your family with it."

Volume 8, Book 79, Number 703:

Narrated Al-Ju'aid bin Abdur-Rahman:

As-Sa'ib bin Yazid said, "The Sa' at the time of the Prophet was equal to one Mudd plus one-third of a Mudd of your time, and then it was increased in the time of Caliph 'Umar bin 'Abdul Aziz."

Volume 8, Book 79, Number 704:

Narrated Nafi:

Ibn Umar used to give the Zakat of Ramadan (Zakat-al-Fitr) according to the Mudd of the Prophet, the first Mudd, and he also used to give things for expiation for oaths according to the Mudd of the Prophet. Abu Qutaiba said, "Malik said to us, 'Our Mudd (i.e., of Medina) is better than yours and we do not see any superiority except in the Mudd of the Prophet!' Malik further said, to me, 'If a ruler came to you and fixed a Mudd smaller than the one of the Prophet, by what Mudd would you measure what you give (for expiation or Zakat-al-Fitr?' I replied, 'We would give it according to the Mudd of the Prophet' On that, Malik said, 'Then, don't you see that we have to revert to the Mudd of the Prophet ultimately?'"

Volume 8, Book 79, Number 705:

Narrated Anas bin Malik:

Allah's Apostle said, "O Allah! Bestow Your Blessings on their measures, Sa' and Mudd (i.e., of the people of Medina) "

Volume 8, Book 79, Number 706:

Narrated Abu Huraira:

The Prophet said, "If somebody manumits a Muslim slave, Allah will save from the Fire every part of his body for freeing the corresponding parts of the slave's body, even his private parts will be saved from the Fire) because of freeing the slave's private parts."

Volume 8, Book 79, Number 707:

Narrated 'Amr:

Jabir said: An Ansari man made his slave a Mudabbar and he had no other property than him. When the Prophet heard of that, he said (to his companions), "Who wants to buy him (i.e., the slave) for me?" Nu'aim bin An-Nahham bought him for eight hundred Dirhams. I heard Jabir saying, "That was a coptic slave who died in the same year."

Volume 8, Book 79, Number 708:

Narrated 'Aisha:

that she intended to buy Barira (a slave girl) and her masters stipulated that they would have her Wala'. When 'Aisha mentioned that to the Prophet ; he said, "Buy her, for the Wala' is for the one who manumits."

Volume 8, Book 79, Number 709:

Narrated Abu Musa Al-Ash'ari:

I went to Allah's Apostle along with a group of people from (the tribe of) Al-Ash'ari, asking for mounts. The Prophet said, "By Allah, I will not give you anything to ride, and I have nothing to mount you on." We stayed there as long as Allah wished, and after that, some camels were brought to the Prophet and he ordered that we be given three camels. When we set out, some of us said to others, "Allah will not bless us, as we all went to Allah's Apostle asking him for mounts, and although he had sworn that he would not give us mounts, he did give us." So we returned to the Prophet; and mentioned that to him. He said, "I have not provided you with mounts, but Allah has. By Allah, Allah willing, if I ever take an oath, and then see that another is better than the first, I make expiration for my (dissolved) oath, and do what is better and make expiration."

Volume 8, Book 79, Number 710:

Narrated Hammad:

the same narration above (i.e. 709), "I make expiation for my dissolved oath, and I do what is better, or do what is better and make expiation."

Volume 8, Book 79, Number 711:

Narrated Abu Huraira:

(The Prophet) Solomon said, "Tonight I will sleep with (my) ninety wives, each of whom will get a male child who will fight for Allah's Cause." On that, his companion (Sufyan said that his companion was an angel) said to him, "Say, "If Allah will (Allah willing)." But Solomon forgot (to say it). He slept with all his wives, but none of the women gave birth to a child, except one who gave birth to a half-boy. Abu Huraira added: The Prophet said, "If Solomon had said, "If Allah will" (Allah willing), he would not have been unsuccessful in his action, and would have attained what he had desired." Once Abu Huraira added: Allah apostle said, "If he had accepted."

Volume 8, Book 79, Number 712:

Narrated Zahdam al-Jarmi:

We were sitting with Abu Musa Al-Ash'sari, and as there were ties of friendship and mutual favors between us and his tribe. His meal was presented before him and there was chicken meat in it. Among those who were present there was a man from Bani Taimillah having a red complexion as a non-Arab freed slave, and that man did not approach the meal. Abu Musa said to him, "Come along! I have seen Allah's Apostle eating of that (i.e., chicken)." The man said, "I have seen it (chickens) eating something I regarded as dirty, and so I have taken an oath that I shall not eat (its meat) chicken." Abu Musa said, "Come along! I will inform you about it (i.e., your oath).

Once we went to Allah's Apostle in company with a group of Ash'airiyin, asking him for mounts while he was distributing some camels from the camels of Zakat. (Aiyub said, "I think he said that the Prophet was in an angry mood at the time.") The Prophet said, 'By Allah! I will not give you mounts, and I have nothing to mount you on.' After we had left, some camels of booty were brought to Allah's Apostle and he said, "Where are those Ash'ariyin? Where are those Ash'ariyin?" So we went (to him) and he gave us five very fat good-looking camels. We mounted them and went away, and then I said to my companions, 'We went to Allah's Apostle to give us mounts, but he took an oath that he would not give us mounts, and then later on he sent for us and gave us mounts, perhaps Allah's Apostle forgot his oath. By Allah, we will never be successful, for we have taken advantage of the fact that Allah's Apostle forgot to fulfill his oath. So let us return to Allah's Apostle to remind him of his oath.' We returned and said, 'O Allah's Apostle! We came to you and asked you for mounts, but you took an oath that you would not give us mounts) but later on you gave us mounts, and we thought or considered that you have forgotten your oath.' The Prophet said, 'Depart, for Allah has given you Mounts. By Allah, Allah willing, if I take an oath and then later find another thing better than that, I do what is better, and make expiation for the oath.' "

Volume 8, Book 79, Number 713:

Narrated Zahdam:

the same narration as above (i.e. No. 712).

Volume 8, Book 79, Number 714:

Narrated Zahdam:

the same narration as above (i.e. No. 712).

Volume 8, Book 79, Number 715:

Narrated 'Abdur-Rahman bin Samura:

Allah's Apostle said, "(O 'Abdur-Rahman!) Do not seek to be a ruler, for, if you are given the authority of ruling without your asking for it, then Allah will help you; but if you are given it by your asking, then you will be held responsible for it (i.e. Allah will not help you) . And if you take an oath to do something and later on find another thing, better than that, then do what is better and make expiation for (the dissolution of) your oath."

Book 80: Laws of Inheritance (Al-Faraa'id)

Volume 8, Book 80, Number 716:

Narrated Jabir bin 'Abdullah:

I became sick so Allah's Apostle and Abu Bakr came on foot to pay me a visit. When they came, I was unconscious. Allah's Apostle performed ablution and he poured over me the water (of his ablution) and I came to my senses and said, "O Allah's Apostle! What shall I do regarding my property? How shall I distribute it?" The Prophet did not reply till the Divine Verses of inheritance were revealed .

Volume 8, Book 80, Number 717:

Narrated Abu Huraira:

Allah's Apostle said, 'Beware of suspicion, for it is the worst of false tales and don't look for the other's faults and don't spy and don't hate each other, and don't desert (cut your relations with) one another O Allah's slaves, be brothers!" (See Hadith No. 90)

Volume 8, Book 80, Number 718:

Narrated 'Aisha:

Fatima and Al 'Abbas came to Abu Bakr, seeking their share from the property of Allah's Apostle and at that time, they were asking for their land at Fadak and their share from Khaibar. Abu Bakr said to them, " I have heard from Allah's Apostle saying, 'Our property cannot be inherited, and whatever we leave is to be spent in charity, but the family of Muhammad may take their provisions from this property." Abu Bakr added, "By Allah, I will not leave the procedure I saw Allah's Apostle following during his lifetime concerning this property." Therefore Fatima left Abu Bakr and did not speak to him till she died.

Volume 8, Book 80, Number 719:

Narrated 'Aisha:

The Prophet said, "Our (Apostles') property should not be inherited, and whatever we leave, is to be spent in charity."

Volume 8, Book 80, Number 720:

Narrated Malik bin Aus:

'I went and entered upon 'Umar, his doorman, Yarfa came saying 'Uthman, 'Abdur-Rahman, Az-Zubair and Sa'd are asking your permission (to see you). May I admit them? 'Umar said, 'Yes.' So he admitted them Then he came again and said, 'May I admit 'Ali and 'Abbas?' He said, 'Yes.' 'Abbas said, 'O, chief of the believers! Judge between me and this man (Ali). 'Umar said, 'I beseech you by Allah by Whose permission both the heaven and the earth exist, do you know that Allah's Apostle said, 'Our (the Apostles') property will not be inherited, and whatever we leave (after our death) is to be spent in charity?' And by that Allah's Apostle meant himself.' The group said, '(No doubt), he said so.' 'Umar then faced 'Ali and 'Abbas and said, 'Do you both know that Allah's Apostle said that?' They replied, '(No doubt), he said so.' 'Umar said, 'So let me talk to you about this matter. Allah favored His Apostle with something of this Fai' (i.e. booty won by the Muslims at war without fighting) which He did not give to anybody else;

Allah said:-- 'And what Allah gave to His Apostle (Fai' Booty) ....to do all things....(59.6) And so that property was only for Allah's Apostle . Yet, by Allah, he neither gathered that property for himself nor withheld it from you, but he gave its income to you, and distributed it among you till there remained the present property out of which the Prophet used to spend the yearly maintenance for his family, and whatever used to remain, he used to spend it where Allah's property is spent (i.e. in charity etc.). Allah's Apostle followed that throughout his life.

Now I beseech you by Allah, do you know all that?' They said, 'Yes.' 'Umar then said to 'Ali and 'Abbas, 'I beseech you by Allah, do you know that?' Both of them said, 'Yes.' 'Umar added, 'And when the Prophet died, Abu Bakr said, ' I am the successor of Allah's Apostle, and took charge of that property and managed it in the same way as Allah's Apostle did.

Then I took charge of this property for two years during which I managed it as Allah's Apostle and Abu Bakr did. Then you both ('Ali and 'Abbas) came to talk to me, bearing the same claim and presenting the same case. (O 'Abbas!) You came to me asking for your share from the property of your nephew, and this man (Ali) came to me, asking for the share of h is wife from the property of her father. I said, 'If you both wish, I will give that to you on that condition (i.e. that you would follow the way of the Prophet and Abu Bakr and as I (Umar) have done in man aging it).' Now both of you seek of me a verdict other than that? Lo! By Allah, by Whose permission both the heaven and the earth exist, I will not give any verdict other than that till the Hour is established. If you are unable to manage it, then return it to me, and I will be sufficient to manage it on your behalf.' "

Volume 8, Book 80, Number 721:

Narrated Abu Huraira:

Allah's Apostle said, "Not even a single Dinar of my property should be distributed (after my deaths to my inheritors, but whatever I leave excluding the provision for my wives and my servants, should be spent in charity."

Volume 8, Book 80, Number 722.

Narrated 'Urwa:

'Aisha said, "When Allah's Apostle died, his wives intended to send 'Uthman to Abu Bakr asking him for their share of the inheritance." Then 'Aisha said to them, "Didn't Allah's Apostle say, 'Our (Apostles') property is not to be inherited, and whatever we leave is to be spent in charity?'"

Volume 8, Book 80, Number 723.

Narrated Abu Huraira:

The Prophet said, "I am more closer to the believers than their own selves, so whoever (of them) dies while being in debt and leaves nothing for its repayment, then we are to pay his debts on his be-half and whoever (among the believers) dies leaving some property, then that property is for his heirs."

Volume 8, Book 80, Number 724.

Narrated Ibn 'Abbas:

The Prophet said, "Give the Fara'id (the shares of the inheritance that are prescribed in the Qur'an) to those who are entitled to receive it. Then whatever remains, should be given to the closest male relative of the deceased ."

Volume 8, Book 80, Number 725.

Narrated Sa'd bin Abi Waqqas:

I was stricken by an ailment that led me to the verge of death. The Prophet came to pay me a visit. I said, "O Allah's Apostle! I have much property and no heir except my single daughter. Shall I give two-thirds of my property in charity?" He said, "No." I said, "Half of it?" He said, "No." I said, "One-third of it?" He said, "You may do so) though one-third is also to a much, for it is better for you to leave your off-spring wealthy than to leave them poor, asking others for help. And whatever you spend (for Allah's sake) you will be rewarded for it, even for a morsel of food which you may put in the mouth of your wife." I said, "O Allah's Apostle! Will I remain behind and fail to complete my emigration?" The Prophet said, "If you are left behind after me, whatever good deeds you will do for Allah's sake, that will upgrade you and raise you high. May be you will have long life so that some people may benefit by you and others (the enemies) be harmed by you." But Allah's Apostle felt sorry for Sa'd bin Khaula as he died in Mecca. (Sufyan, a sub-narrator said that Sa'd bin Khaula was a man from the tribe of Bani 'Amir bin Lu'ai.)

Volume 8, Book 80, Number 726:

Narrated Al-Aswad bin Yazid:

Mu'adh bin Jabal came to us in Yemen as a tutor and a ruler, and we (the people of Yemen) asked him about (the distribution of the property of) a man who had died leaving a daughter and a sister. Mu'adh gave the daughter one-half of the property and gave the sister the other half.

Volume 8, Book 80, Number 727:

Narrated Ibn 'Abbas:

Allah's Apostle said, "Give the Fara'id (shares prescribed in the Qur'an) to those who are entitled to receive it; and whatever remains, should be given to the closest male relative of the deceased.'

Volume 8, Book 80, Number 728:

Narrated Huzail bin Shirahbil:

Abu Musa was asked regarding (the inheritance of) a daughter, a son's daughter, and a sister. He said, "The daughter will take one-half and the sister will take one-half. If you go to Ibn Mas'ud, he will tell you the same." Ibn Mas'ud was asked and was told of Abu Musa's verdict. Ibn Mas'ud then said, "If I give the same verdict, I would stray and would not be of the rightly-guided. The verdict I will give in this case, will be the same as the Prophet did, i.e. one-half is for daughter, and one-sixth for the son's daughter, i.e. both shares make two-thirds of the total property; and the rest is for the sister." Afterwards we cams to Abu Musa and informed him of Ibn Mas'ud's verdict, whereupon he said, "So, do not ask me for verdicts, as long as this learned man is among you."

Volume 8, Book 80, Number 729:

Narrated Ibn 'Abbas:

The Prophet said, "Give the Fara'id, (the shares prescribed in the Qur'an) to those who are entitled to receive it, and then whatever remains, should be given to the closest male relative of the deceased."

Volume 8, Book 80, Number 730:

Narrated Ibn 'Abbas:

The person about whom Allah's Apostle said, "If I were to take a Khalil from this nation (my followers), then I would have taken him (i.e., Abu Bakr), but the Islamic Brotherhood is better (or said, good)," regarded a grandfather as the father himself (in inheritance).

Volume 8, Book 80, Number 731:

Narrated Ibn 'Abbas:

(During the early days of Islam), the inheritance used to be given to one's offspring and legacy used to be bequeathed to the parents, then Allah cancelled what He wished from that order and decreed that the male should be given the equivalent of the portion of two females, and for the parents one-sixth for each of them, and for one's wife one-eighth (if the deceased has children) and one-fourth (if he has no children), for one's husband one-half (if the deceased has no children) and one-fourth (if she has children)."

Volume 8, Book 80, Number 732:

Narrated Abu Huraira:

Allah's Apostle gave the judgment that a male or female slave should be given in Qisas for an abortion case of a woman from the tribe of Bani Lihyan (as blood money for the fetus) but the lady on whom the penalty had been imposed died, so the Prophets ordered that her property be inherited by her offspring and her husband and that the penalty be paid by her Asaba.

Volume 8, Book 80, Number 733:

Narrated Al-Aswad:

Mu'adh bin Jabal gave this verdict for us in the lifetime of Allah's Apostle. One-half of the inheritance is to be given to the daughter and the other half to the sister. Sulaiman said, Mu'adh gave a verdict for us, but he did not mention that it was so in the lifetime of Allah's Apostle.

Volume 8, Book 80, Number 734:

Narrated Huzail:

'Abdullah said, "The judgment I will give in this matter will be like the judgment of the Prophet, i.e. one-half is for the daughter and one-sixth for the son's daughter and the rest of the inheritance for the sister."

Volume 8, Book 80, Number 735:

Narrated Jabir:

While I was sick, the Prophet entered upon me and asked for some water to perform ablution, and after he had finished his ablution, he sprinkled some water of his ablution over me, whereupon I became conscious and said, "O Allah's Apostle! I have sisters." Then the Divine Verses regarding the laws of inheritance were revealed.

Volume 8, Book 80, Number 736:

Narrated Al-Bara:

The last Quranic Verse that was revealed (to the Prophet) was the final Verse of Surat-an-Nisa, i.e., 'They ask you for a legal verdict Say: Allah directs (thus) About those who leave No descendants or ascendants as heirs....' (4.176)

Volume 8, Book 80, Number 737:

Narrated Abu Huraira:

Allah's Apostle said, "I am more closer to the believers than their ownselves, so whoever (among them) dies leaving some inheritance, his inheritance will be given to his 'Asaba, and whoever dies leaving a debt or dependants or destitute children, then I am their supporter."

Volume 8, Book 80, Number 738:

Narrated Ibn 'Abbas:

The Prophet said, "Give the Fara'id (the shares of the inheritance that are prescribed in the Qur'an) to those who are entitled to receive it; and whatever is left should be given to the closest male relative of the deceased."

Volume 8, Book 80, Number 739:

Narrated Ibn 'Abbas: regarding the Holy Verse:--'And to everyone, We have appointed heirs.'

When the emigrants came to Medina, the Ansar used to be the heir of the emigrants (and vice versa) instead of their own kindred by blood (Dhawl-1-arham), and that was because of the bond of brotherhood which the Prophet had established between them, i.e. the Ansar and the emigrants. But when the Divine Verse:--

'And to everyone We have appointed heirs,' (4.33) was revealed, it cancelled the other, order i.e. 'To those also, to whom Your right hands have pledged.'

Volume 8, Book 80, Number 740:

Narrated Ibn 'Umar:

A man and his wife had a case of Lian (or Mula'ana) during the lifetime of the Prophet and the man denied the paternity of her child. The Prophet gave his verdict for their separation (divorce) and then the child was regarded as belonging to the wife only.

Volume 8, Book 80, Number 741:

Narrated 'Aisha:

'Utba (bin Abi Waqqas) said to his brother Sa'd, "The son of the slave girl of Zam'a is my son, so be his custodian." So when it was the year of the Conquest of Mecca, Sa'd took that child and said, "He is my nephew, and my brother told me to be his custodian." On that, 'Abu bin Zam'a got up and said, 'but the child is my brother, and the son of my father's slave girl as he was born on his bed." So they both went to the Prophet. Sa'd said, "O Allah's Apostle! (This is) the son of my brother and he told me to be his custodian." Then 'Abu bin Zam'a said, "(But he is) my brother and the son of the slave girl of my father, born on his bed." The Prophet said, "This child is for you. O 'Abu bin Zam'a, as the child is for the owner of the bed, and the adulterer receives the stones." He then ordered (his wife) Sauda bint Zam'a to cover herself before that boy as he noticed the boy's resemblance to 'Utba. Since then the boy had never seen Sauda till he died.

Volume 8, Book 80, Number 742:

Narrated Abu Huraira:

The Prophet said, "The boy is for the owner of the bed."

Volume 8, Book 80, Number 743:

Narrated 'Aisha:

I bought Barira (a female slave). The Prophet said (to me), "Buy her as the Wala' is for the manu-mitted." Once she was given a sheep (in charity). The Prophet said, "It (the sheep) is a charitable gift for her (Barira) and a gift for us." Al-Hakam said, "Barira's husband was a free man." Ibn 'Abbas said, 'When I saw him, he was a slave."

Volume 8, Book 80, Number 744:

Narrated Ibn 'Umar:

The Prophet said, "The Wala' is for the manumitted (of the slave)."

Volume 8, Book 80, Number 745:

Narrated 'Abdullah:

The Muslims did not free slaves as Sa'iba, but the People of the Pre-Islamic Period of Ignorance used to do so.

Volume 8, Book 80, Number 746:

Narrated Al-Aswad:

'Aisha bought Barira in order to manumit her, but her masters stipulated that her Wala' (after her death) would be for them. 'Aisha said, "O Allah's Apostle! I have bought Barira in order to manumit her, but her masters stipulated that her Wala' will be for them." The Prophet said, "Manumit her as the Wala is for the one who manumits (the slave)," or said, "The one who pays her price." Then 'Aisha bought and manumitted her. After that, Barira was given the choice (by the Prophet) (to stay with her husband or leave him). She said, "If he gave me so much and so much (money) I would not stay with him." (Al-Aswad added: Her husband was a free man.) The sub-narrator added: The series of the narrators of Al-Aswad's statement is incomplete. The statement of Ibn Abbas, i.e., when I saw him he was a slave, is more authentic.

Volume 8, Book 80, Number 747:

Narrated 'Ali:

We have no Book to recite except the Book of Allah (Qur'an) and this paper. Then 'Ali took out the paper, and behold ! There was written in it, legal verdicts about the retaliation for wounds, the ages of the camels (to be paid as Zakat or as blood money). In it was also written: 'Medina is a sanctuary from Air (mountain) to Thaur (mountain). So whoever innovates in it an heresy (something new in religion) or commits a crime in it or gives shelter to such an innovator, will incur the curse of Allah, the angels and all the people, and none of his compulsory or optional good deeds will be accepted on the Day of Resurrection. And whoever (a freed slave) takes as his master (i.e. be-friends) some people other than hi real masters without the permission of his real masters, will incur the curse of Allah, the angels and all the people, and none of his compulsory, or optional good deeds will be accepted on the Day of Resurrection. And the asylum granted by any Muslim is to be secured by all the Muslims, even if it is granted by one of the lowest social status among them; and whoever betrays a Muslim, in this respect will incur the curse of Allah, the angels, and all the people, and none of his Compulsory or optional good deeds will be accepted on the Day of Resurrection."

Volume 8, Book 80, Number 748:

Narrated Ibn 'Umar:

The Prophet forbade the selling of the Wala' (of slaves) or giving it as a present.

Volume 8, Book 80, Number 749:

Narrated Ibn Umar:

That Aisha, the mother of the Believers, intended to buy a slave girl in order to manumit her. The slave girl's master said, "We are ready to sell her to you on the condition that her Wala should be for us." Aisha mentioned that to Allah's Apostle who said, "This (condition) should not prevent you from buying her, for the Wala is for the one who manumits (the slave)."

Volume 8, Book 80, Number 750:

Narrated Al-Aswad:

Aisha said, "I bought Barira and her masters stipulated that the Wala would be for them." Aisha mentioned that to the Prophet and he said, "Manumit her, as the Wala is for the one who gives the silver (i.e. pays the price for freeing the slave)." Aisha added, "So I manumitted her. After that, the Prophet caller her (Barira) and gave her the choice to go back to her husband or not. She said, "If he gave me so much and so much (money) I would not stay with him." So she selected her ownself (i.e. refused to go back to her husband)."

Volume 8, Book 80, Number 751:

Narrated Ibn Umar:

When Aisha intended to buy Barira, she said to the Prophet, "Barira's masters stipulated that they will have the Wala." The Prophet said (to Aisha), "Buy her, as the Wala is for the one who manumits."

Volume 8, Book 80, Number 752:

Narrated Aisha:

Allah's Apostle said, "The wala is for the one who gives the silver (pays the price) and does the favor (of manumission after paying the price)."

Volume 8, Book 80, Number 753:

Narrated Anas bin Malik:

The Prophet said, "The freed slave belongs to the people who have freed him," or said something similar.

Volume 8, Book 80, Number 754:

Narrated Anas bin Malik:

The Prophet said, "The son of the sister of some people is from them or from their own selves."

Volume 8, Book 80, Number 755:

Narrated Abu Huraira:

The Prophet said, " If somebody dies (among the Muslims) leaving some property, the property will go to his heirs; and if he leaves a debt or dependants, we will take care of them."

Volume 8, Book 80, Number 756:

Narrated Usama bin Zaid:

the Prophet said, "A Muslim cannot be the heir of a disbeliever, nor can a disbeliever be the heir of a Muslim."

Volume 8, Book 80, Number 757:

Narrated 'Aisha:

Sa'd bin Abi Waqqas and 'Abu bin Zam'a had a dispute over a boy. Sa'd said, "O Allah's Apostle! This (boy) is the son of my brother, 'Utba bin Abi Waqqas who told me to be his custodian as he was his son. Please notice to whom he bears affinity." And 'Abu bin Zam'a said, "This is my brother, O Allah's Apostle! He was born on my father's bed by his slave girl." Then the Prophet looked at the boy and noticed evident resemblance between him and 'Utba, so he said, "He (the toy) is for you, O 'Abu bin Zam'a, for the boy is for the owner of the bed, and the stone is for the adulterer. Screen yourself before the boy, O Sauda bint Zam'a." 'Aisha added: Since then he had never seen Sauda.

Volume 8, Book 80, Number 758:

Narrated Sa'd:

I heard the Prophet saying, "Whoever claims to be the son of a person other than his father, and he knows that person is not his father, then Paradise will be forbidden for him." I mentioned that to Abu Bakra, and he said, "My ears heard that and my heart memorized it from Allah's Apostle

Volume 8, Book 80, Number 759:

Narrated Abu Huraira:

The Prophet said, "Do not deny your fathers (i.e. claim to be the sons of persons other than your fathers), and whoever denies his father, is charged with disbelief."

Volume 8, Book 80, Number 760:

Narrated Abu Huraira:

Allah's Apostle said, "There were two women with whom there were their two sons. A wolf came and took away the son of one of them. That lady said to her companion, 'The wolf has taken your son.' The other said, 'But it has taken your son.' So both of them sought the judgment of (the Prophet) David who judged that the boy should be given to the older lady. Then both of them went to (the Prophet) Solomon, son of David and informed him of the case. Solomon said, 'Give me a knife so that I may cut the child into two portions and give one half to each of you.' The younger lady said, 'Do not do so; may Allah bless you ! He is her child.' On that, he gave the child to the younger lady." Abu Huraira added: By Allah! I had never heard the word 'Sakkin' as meaning knife, except on that day, for we used to call it 'Mudya"

Volume 8, Book 80, Number 761:

Narrated 'Aisha:

Allah's Apostle once entered upon me in a very happy mood, with his features glittering with joy, and said, "O 'Aisha! won't you see that Mujazziz (a Qa'if) looked just now at Zaid bin Haritha and Usama bin Zaid and said, 'These feet (of Usama and his father) belong to each other." (See Hadith No. 755, Vol. 4)

Volume 8, Book 80, Number 762:

Narrated 'Aisha:

Once Allah's Apostle entered upon me and he was in a very happy mood and said, "O 'Aisha: Don't you know that Mujazziz Al-Mudliji entered and saw Usama and Zaid with a velvet covering on them and their heads were covered while their feet were uncovered. He said, 'These feet belong to each other.'

Book 81: Limits and Punishments set by Allah (Hudood)

Volume 8, Book 81, Number 763:

Narrated Abu Huraira:

Allah's Apostle said, "When an adulterer commits illegal sexual intercourse, then he is not a believer at the time he is doing it; and when somebody drinks an alcoholic drink, then he is not believer at the time of drinking, and when a thief steals, he is not a believer at the time when he is stealing; and when a robber robs and the people look at him, then he is not a believer at the time of doing it." Abu Huraira in another narration, narrated the same from the Prophet with the exclusion of robbery.

Volume 8, Book 81, Number 764:

Narrated Anas bin Malik:

The Prophet beat a drunk with palm-leaf stalks and shoes. And Abu Bakr gave (such a sinner) forty lashes.

Volume 8, Book 81, Number 765:

Narrated 'Uqba bin Al-Harith:

An-Nu'man or the son of An-Nu'man was brought to the Prophet on a charge of drunkenness. So the Prophet ordered all the men present in the house, to beat him. So all of them beat him, and I was also one of them who beat him with shoes.

Volume 8, Book 81, Number 766:

Narrated' Uqba bin Al-Harith:

An-Nu'man or the son of An-Nu'man was brought to the Prophet in a state of intoxication. The Prophet felt it hard (was angry) and ordered all those who were present in the house, to beat him. And they beat him, using palm-leaf stalks and shoes, and I was among those who beat him.

Volume 8, Book 81, Number 767:

Narrated Anas:

The Prophet lashed a drunk with dateleaf stalks and shoes. And Abu Bakr gave a drunk forty lashes.

Volume 8, Book 81, Number 768:

Narrated Abu Salama:

Abu Huraira said, "A man who drank wine was brought to the Prophet. The Prophet said, 'Beat him!' Abu Huraira added, "So some of us beat him with our hands, and some with their shoes, and some with their garments (by twisting it) like a lash, and then when we finished, someone said to him, 'May Allah disgrace you!' On that the Prophet said, 'Do not say so, for you are helping Satan to overpower him.' "

Volume 8, Book 81, Number 769:

Narrated 'Ali bin Abi Talib:

I would not feel sorry for one who dies because of receiving a legal punishment, except the drunk, for if he should die (when being punished), I would give blood money to his family because no fixed punishment has been ordered by Allah's Apostle for the drunk.

Volume 8, Book 81, Number 770:

Narrated As-Sa'ib bin Yazid:

We used to strike the drunks with our hands, shoes, clothes (by twisting it into the shape of lashes) during the lifetime of the Prophet, Abu Bakr and the early part of 'Umar's caliphate. But during the last period of 'Umar's caliphate, he used to give the drunk forty lashes; and when drunks became mischievous and disobedient, he used to scourge them eighty lashes.

Volume 8, Book 81, Number 771:

Narrated 'Umar bin Al-Khattab:

During the lifetime of the Prophet there was a man called 'Abdullah whose nickname was Donkey, and he used to make Allah's Apostle laugh. The Prophet lashed him because of drinking (alcohol). And one-day he was brought to the Prophet on the same charge and was lashed. On that, a man among the people said, "O Allah, curse him ! How frequently he has been brought (to the Prophet on such a charge)!" The Prophet said, "Do not curse him, for by Allah, I know for he loves Allah and His Apostle."

Volume 8, Book 81, Number 772.

Narrated Abu Huraira.

A drunk was brought to the Prophet and he ordered him to be beaten (lashed). Some of us beat him with our hands, and some with their shoes, and some with their garments (twisted in the form of a lash). When that drunk had left, a man said, "What is wrong with him? May Allah disgrace him!" Allah's Apostle said, "Do not help Satan against your (Muslim) brother."

Volume 8, Book 81, Number 773.

Narrated Ibn 'Abbas.

The Prophet said, "When (a person) an adulterer commits illegal sexual intercourse then he is not a believer at the time he is doing it; and when somebody steals, then he is not a believer at the time he is stealing."

Volume 8, Book 81, Number 774.

Narrated Abu Huraira.

The Prophet said, "Allah curses a man who steals an egg and gets his hand cut off, or steals a rope and gets his hands cut off." Al-A'mash said, "People used to interpret the Baida as an iron helmet, and they used to think that the rope may cost a few dirhams."

Volume 8, Book 81, Number 775.

Narrated 'Ubada bin As-Samit.

We were with the Prophet in a gathering and he said, 'Swear allegiance to me that you will not worship anything besides Allah, Will not steal, and will not commit illegal sexual intercourse." And then (the Prophet) recited the whole Verse (i.e. 60.12). The Prophet added, 'And whoever among you fulfills his pledge, his reward is with Allah; and whoever commits something of such sins and receives the legal punishment for it, that will be considered as the expiation for that sin, and whoever commits something of such sins and Allah screens him, it is up to Allah whether to excuse or punish him."

Volume 8, Book 81, Number 776.

Narrated Abdullah.

Allah Apostle said in Hajjat-al-Wada, "Which month (of the year) do you think is most sacred?" The people said, "This current month of ours (the month of Dhull-Hijja)." He said, "Which town (country) do you think is the most sacred?" They said, "This city of ours (Mecca)." He said, "Which day do you think is the most sacred?" The people said, "This day of ours." He then said, "Allah, the Blessed, the Supreme, has made your blood, your property and your honor as sacred as this day of yours in this town of yours, in this month of yours (and such protection cannot be slighted) except rightfully." He then said thrice, "Have I conveyed Allah's Message (to you)?" The people answered him each time saying, 'Yes." The Prophet added, 'May Allah be merciful to you (or, woe on you)! Do not revert to disbelief after me by cutting the necks of each other.'

Volume 8, Book 81, Number 777:

Narrated Aisha:

Whenever the Prophet was given an option between two things, he used to select the easier of the two as long as it was not sinful; but if it was sinful, he would remain far from it. By Allah, he never took revenge for himself concerning any matter that was presented to him, but when Allah's Limits were transgressed, he would take revenge for Allah's Sake.

Volume 8, Book 81, Number 778:

Narrated 'Aisha:

Usama approached the Prophet on behalf of a woman (who had committed theft). The Prophet said, "The people before you were destroyed because they used to inflict the legal punishments on the poor and forgive the rich. By Him in Whose Hand my soul is! If Fatima (the daughter of the Prophet) did that (i.e. stole), I would cut off her hand."

Volume 8, Book 81, Number 779:

Narrated 'Aisha:

The Quraish people became very worried about the Makhzumiya lady who had committed theft. They said, "Nobody can speak (in favor of the lady) to Allah's Apostle and nobody dares do that except Usama who is the favorite of Allah's Apostle. " When Usama spoke to Allah's Apostle about that matter, Allah's Apostle said, "Do you intercede (with me) to violate one of the legal punishment of Allah?" Then he got up and addressed the people, saying, "O people! The nations before you went astray because if a noble person committed theft, they used to leave him, but if a weak person among them committed theft, they used to inflict the legal punishment on him. By Allah, if Fatima, the daughter of Muhammad committed theft, Muhammad will cut off her hand.!"

Volume 8, Book 81, Number 780:

Narrated 'Aisha:

The Prophet said, "The hand should be cut off for stealing something that is worth a quarter of a Dinar or more."

Volume 8, Book 81, Number 781:

Narrated 'Aisha:

The Prophet said, "The hand of a thief should be cut off for stealing a quarter of a Dinar."

Volume 8, Book 81, Number 782:

Narrated 'Aisha:

The Prophet said, "The hand should be cut off for stealing a quarter of a Dinar."

Volume 8, Book 81, Number 783:

Narrated 'Aisha:

The hand of a thief was not cut off during the lifetime of the Prophet except for stealing something equal to a shield in value.

Volume 8, Book 81, Number 784:

Narrated 'Aisha:

as above (783).

Volume 8, Book 81, Number 785:

Narrated 'Aisha:

A thief's hand was not cut off for stealing something cheaper than a Hajafa or a Turs (two kinds of shields), each of which was worth a (respectable) price.

Volume 8, Book 81, Number 786:

Narrated 'Aisha:

A thief's hand was not cut off for stealing something worth less than the price of a shield, whether a Turs or Hajafa (two kinds of shields), each of which was worth a (respectable) price.

Volume 8, Book 81, Number 787:

Narrated Ibn 'Umar:

Allah's Apostle cut off the hand of a thief for stealing a shield that was worth three Dirhams.

Volume 8, Book 81, Number 788.

Narrated Ibn 'Umar.

The Prophet cut off the hand of a thief for stealing a shield that was worth three Dirhams.

Volume 8, Book 81, Number 789.

Narrated 'Abdullah bin 'Umar.

The Prophet cut off the hand of a thief for stealing a shield that was worth three Dirhams.

Volume 8, Book 81, Number 790.

Narrated 'Abdullah bin 'Umar.

The Prophet cutoff the hand of a thief for stealing a shield that was worth three Dirhams.

Volume 8, Book 81, Number 791.

Narrated Abu Huraira.

Allah 's Apostle said, "Allah curses the thief who steals an egg (or a helmet) for which his hand is to be cut off, or steals a rope, for which his hand is to be cut off."

Volume 8, Book 81, Number 792.

Narrated 'Aisha.

The Prophet cut off the hand of a lady, and that lady used to come to me, and I used to convey her message to the Prophet and she repented, and her repentance was sincere.

Volume 8, Book 81, Number 793.

Narrated Ubada bin As-Samit.

I gave the pledge of allegiance to the Prophet with a group of people, and he said, "I take your pledge that you will not worship anything besides Allah, will not steal, will not commit infanticide, will not slander others by forging false statements and spreading it, and will not disobey me in anything good. And whoever among you fulfill all these (obligations of the pledge), his reward is with Allah. And whoever commits any of the above crimes and receives his legal punishment in this world, that will be his expiation and purification. But if Allah screens his sin, it will be up to Allah, Who will either punish or forgive him according to His wish." Abu Abdullah said. "If a thief repents after his hand has been cut off, the his witness well be accepted. Similarly, if any person upon whom any legal punishment has been inflicted, repents, his witness will be accepted."

Book 82: Punishment of Disbelievers at War with Allah and His Apostle

Volume 8, Book 82, Number 794:

Narrated Anas:

Some people from the tribe of 'Ukl came to the Prophet and embraced Islam. The climate of Medina did not suit them, so the Prophet ordered them to go to the (herd of milch) camels of charity and to drink, their milk and urine (as a medicine). They did so, and after they had recovered from their ailment (became healthy) they turned renegades (reverted from Islam) and killed the shepherd of the camels and took the camels away. The Prophet sent (some people) in their pursuit and so they were (caught and) brought, and the Prophets ordered that their hands and legs should be cut off and that their eyes should be branded with heated pieces of iron, and that their cut hands and legs should not be cauterized, till they die.

Volume 8, Book 82, Number 795:

Narrated Anas:

The Prophet cut off the hands and feet of the men belonging to the tribe of 'Uraina and did not cauterise (their bleeding limbs) till they died.

Volume 8, Book 82, Number 796:

Narrated Anas:

A group of people from 'Ukl (tribe) came to the Prophet and they were living with the people of As-Suffa, but they became ill as the climate of Medina did not suit them, so they said, "O Allah's Apostle! Provide us with milk." The Prophet said, I see no other way for you than to use the camels of Allah's Apostle." So they went and drank the milk and urine of the camels, (as medicine) and became healthy and fat. Then they killed the shepherd and took the camels away. When a help-seeker came to Allah's Apostle, he sent some men in their pursuit, and they were captured and brought before mid day. The Prophet ordered for some iron pieces to be made red hot, and their eyes were branded with them and their hands and feet were cut off and were not cauterized. Then they were put at a place called Al-Harra, and when they asked for water to drink they were not given till they died. (Abu Qilaba said, "Those people committed theft and murder and fought against Allah and His Apostle.")

Volume 8, Book 82, Number 797:

Narrated Anas bin Malik:

A group of people from 'Ukl (or 'Uraina) tribe ----but I think he said that they were from 'Ukl came to Medina and (they became ill, so) the Prophet ordered them to go to the herd of (Milch) she-camels and told them to go out and drink the camels' urine and milk (as a medicine). So they went and drank it, and when they became healthy, they killed the shepherd and drove away the camels. This news reached the Prophet early in the morning, so he sent (some) men in their pursuit and they were captured and brought to the Prophet before midday. He ordered to cut off their hands and legs and their eyes to be branded with heated iron pieces and they were thrown at Al-Harra, and when they asked for water to drink, they were not given water. (Abu Qilaba said, "Those were the people who committed theft and murder and reverted to disbelief after being believers (Muslims), and fought against Allah and His Apostle").

Volume 8, Book 82, Number 798:

Narrated Abu Huraira:

The Prophet said, "Seven (people) will be shaded by Allah by His Shade on the Day of Resurrection when there will be no shade except His Shade. (They will be), a just ruler, a young man who has been brought up in the worship of Allah, a man who remembers Allah in seclusion and his eyes are then flooded with tears, a man whose heart is attached to mosques (offers his compulsory congregational prayers in the mosque), two men who love each other for Allah's Sake, a man who is called by a charming lady of noble birth to commit illegal sexual intercourse with her, and he says, 'I am afraid of Allah,' and (finally), a man who gives in charity so secretly that his left hand does not know what his right hand has given."

Volume 8, Book 82, Number 799:

Narrated Sahl bin Sa'd:

The Prophet said, "Whoever guarantees me (the chastity of) what is between his legs (i.e. his private parts), and what is between his jaws (i.e., his tongue), I guarantee him Paradise."

Volume 8, Book 82, Number 800i:

Narrated Anas:

I will narrate to you a narration which nobody will narrate to you after me. I heard that form the Prophet. I heard the Prophet saying, "The Hour sill not be established" or said: "From among the portents of the Hour is that the religious knowledge will betaken away (by the death of religious Scholars) and general ignorance (of religion) will appear; and the drinking of alcoholic drinks will be very common, and (open) illegal sexual intercourse will prevail, and men will decrease in number while women will increase so much so that, for fifty women there will only be one man to look after them."

Volume 8, Book 82, Number 800e:

Narrated 'Ikrima from Ibn 'Abbas:

Allah's Apostles said, "When a slave (of Allah) commits illegal sexual intercourse, he is not a believer at the time of committing it; and if he steals, he is not a believer at the time of stealing; and if he drinks an alcoholic drink, when he is not a believer at the time of drinking it; and he is not a believer when he commits a murder," 'Ikrima said: I asked Ibn Abbas, "How is faith taken away from him?" He said, Like this," by clasping his hands and then separating them, and added, "But if he repents, faith returns to him like this, by clasping his hands again.

Volume 8, Book 82, Number 801:

Narrated Abu Huraira:

The Prophet said, "The one who commits an illegal sexual intercourse is not a believer at the time of committing illegal sexual intercourse and a thief is not a believer at the time of committing theft and a drinker of alcoholic drink is not a believer at the time of drinking. Yet, (the gate of) repentance is open thereafter."

Volume 8, Book 82, Number 802:

Narrated 'Abdullah bin Mas'ud:

I said, "O Allah's Apostle! Which is the biggest sin?" He said, "To set up rivals to Allah by worshipping others though He alone has created you." I asked, "What is next?" He said, "To kill your child lest it should share your food." I asked, "What is next?" He said, "To commit illegal sexual intercourse with the wife of your neighbor."

Volume 8, Book 82, Number 803:

Narrated Ash-Sha'bi:

from 'Ali when the latter stoned a lady to death on a Friday. 'Ali said, "I have stoned her according to the tradition of Allah's Apostle."

Volume 8, Book 82, Number 804:

Narrated Ash Shaibani:

I asked 'Abdullah bin Abi Aufa, 'Did Allah's Apostle carry out the Rajam penalty (i.e., stoning to death)?' He said, "Yes." I said, "Before the revelation of Surat-ar-Nur or after it?" He replied, "I don't Know."

Volume 8, Book 82, Number 805:

Narrated Jabir bin Abdullah Al-Ansari:

A man from the tribe of Bani Aslam came to Allah's Apostle and Informed him that he had committed illegal sexual intercourse and bore witness four times against himself. Allah's Apostle ordered him to be stoned to death as he was a married Person.

Volume 8, Book 82, Number 806:

Narrated Abu Huraira:

A man came to Allah's Apostle while he was in the mosque, and he called him, saying, "O Allah's Apostle! I have committed illegal sexual intercourse.'" The Prophet turned his face to the other side, but that man repeated his statement four times, and after he bore witness against himself four times, the Prophet called him, saying, "Are you mad?" The man said, "No." The Prophet said, "Are you married?" The man said, "Yes." Then the Prophet said, 'Take him away and stone him to death." Jabir bin 'Abdullah said: I was among the ones who participated in stoning him and we stoned him at the Musalla. When the stones troubled him, he fled, but we over took him at Al-Harra and stoned him to death.

Volume 8, Book 82, Number 807:

Narrated 'Aisha:

Sa'd bin Abi Waqqas and 'Abd bin Zam'a quarrelled with each other (regarding a child). The Prophet said, "The boy is for you, O 'Abd bin Zam'a, for the boy is for (the owner) of the bed. O Sauda ! Screen yourself from the boy." The sub-narrator, Al-Laith added (that the Prophet also said), "And the stone is for the person who commits an illegal sexual intercourse."

Volume 8, Book 82, Number 808:

Narrated Abu Huraira:

The Prophet said, "The boy is for (the owner of) the bed and the stone is for the person who commits illegal sexual intercourse.'

Volume 8, Book 82, Number 809:

Narrated Ibn 'Umar:

A Jew and a Jewess were brought to Allah's Apostle on a charge of committing an illegal sexual intercourse. The Prophet asked them. "What is the legal punishment (for this sin) in your Book (Torah)?" They replied, "Our priests have innovated the punishment of blackening the faces with charcoal and Tajbiya." 'Abdullah bin Salam said, "O Allah's Apostle, tell them to bring the Torah." The Torah was brought, and then one of the Jews put his hand over the Divine Verse of the Rajam (stoning to death) and started reading what preceded and what followed it. On that, Ibn Salam said to the Jew, "Lift up your hand." Behold! The Divine Verse of the Rajam was under his hand. So Allah's Apostle ordered that the two (sinners) be stoned to death, and so they were stoned. Ibn 'Umar added: So both of them were stoned at the Balat and I saw the Jew sheltering the Jewess.

Volume 8, Book 82, Number 810:

Narrated Jabir:

A man from the tribe of Aslam came to the Prophet and confessed that he had committed an illegal sexual intercourse. The Prophet turned his face away from him till the man bore witness against himself four times. The Prophet said to him, "Are you mad?" He said "No." He said, "Are you married?" He said, "Yes." Then the Prophet ordered that he be stoned to death, and he was stoned to death at the Musalla. When the stones troubled him, he fled, but he was caught and was stoned till he died. The Prophet spoke well of him and offered his funeral prayer.

Volume 8, Book 82, Number 811d:

Narrated Abu Huraira:

A person had sexual relation with his wife in the month of Ramadan (while he was fasting), and he came to Allah's Apostle seeking his verdict concerning that action. The Prophet said (to him), "Can you afford to manumit a slave?" The man said, "No." The Prophet said, "Can you fast for two successive months?" He said, "No." The Prophet said, "Then feed sixty poor persons."

Volume 8, Book 82, Number 811e:

Narrated 'Aisha:

A man came to the Prophet in the mosque and said, "I am burnt (ruined)!" The Prophet asked him, "With what (what have you done)?" He said, "I have had sexual relation with my wife in the month of Ramadan (while fasting)." The Prophet said to him, "Give in charity." He said, "I have nothing." The man sat down, and in the meantime there came a person driving a donkey carrying food to the Prophet ..... (The sub-narrator, 'Abdur Rahman added: I do not know what kind of food it was). On that the Prophet said, "Where is the burnt person?" The man said, "Here I am." The Prophet said to him, "Take this (food) and give it in charity (to someone)." The man said, "To a poorer person than I? My family has nothing to eat." Then the Prophet said to him, "Then eat it yourselves."

Volume 8, Book 82, Number 812:

Narrated Anas bin Malik:

While I was with the Prophet a man came and said, "O Allah's Apostle! I have committed a legally punishable sin; please inflict the legal punishment on me'.' The Prophet did not ask him what he had done. Then the time for the prayer became due and the man offered prayer along with the Prophet, and when the Prophet had finished his prayer, the man again got up and said, "O Allah's Apostle! I have committed a legally punishable sin; please inflict the punishment on me according to Allah's Laws." The Prophet said, "Haven't you prayed with us?' He said, "Yes." The Prophet said, "Allah has forgiven your sin." or said, "....your legally punishable sin."

Volume 8, Book 82, Number 813:

Narrated Ibn 'Abbas:

When Ma'iz bin Malik came to the Prophet (in order to confess), the Prophet said to him, "Probably you have only kissed (the lady), or winked, or looked at her?" He said, "No, O Allah's Apostle!" The Prophet said, using no euphemism, "Did you have sexual intercourse with her?" The narrator added: At that, (i.e. after his confession) the Prophet ordered that he be stoned (to death).

Volume 8, Book 82, Number 814:

Narrated Abu Huraira:

A man from among the people, came to Allah's Apostle while Allah's Apostle was sitting in the mosque, and addressed him, saying, "O Allah's Apostle! I have committed an illegal sexual inter-course." The Prophet turned his face away from him. The man came to that side to which the Prophet had turned his face, and said, "O Allah's Apostle! I have committed an illegal intercourse." The Prophet turned his face to the other side, and the man came to that side, and when he confessed four times, the Prophet called him and said, "Are you mad?" He said, "No, O Allah's Apostle!" The Prophet said, "Are you married?" He said, "Yes, O Allah's Apostle." The Prophet said (to the people), "Take him away and stone him to death." Ibn Shihab added, "I was told by one who heard Jabir, that Jabir said, 'I was among those who stoned the man, and we stoned him at the Musalla ('Id praying Place), and when the stones troubled him, he jumped quickly and ran away, but we overtook him at Al-Harra and stoned him to death (there).' "

Volume 8, Book 82, Number 815:

Narrated Abu Huraira and Zaid bin Khalid:

While we were with the Prophet , a man stood up and said (to the Prophet), "I beseech you by Allah, that you should judge us according to Allah's Laws." Then the man's opponent who was wiser than him, got up saying (to Allah's Apostle) "Judge us according to Allah's Law and kindly allow me (to speak)." The Prophet said, "'Speak." He said, "My son was a laborer working for this man and he committed an illegal sexual intercourse with his wife, and I gave one-hundred sheep and a slave as a ransom for my son's sin. Then I asked a learned man about this case and he informed me that my son should receive one hundred lashes and be exiled for one year, and the man's wife should be stoned to death." The Prophet said, "By Him in Whose Hand my soul is, I will judge you according to the Laws of Allah. Your one-hundred sheep and the slave are to be returned to you, and your son has to receive one-hundred lashes and be exiled for one year. O Unais! Go to the wife of this man, and if she confesses, then stone her to death." Unais went to her and she confessed. He then stoned her to death.

Volume 8, Book 82, Number 816:

Narrated Ibn 'Abbas:

'Umar said, "I am afraid that after a long time has passed, people may say, "We do not find the Verses of the Rajam (stoning to death) in the Holy Book," and consequently they may go astray by leaving an obligation that Allah has revealed. Lo! I confirm that the penalty of Rajam be inflicted on him who commits illegal sexual intercourse, if he is already married and the crime is proved by witnesses or pregnancy or confession." Sufyan added, "I have memorized this narration in this way." 'Umar added, "Surely Allah's Apostle carried out the penalty of Rajam, and so did we after him."

Volume 8, Book 82, Number 817:

Narrated Ibn 'Abbas:

I used to teach (the Qur'an to) some people of the Muhajirln (emigrants), among whom there was 'Abdur Rahman bin 'Auf. While I was in his house at Mina, and he was with 'Umar bin Al-Khattab during 'Umar's last Hajj, Abdur-Rahman came to me and said, "Would that you had seen the man who came today to the Chief of the Believers ('Umar), saying, 'O Chief of the Believers! What do you think about so-and-so who says, 'If 'Umar should die, I will give the pledge of allegiance to such-and-such person, as by Allah, the pledge of allegiance to Abu Bakr was nothing but a prompt sudden action which got established afterwards.' 'Umar became angry and then said, 'Allah willing, I will stand before the people tonight and warn them against those people who want to deprive the others of their rights (the question of rulership)."

'Abdur-Rahman said, "I said, 'O Chief of the believers! Do not do that, for the season of Hajj gathers the riff-raff and the rubble, and it will be they who will gather around you when you stand to address the people. And I am afraid that you will get up and say something, and some people will spread your statement and may not say what you have actually said and may not understand its meaning, and may interpret it incorrectly, so you should wait till you reach Medina, as it is the place of emigration and the place of Prophet's Traditions, and there you can come in touch with the learned and noble people, and tell them your ideas with confidence; and the learned people will understand your statement and put it in its proper place.' On that, 'Umar said, 'By Allah! Allah willing, I will do this in the first speech I will deliver before the people in Medina."

Ibn Abbas added: We reached Medina by the end of the month of Dhul-Hijja, and when it was Friday, we went quickly (to the mosque) as soon as the sun had declined, and I saw Sa'id bin Zaid bin 'Amr bin Nufail sitting at the corner of the pulpit, and I too sat close to him so that my knee was touching his knee, and after a short while 'Umar bin Al-Khattab came out, and when I saw him coming towards us, I said to Said bin Zaid bin 'Amr bin Nufail "Today 'Umar will say such a thing as he has never said since he was chosen as Caliph." Said denied my statement with astonishment and said, "What thing do you expect 'Umar to say the like of which he has never said before?"

In the meantime, 'Umar sat on the pulpit and when the callmakers for the prayer had finished their call, 'Umar stood up, and having glorified and praised Allah as He deserved, he said, "Now then, I am going to tell you something which (Allah) has written for me to say. I do not know; perhaps it portends my death, so whoever understands and remembers it, must narrate it to the others wherever his mount takes him, but if somebody is afraid that he does not understand it, then it is unlawful for him to tell lies about me. Allah sent Muhammad with the Truth and revealed the Holy Book to him, and among what Allah revealed, was the Verse of the Rajam (the stoning of married person (male & female) who commits illegal sexual intercourse, and we did recite this Verse and understood and memorized it. Allah's Apostle did carry out the punishment of stoning and so did we after him.

I am afraid that after a long time has passed, somebody will say, 'By Allah, we do not find the Verse of the Rajam in Allah's Book,' and thus they will go astray by leaving an obligation which Allah has revealed. And the punishment of the Rajam is to be inflicted to any married person (male & female), who commits illegal sexual intercourse, if the required evidence is available or there is conception or confession. And then we used to recite among the Verses in Allah's Book: 'O people! Do not claim to be the offspring of other than your fathers, as it is disbelief (unthankfulness) on your part that you claim to be the offspring of other than your real father.' Then Allah's Apostle said, 'Do not praise me excessively as Jesus, son of Marry was praised, but call me Allah's Slave and His Apostles.' (O people!) I have been informed that a speaker amongst you says, 'By Allah, if 'Umar should die, I will give the pledge of allegiance to such-and-such person.' One should not deceive oneself by saying that the pledge of allegiance given to Abu Bakr was given suddenly and it was successful. No doubt, it was like that, but Allah saved (the people) from its evil, and there is none among you who has the qualities of Abu Bakr. Remember that whoever gives the pledge of allegiance to anybody among you without consulting the other Muslims, neither that person, nor the person to whom the pledge of allegiance was given, are to be supported, lest they both should be killed.

And no doubt after the death of the Prophet we were informed that the Ansar disagreed with us and gathered in the shed of Bani Sa'da. 'Ali and Zubair and whoever was with them, opposed us, while the emigrants gathered with Abu Bakr. I said to Abu Bakr, 'Let's go to these Ansari brothers of ours.' So we set out seeking them, and when we approached them, two pious men of theirs met us and informed us of the final decision of the Ansar, and said, 'O group of Muhajirin (emigrants) ! Where are you going?' We replied, 'We are going to these Ansari brothers of ours.' They said to us, 'You shouldn't go near them. Carry out whatever we have already decided.' I said, 'By Allah, we will go to them.' And so we proceeded until we reached them at the shed of Bani Sa'da. Behold! There was a man sitting amongst them and wrapped in something. I asked, 'Who is that man?' They said, 'He is Sa'd bin 'Ubada.' I asked, 'What is wrong with him?' They said, 'He is sick.' After we sat for a while, the Ansar's speaker said, 'None has the right to be worshipped but Allah,' and praising Allah as He deserved, he added, 'To proceed, we are Allah's Ansar (helpers) and the majority of the Muslim army, while you, the emigrants, are a small group and some people among you came with the intention of preventing us from practicing this matter (of caliphate) and depriving us of it.'

When the speaker had finished, I intended to speak as I had prepared a speech which I liked and which I wanted to deliver in the presence of Abu Bakr, and I used to avoid provoking him. So, when I wanted to speak, Abu Bakr said, 'Wait a while.' I disliked to make him angry. So Abu Bakr himself gave a speech, and he was wiser and more patient than I. By Allah, he never missed a sentence that I liked in my own prepared speech, but he said the like of it or better than it spontaneously. After a pause he said, 'O Ansar! You deserve all (the qualities that you have attributed to yourselves, but this question (of Caliphate) is only for the Quraish as they are the best of the Arabs as regards descent and home, and I am pleased to suggest that you choose either of these two men, so take the oath of allegiance to either of them as you wish. And then Abu Bakr held my hand and Abu Ubada bin Abdullah's hand who was sitting amongst us. I hated nothing of what he had said except that proposal, for by Allah, I would rather have my neck chopped off as expiator for a sin than become the ruler of a nation, one of whose members is Abu Bakr, unless at the time of my death my own-self suggests something I don't feel at present.'

And then one of the Ansar said, 'I am the pillar on which the camel with a skin disease (eczema) rubs itself to satisfy the itching (i.e., I am a noble), and I am as a high class palm tree! O Quraish. There should be one ruler from us and one from you.'

Then there was a hue and cry among the gathering and their voices rose so that I was afraid there might be great disagreement, so I said, 'O Abu Bakr! Hold your hand out.' He held his hand out and I pledged allegiance to him, and then all the emigrants gave the Pledge of allegiance and so did the Ansar afterwards. And so we became victorious over Sa'd bin Ubada (whom Al-Ansar wanted to make a ruler). One of the Ansar said, 'You have killed Sa'd bin Ubada.' I replied, 'Allah has killed Sa'd bin Ubada.' Umar added, "By Allah, apart from the great tragedy that had happened to us (i.e. the death of the Prophet), there was no greater problem than the allegiance pledged to Abu Bakr because we were afraid that if we left the people, they might give the Pledge of allegiance after us to one of their men, in which case we would have given them our consent for something against our real wish, or would have opposed them and caused great trouble. So if any person gives the Pledge of allegiance to somebody (to become a Caliph) without consulting the other Muslims, then the one he has selected should not be granted allegiance, lest both of them should be killed."

Volume 8, Book 82, Number 818:

Narrated Zaid bin Khalid Al-Jihani:

I heard the Prophet ordering that an unmarried person guilty of illegal sexual intercourse be flogged one-hundred stripes and be exiled for one year. Umar bin Al-Khattab also exiled such a person, and this tradition is still valid.

Volume 8, Book 82, Number 819:

Narrated Abu Huraira:

Allah's Apostle judged that the unmarried person who was guilty of illegal sexual intercourse be exiled for one year and receive the legal punishment (i.e., be flogged with one-hundred stripes) .

Volume 8, Book 82, Number 820:

Narrated Ibn 'Abbas:

The Prophet cursed the effeminate men and those women who assume the similitude (manners) of men. He also said, "Turn them out of your houses." He turned such-and-such person out, and 'Umar also turned out such-and-such person.

Volume 8, Book 82, Number 821:

Narrated Abu Huraira and Zaid bin Khalid:

A bedouin came to the Prophet while he (the Prophet) was sitting, and said, "O Allah's Apostle! Give your verdict according to Allah's Laws (in our case)." Then his opponent got up and said, "He has told the truth, O Allah's Apostle! Decide his case according to Allah's Laws. My son was a laborer working for this person, and he committed illegal sexual intercourse with his wife, and the people told me that my son should be stoned to death, but I offered one-hundred sheep and a slave girl as a ransom for him. Then I asked the religious learned people, and they told me that my son should be flogged with one-hundred stripes and be exiled for one year." The Prophet said, "By Him in Whose Hand my soul is, I will judge you according to Allah's Laws. The sheep and the slave girl will be returned to you and your son will be flogged one-hundred stripes and be exiled for one year. And you,

O Unais! Go to the wife of this man (and if she confesses), stone her to death." So Unais went in the morning and stoned her to death (after she had confessed).

Volume 8, Book 82, Number 822:

Narrated Abu Huraira and Said bin Khalid:

The verdict of Allah's Apostle was sought about an unmarried slave girl guilty of illegal intercourse. He replied, "If she commits illegal sexual intercourse, then flog her (fifty stripes), and if she commits illegal sexual intercourse (after that for the second time), then flog her (fifty stripes), and if she commits illegal sexual intercourse (for the third time), then flog her (fifty stripes) and sell her for even a hair rope." Ibn Shihab said, "I am not sure whether the Prophet ordered that she be sold after the third or fourth time of committing illegal intercourse."

Volume 8, Book 82, Number 823:

Narrated Abu Huraira:

The Prophet said, "If a lady slave commits illegal sexual intercourse and she is proved guilty of illegal sexual intercourse, then she should be flogged (fifty stripes) but she should not be admonished; and if she commits illegal sexual intercourse again, then she should be flogged again but should not be admonished; and if she commits illegal sexual intercourse for the third time, then she should be sold even for a hair rope."

Volume 8, Book 82, Number 824:

Narrated Ash-Shaibani:

I asked 'Abdullah bin Abi 'Aufa about the Rajam (stoning somebody to death for committing illegal sexual intercourse). He replied, "The Prophet carried out the penalty of Rajam," I asked, "Was that before or after the revelation of Surat-an-Nur?" He replied, "I do not know."

Volume 8, Book 82, Number 825:

Narrated Abdullah bin Umar:

The jews came to Allah's Apostle and mentioned to him that a man and a lady among them had committed illegal sexual intercourse. Allah's Apostle said to them, "What do you find in the Torah regarding the Rajam?" They replied, "We only disgrace and flog them with stripes." 'Abdullah bin Salam said to them, 'You have told a lie the penalty of Rajam is in the Torah.' They brought the Torah and opened it. One of them put his hand over the verse of the Rajam and read what was before and after it. Abdullah bin Salam said to him, "Lift up your hand." Where he lifted it there appeared the verse of the Rajam. So they said, "O Muhammad! He has said the truth, the verse of the Rajam is in it (Torah)."

Then Allah's Apostle ordered that the two persons (guilty of illegal sexual intercourse) be stoned to death, and so they were stoned, and I saw the man bending over the woman so as to protect her from the stones.

Volume 8, Book 82, Number 826:

Narrated Abu Huraira and Zaid bin Khalid:

Two men had a dispute in the presence of Allah's Apostle. One of them said, "Judge us according to Allah's Laws." The other who was more wise said, "Yes, Allah's Apostle, judge us according to Allah's Laws and allow me to speak (first)" The Prophet said to him, 'Speak " He said, "My son was a laborer for this man, and he committed illegal sexual intercourse with his wife, and the people told me that my son should be stoned to death, but I have given one-hundred sheep and a slave girl as a ransom (expiation) for my son's sin. Then I asked the religious learned people (about It), and they told me that my son should he flogged one-hundred stripes and should be exiled for one year, and only the wife of this man should be stoned to death " Allah's Apostle said, "By Him in Whose Hand my soul is, I will judge you according to Allah's Laws: O man, as for your sheep and slave girl, they are to be returned to you." Then the Prophet had the man's son flogged one hundred stripes and exiled for one year, and ordered Unais Al-Aslami to go to the wife of the other man, and if she confessed, stone her to death. She confessed and was stoned to death.

Volume 8, Book 82, Number 827:

Narrated 'Aisha:

Abu Bakr came to me while Allah's Apostle was sleeping with his head on my thigh. Abu Bakr said (to me), "You have detained Allah's Apostle and the people, and there is no water in this place." So he admonished me and struck my flanks with his hand, and nothing could stop me from moving except the reclining of Allah's Apostle (on my thigh), and then Allah revealed the Divine Verse of Tayammum.

Volume 8, Book 82, Number 828:

Narrated Aisha:

Abu Bakr came to towards me and struck me violently with his fist and said, "You have detained the people because of your necklace." But I remained motionless as if I was dead lest I should awake Allah's Apostle although that hit was very painful.

Volume 8, Book 82, Number 829:

Narrated Al-Mughira:

Sa'd bin Ubada said, "If I found a man with my wife, I would kill him with the sharp side of my sword." When the Prophet heard that he said, "Do you wonder at Sa'd's sense of ghira (self-respect)? Verily, I have more sense of ghira than Sa'd, and Allah has more sense of ghira than I."

Volume 8, Book 82, Number 830:

Narrated Abu Huraira:

A bedouin came to Allah's Apostle and said, "My wife has delivered a black child." The Prophet said to him, "Have you camels?" He replied, "Yes." The Prophet said, "What color are they?" He replied, "They are red." The Prophet further asked, "Are any of them gray in color?" He replied, "Yes." The Prophet asked him, "Whence did that grayness come?" He said, "I thing it descended from the camel's ancestors." Then the Prophet said (to him), "Therefore, this child of yours has most probably inherited the color from his ancestors."

Volume 8, Book 82, Number 831:

Narrated Abu Burda:

The Prophet used to say, "Nobody should be flogged more than ten stripes except if he is guilty of a crime, the legal punishment of which is assigned by Allah."

Volume 8, Book 82, Number 832:

Narrated 'Abdur-Rahman bin Jabir:

On the authority of others, that the Prophet said, "No Punishment exceeds the flogging of the ten stripes, except if one is guilty of a crime necessitating a legal punishment prescribed by Allah."

Volume 8, Book 82, Number 833:

Narrated Abu Burda Al-Ansari:

I heard the Prophet saying, "Do not flog anyone more than ten stripes except if he is involved in a crime necessitating Allah's legal Punishment."

Volume 8, Book 82, Number 834:

Narrated Abu Huraira:

Allah's Apostle forbade Al-Wisal (fasting continuously for more than one day without taking any meals). A man from the Muslims said, "But you do Al-Wisal, O Allah's Apostle!" Allah's Apostle I said, "Who among you is similar to me? I sleep and my Lord makes me eat and drink." When the people refused to give up Al-Wisal, the Prophet fasted along with them for one day, and did not break his fast but continued his fast for another day, and when they saw the crescent, the Prophet said, "If the crescent had not appeared, I would have made you continue your fast (for a third day)," as if he wanted to punish them for they had refused to give up Al-Wisal.

Volume 8, Book 82, Number 835:

Narrated 'Abdullah bin 'Umar:

Those people who used to buy foodstuff at random (without weighing or measuring it) were beaten in the lifetime of Allah's Apostle if they sold it at the very place where they had bought it, till they carried it to their dwelling places.

Volume 8, Book 82, Number 836:

Narrated 'Aisha:

Allah's Apostle never took revenge for his own self in any matter presented to him till Allah's limits were exceeded, in which case he would take revenge for Allah's sake.

Volume 8, Book 82, Number 837:

Narrated Sahl bin Sa'd:

I witnessed the case of Lian (the case of a man who charged his wife for committing illegal sexual intercourse when I was fifteen years old. The Prophet ordered that they be divorced, and the husband said, "If I kept her, I would be a liar." I remember that Az-Zubair also said, "(It was said) that if that woman brought forth the child with such-and-such description, her husband would prove truthful, but if she brought it with such-and-such description looking like a Wahra (a red insect), he would prove untruthful." I heard Az-Zubair also saying, "Finally she gave birth to a child of description which her husband disliked .

Volume 8, Book 82, Number 838:

Narrated Al-Qasim bin Muhammad:

Ibn 'Abbas mentioned the couple who had taken the oath of Lian. 'Abdullah bin Shaddad said (to him), "Was this woman about whom Allah's Apostle said, 'If I were ever to stone to death any woman without witnesses. (I would have stoned that woman to death)?' Ibn 'Abbas replied," No, that lady exposed herself (by her suspicious behavior)."

Volume 8, Book 82, Number 839:

Narrated Ibn Abbas:

Lian was mentioned in the presence of the Prophet, Asim bin Adi said a statement about it, and when he left, a man from his tribe came to him complaining that he had seen a man with his wife. Asim said, "I have been put to trial only because of my statement." So he took the man to the Prophet and the man told him about the incident. The man (husband) was of yellow complexion, thin, and of lank hair, while the man whom he had accused of having been with his wife, was reddish brown with fat thick legs and fat body. The Prophet said, "O Allah! Reveal the truth." Later on the lady delivered a child resembling the man whom the husband had accused of having been with her. So the Prophet made them take the oath of Lian. A man said to Ibn Abbas in the gathering, "Was that the same lady about whom the Prophet said, "If I were to stone any lady (for committing illegal sexual intercourse) to death without witnesses, I would have stoned that lade to death?" Ibn Abbas said, "No, that was another lady who used to behave in such a suspicious way among the Muslims that one might accuse her of committing illegal sexual intercourse."

Volume 8, Book 82, Number 840:

Narrated Abu Huraira:

The Prophet said, "Avoid the seven great destructive sins." They (the people!) asked, "O Allah's Apostle! What are they?" He said, "To join partners in worship with Allah; to practice sorcery; to kill the life which Allah has forbidden except for a just cause (according to Islamic law); to eat up usury (Riba), to eat up the property of an orphan; to give one's back to the enemy and freeing from the battle-field at the time of fighting and to accuse chaste women who never even think of anything touching chastity and are good believers."

Volume 8, Book 82, Number 841:

Narrated Abu Huraira:

I heard Abu-l-Qasim (the Prophet) saying, "If somebody slanders his slave and the slave is free from what he says, he will be flogged on the Day of Resurrection unless the slave is really as he has described him."

Volume 8, Book 82, Number 842:

Narrated Abu Huraira and Zaid bin Khalid Al-Juhani:

A man came to the Prophet and said, "I beseech you to judge us according to Allah's Laws." Then his opponent who was wiser than he, got up and said, "He has spoken the truth. So judge us according to Allah's Laws and please allow me (to speak), O Allah's Apostle." The Prophet said, "Speak." He said, "My son was a laborer for the family of this man and he committed illegal sexual intercourse with his wife, and I gave one-hundred sheep and a slave as a ransom (for my son), but I asked the religious learned people (regarding this case), and they informed me that my son should be flogged one-hundred stripes, and be exiled for one year, and the wife of this man should be stoned (to death)."The Prophet said, "By Him in Whose Hand my soul is, I will Judge you (in this case) according to Allah's Laws. The one-hundred (sheep) and the slave shall be returned to you and your son shall be flogged one-hundred stripes and be exiled for one year. And O Unais! Go in the morning to the wife of this man and ask her, and if she confesses, stone her to death." She confessed and he stoned her to death.